
The Contracting Organization

The Contracting Organization

A Strategic Guide to Outsourcing

SIMON DOMBERGER

OXFORD UNIVERSITY PRESS

1998

Oxford University Press, Great Clarendon Street, Oxford OX2 6DP

Oxford New York

Athens Auckland Bangkok Bogotá Buenos Aires Calcutta
Cape Town Chennai Dar es Salaam Delhi Florence Hong Kong Istanbul
Karachi Kuala Lumpur Madrid Melbourne Mexico City Mumbai
Nairobi Paris São Paulo Singapore Taipei Tokyo Toronto Warsaw

and associated companies in Berlin Ibadan

Oxford is a registered trade mark of Oxford University Press

Published in the United States
by Oxford University Press Inc., New York

British Library Cataloguing in Publication Data
Data available

Library of Congress Cataloging in Publication Data
Domberger, Simon.
The contracting organization: a strategic guide to outsourcing/
Simon Domberger.
p. cm.
Includes bibliographical references and index.
1. Contracting out. 2. Subcontracting. 3. Make-or-buy decisions.
4. Industrial procurement. 5. Contracting out—Case studies.
I. Title.
HD2365.D65 1998
658.7'2—dc21 98-27578

ISBN 0-19-877458-3
ISBN 0-19-877457-5 (pbk)

10 9 8 7 6 5 4 3 2 1

Typeset in 9½/12 Utopia
by Cambrian Typesetters, Frimley, Surrey

Printed in Great Britain
on acid-free paper by
Biddles Limited, Guildford and King's Lynn

PREFACE

IN the mid-1980s, while at the London Business School, I embarked on a study which was to determine the course of my research endeavours for the next thirteen years. The purpose of the investigation, conducted with David Thompson and Shirley Meadowcroft of the Institute for Fiscal Studies, was to establish whether the contracting out of refuse collection saved local councils any money. The answer turned out to be around 20 per cent of previous expenditure. Other studies, for different services, suggested similar results, and policy makers jumped enthusiastically on the contracting bandwagon. In local government, health and white-collar services contracting was to unleash market forces, as a means to cheaper and better-quality services.

In the private sector similar developments were occurring under the name of outsourcing. Touted as the latest management fad, outsourcing extended its reach to many services and activities hitherto kept firmly in-house. These parallel developments raised the question of the appropriateness of such public policies and business policies, and their sustainability over time. The persistence of contracting and outsourcing activity was certainly a clue that something more than transitory was going on. But it also raised the question of where the limits of contracting lie, for limits there must surely be.

At the same time exciting new developments were taking place in the theory of the firm, led by Oliver Hart of Harvard University. They shed light on questions such as when should activities be integrated under single firm ownership, and when are arm's-length market transactions more efficient? This work is highly relevant to the contracting decision, although it is theoretical in nature and not easily accessible to non-specialist readers.

For practitioners, the question of what to outsource and what to keep in-house superficially appeared to boil down to a matter of cost comparison. If it costs more to do in-house, contract out. Admittedly, an important influence on contracting decisions in the public sector was the pursuit of smaller government, using private sector expertise wherever possible. Efficiency—and budget—considerations lay at the heart of this trend. But a simple cost comparison is not adequate to reach such decisions. What of the opportunity costs of managing the in-house operation? Should they not be counted in the assessment? Interestingly, one major company representative interviewed in the course of the research for this book commented that if a contracting decision was cost neutral, meaning that the in-house provider's costs were line ball with the external contractor, the outsourcing decision would prevail.

Other complications arise. These include strategic issues concerning potential loss of skills or expertise, and management issues concerning organizational change. They have the effect of broadening the decision-making framework well beyond simple cost comparisons. This book was written to address the questions which lie behind the numbers; to improve understanding, and provide an analytical framework for contracting decisions which can be applied in both the private and the public sectors. It is the culmination of over a decade of research which started in the UK, continued in Australia, and encompassed several countries in which contracting and outsourcing have been widespread.

The book is divided into four parts. Part I begins by considering the 'make or buy' decision. This is followed by a discussion of the shifting boundaries of organizations, which revisits some of the critical issues underlying the theory of the firm: why do firms exist and what forces determine their boundaries. As was pointed out earlier, this is an area in which research is yielding useful new insights about the optimal economic structures of organizations. Part II examines in detail the benefits and costs of contracting. The approach taken in these two chapters is taxonomic: it is merely an overview of what factors determine the costs and the benefits, and does not contain a discussion of how such benefits could be maximized or contracting costs brought under control.

These strategic aspects of contracting, involving the implementation of actual policies, are closely examined in Part III, entitled 'contracting strategies'. The next four chapters cover the key elements of contracting: why specialization lies at the heart of contracting strategies (Chapter 5); how to capture the added value generated by specialization (Chapter 6); how to achieve control and flexibility in contractual relationships (Chapter 7); and lastly, in Chapter 8, how to steer through the organizational change minefield associated with contracting with the minimum of disruption and industrial disputation.

Lastly Part IV looks at structural change associated with contracting, at the level of both individual sectors and the whole economy. The important changes that have occurred in the public sector are discussed in Chapter 9, and Chapter 10 takes a 'whole economy' view of the links between contracting and the growth of the service economy. In particular, it looks at recent structural changes in the UK, USA, and Australia and some of the economic forces propelling them. Chapters 11 and 12 sum up the arguments by examining current trends and future projections, as well as the lessons learnt from past experience for business and public policy.

Case studies and specific illustrations are used extensively throughout the book. There are over thirty case studies scattered in boxes and in the text of most chapters. They highlight particular points and inform the reader on what was done in particular circumstances and why. The cases span several countries, including the UK, USA, Australia, New Zealand, Germany, Italy, Japan, Korea, and Brazil, making the coverage of this material truly international.

The book is intended for business students and MBAs in particular, strategic analysts, consultants, policy makers, public sector managers, CEOs, and CFOs as well as those wishing to enhance their understanding of the factors which determine successful contracting. Although many of the concepts used in this book stem from the field of economics, the study draws heavily on the cognate disciplines of management and public administration. If the book succeeds in distilling the relevant concepts from those disciplines in an accessible non-technical way, then its purpose will have been well served.

Now to the acknowledgements. The book could not have been written without the efforts and cooperation of many individuals and organizations. In case some have been missed, I apologize to them in advance. My greatest debt in the completion of this project is owed to Paul Jensen, who, as Research Associate, masterminded the literature review, wrote many of the case studies, compiled the bibliography, and commented on every single draft chapter. His contribution has been immense, and deserves special recognition.

Others on my research team who made a significant contribution include Christine Hall, who was the team leader, Geesche Jacobsen, Paula Callen, Kuru Pancharatnam, and Daniel Domberger. When the pressure of time was most intense, other family members were coopted to the enterprise, namely my wife Brenda and my daughter Shelley, who provided assistance with figures and tables. To my wife I am also grateful for her unwavering support and boundless patience during the many months of writing.

Those who provided helpful comments on early drafts of selected chapters include John Kay of Oxford, Oliver Hart of Harvard, Robert Grant of Georgetown University, Stephen Rimmer of the Industry Commission in Melbourne, and Frank Theophile of the Serco Institute in Sydney. Useful discussions with, and inputs by, Richard White, Richard Nicholls, Chris Wood, John Oughton, Paddy Doyle, Phil Braithwaite, Stanley Goodchild, Anthony Geeson, Dr Ian Leigh, John Meacock, Andrew Rich, Chris Bowman, Shane Hodson, Mike McNamara, and Patrick Fernandez are also gratefully acknowledged. The New Zealand Department of Corrections kindly provided a copy of their advertisement seeking expressions of interest in the provision of custodial services.

To David Musson, my publisher at Oxford University Press, special thanks for useful comments and encouragement throughout the long gestation of this book, which was lengthened even further by a bout of illness. I am also grateful to Sarah Dobson and Hilary Walford for expert editorial assistance. Lastly, acknowledgement is due to the Australian Research Council and also to the New South Wales Treasury, which, under the stewardship of its erstwhile secretary, Michael Lambert, co-funded the large research project that made it possible to write this book.

S. D.

CONTENTS

LIST OF CASE STUDIES

LIST OF FIGURES

LIST OF ILLUSTRATIONS

LIST OF TABLES

I

ORGANIZATIONS AND MARKETS

This section of the book introduces the central issues by asking 'why make when you can buy?' It begins in Chapter 1 by outlining a handful of contracting examples, most of which have been successful but including one outright failure. It then goes on to suggest what may have been the crucial elements of contracting decisions which resulted in success or failure. This provides an initial glimpse of the themes, the development of which is the main purpose of the book. Chapter 1 also outlines the approach that will be taken in this book, which is not a contracting manual, but an analytical tool to facilitate strategic thinking about contracting.

Chapter 2 examines the shifting boundaries of organizations—what they choose to do for themselves and what they increasingly rely on the market for. The chapter briefly considers the changes in horizontal as well as vertical boundaries of firms. Horizontal boundaries determine what range of output markets firms choose to be in, over and above their principal business activity. Vertical boundaries are determined by the proportion of activities in a firm's value chain let out to external providers of goods and services. This chapter also examines the underlying factors behind these organizational changes, in both the private and the public sectors. In addition, it contains a brief overview of international contracting trends in the G5 economies and in Australia.

1

Why Make When You Can Buy?

Outsource: contract (work) out.
(Concise Oxford Dictionary)

Contract: to enter into or make a contract. From the Latin *contractus*, the past participle of *contrahere*, to draw together, bring about or enter into an agreement: *con*, together + *trahere*, to draw.
(Webster's English Dictionary)

Why did Microsoft Corporation decide to contract out the customer support function for its Windows 95 software? Why did Mambo Graphics, an Australian design and sports apparel company, achieve compound sales and profit growth after it took the strategic decision to outsource the entire manufacturing process and distribution of its products? How does Marks & Spencer secure the lasting and successful contractual relationships with its suppliers which are a source of its competitive advantage? And what caused Fairfax County, in the state of Virginia, to terminate a major vehicle maintenance contract within four months of awarding it?

The answers to these questions lie in two key strategic choices that all organizations have to make. The first concerns the location of organizational *boundaries*. In practical terms this means: what should the organization produce itself, and what should it obtain through the market? Both Microsoft and Mambo chose to contract out activities that, while critical to the commercial success of their operations, were not considered to lie within their special capabilities. The second choice involves the *structure* of contractual relationships. Here there are numerous possibilities, but organizations tend to adopt different styles, some of which are more successful than others. Thus Marks & Spencer has developed a particular contracting style based on trust and long-term relationships with suppliers. It appears to work so well that the company has become an archetype for others to follow and for management scholars to study. By contrast, Fairfax County, a relative newcomer to contracting, struck a particular contract with its supplier which quickly became untenable.

Before describing the specific issues that will be addressed in this book, it is useful to consider, in greater detail, the contracting experiences which were briefly outlined in the opening paragraphs. It is also useful to review recent international contracting trends and their likely effects on industries and markets.

Microsoft Corporation: Redmond, USA

Microsoft Corporation recognized early that its distinctive capability lay in the development of software and computer operating systems. It therefore made the strategic decision to contract out peripheral functions, ranging from customer and technical support to production, distribution, and warehousing. When Windows 95 was released, customer support was provided by means of free telephone assistance to those wishing to update their operating systems for ninety days after purchase. This service complemented Microsoft's marketing campaign, which was designed to facilitate the switch from its previous operating system, Windows 3.1. Microsoft chose to harness the capability of outside contractors, instead of temporarily bolstering its in-house customer support function.

The high volume of calls was expected for only a limited period of time (the ninety-day free assistance period). It was expected that, once the initial period had lapsed, high staffing levels for customer support would no longer be required, although paid assistance would remain available. Microsoft's strategy was to use the market in dealing with this peak demand.

UCA&L was one of the companies which provided much of the before- and after-sales service to Microsoft, with the release of Windows 95. Pre-sales assistance included information about the product, systems requirements, and the like. Hence this service complemented Microsoft's marketing drive. Its after-sales service included providing assistance to software users. UCA&L's attraction to Microsoft was its staffing flexibility; the ability to accommodate peaks and troughs in service calls.

The contractor's service staff were given the same extensive training in Windows 95 as Microsoft's own telemarketing personnel. The system works in such a way that telephone calls to Microsoft are rerouted to one of the contractors. As far as the customer is concerned, Microsoft staff become indistinguishable from those of the contractor.

The decision to contract out customer support functions for a new computer application is generally risky because the contractor's knowledge of the software is likely to be incomplete. Microsoft's reputation could have been adversely affected if customers became aware of this deficiency and attributed it, wrongly, to the software developer. But, as will be argued in Chapter 3, it can make good economic sense for Microsoft to continue to specialize in the activity from which it can extract greatest value—software development.

Mambo Graphics: Sydney, Australia

Mambo is one of the success stories of the surf/leisure clothing industry, which is estimated to be worth more than $100 million in Australia alone. From humble beginnings as a screen-printing business employing 120 people in suburban Sydney, Mambo has undergone a metamorphosis into a global design company which produces such diverse products as clothing, swimwear, watches, skiwear, and other accessories. In 1995, Mambo's annual turnover was in excess of $A25 million, and their first store in London, which opened in June 1995, has been so successful that it has had to move into new premises to cater for the demand.

A large part of Mambo's success can be attributed to the realignment of its business operation that occurred in 1989. Set up in 1984, Mambo grew relatively modestly, as a designer and screen printer of surfing apparel: shorts, T-shirts, and swimming costumes. By 1988 it had secured a number of lucrative contracts and had a sizeable production facility, but still there were problems. First, Mambo realized that, while there was an abundance of potential garment manufacturers, there were very few companies specializing in the highly creative design facet of the production process. Secondly, there was the issue of increasing financial pressure—as the screen-printing business grew, Mambo needed more capital, but was not prepared to sacrifice artistic integrity or the design capacity of the company by taking on an equity partner.

The two owners of Mambo, Dare Jennings and Andrew Rich, slowly came to the realization that their area of expertise was in design rather than production. A strategic decision was then made which led to a clearer separation between downstream (production) and upstream (design) operations. In effect, Mambo decided to outsource the production side of its business. Mambo consequently sold off the screen printing side of its operations and focused on fostering its small network of creative designers. Mambo has also maintained control of marketing, which it believes is all-important, to the point that it even controls which shops its products will be sold in. Department stores, for example, do not suit the image Mambo wants to project.

Mambo then struck a deal with Gazal Apparel whereby Mambo would keep control of its trademark and continue to design its range of products and oversee market positioning of the goods, while Gazal would take over the production and distribution of the clothing. For other stock, it outsourced production to low-cost producers in South-East Asia.

Mambo has carefully nurtured its relationships with the small network of both internal and external artists who undertake the graphic design. In addition to financial compensation they are given a firm and credible guarantee that their artistic integrity will be assured. As a result, Mambo's graphics are known for their quirky and idiosyncratic style.

The company's story is a classic one of how, by outsourcing production, it has been possible to focus on and develop key design and marketing capabilities. Not only has it prospered as a result, but its main supplier, Gazal Apparel, has also done very well.

Marks & Spencer: London, UK

From humble beginnings in 1884, Marks & Spencer (M&S) has expanded to become one of the UK's leading retailers, with an annual turnover in 1996 of £7,231.6 million and profits of £940.2 million. In 1991, a survey of companies in *The Economist* found M&S to be the second most admired company in Europe, based on the quality of its products, and the perceived calibre of its management. Today the company operates 368 stores, 280 of which are in Britain, and further international expansion is constantly taking place. Its entire product range carries the *St Michael* brand name, but M&S does not manufacture the products it retails under its own brand name. Instead, the production and distribution of its goods are sourced from a wide network of suppliers and contractors. The distinctive feature of the relationship M&S has with its suppliers is a large element of trust.

M&S has been described as a manufacturer without factories, and its suppliers referred to as 'retailers without stores'. Since the 1920s the retailer has been buying directly from its suppliers, to exacting specifications. M&S and its suppliers agree on matters ranging from the raw materials which should be used in manufacturing, to the product specifications themselves and the methods of production. The primary role taken by the company's management is the coordination of its independent suppliers, including goods manufacturers, raw material suppliers, and transport and store maintenance management contractors.

M&S invests heavily in the development of contractual relationships. For example, managerial and technical assistance is often offered to suppliers during difficult trading times. This binds the parties together and creates strong incentives to maintain performance. The company has lost no more than two suppliers every decade, an attrition rate which is indicative of the loyalty and longevity of supply relationships. And when the company introduces a new product line, it encourages existing suppliers to undertake the necessary investment, rather than forming alliances with new contractors.

The relationship M&S has with Claremont Garments is representative of its contractual style. Claremont, a company whose turnover was £300 million in 1995, supplies 4 per cent of all the clothing sold by M&S. Ninety per cent of Claremont's production is dedicated to M&S, which clearly makes it vulnerable to a potential loss of the contract with the retailer. However, the relationship has been largely trouble free since it first began in 1967, when the company was founded as Charnos Garments.

Claremont's approach to maintaining its relationship with M&S is to improve long-term manufacturing efficiency. This is achieved by continuously investing in new technology, and by a continuous search for reductions in unit costs. A recent innovation by Claremont was the introduction of a computer aided design (CAD) system which enables designers to create concept garments on screen, a faster and more efficient method than the conventional way of creating samples. When combined with the latest printing technology, it facilitates much quicker fabric design. This faster response speed is important to M&S, because it needs to adapt quickly to changes in fashions and consumer preferences. The relationship between Claremont and M&S is based on trust and reciprocity: the retailer remains loyal to the garment manufacturer, who in turn maintains a heavy investment programme which improves the product and benefits the customer.

M&S is truly a 'contracting organization', having a distinctive capability in the development and maintenance of long-term contractual relationships. This reputation is so well established that suppliers know they have little to fear, and much to gain, from contracts with the retailer. It gives M&S a distinct competitive advantage in its principal commercial activity—retail merchandise trade.

Fairfax County: Virginia, USA

In 1994, Fairfax County embarked on an ambitious project to contract out one of four garages that provided maintenance of County-operated vehicles. The four garages were operated under the responsibility of the Equipment Management Transportation Agency (EMPTA). One of the principal services provided by EMPTA was maintenance of the County's 1,300 school buses. EMPTA had previously been restructured; its staff had been cut by approximately 170 positions, significantly reducing the 'fat' left on EMPTA's operating budget.

Extensive research was undertaken by Fairfax County to identify which of the garages was most suitable for contracting out. The garage selected, West Ox Road, was chosen because it had a mix of vehicles which provided the most challenging environment for the new contractor. Fairfax County effectively minimized its exposure to risk by selecting only one garage for market testing in the first instance. Care was also taken to ensure that the specification was both clear and comprehensive.

The contract was designed to provide two strong incentive mechanisms to the contractor. First, a target cost was established for each year of the contract. This represented the maximum amount that the County would pay each year. Any costs above the target would be absorbed by the contractor, while 40 per cent of any savings realized would be passed on to the client if the contractor came in under the target cost. Secondly, as an incentive to minimize the number of buses which were not in operation due to mechanical problems, the contractor would be fined $800 per day for each bus which was inoperable for twenty-four hours. The fine would apply only when the number of buses exceeded 5 per cent of the total number of buses maintained by the contractor.

The three-year, $11 million contract was awarded to Johnson Controls in January 1994 and the contract commenced in March the same year. Problems

emerged from the outset. By April, the proportion of buses requiring maintenance ranged from one-quarter to one-third, for reasons that were not immediately clear. The management of Johnson Controls argued that there were
three principal causes: poor maintenance scheduling; the fact that repairs had
not been performed prior to contract commencement; and overly critical
safety inspections. However, it was also apparent that Johnson Controls did
not have a sufficient number of skilled bus mechanics to perform all of the
necessary work. The end result was that hundreds of schoolchildren were late
for school or left stranded at bus stops.

In July, Fairfax County terminated the contract with Johnson Controls. In
hindsight, there were a number of reasons for the contract's failure. First, the
County failed to obtain consensus among the County supervisors that
contracting out maintenance of a highly visible service such as school buses
was a step in the right direction. This made the decision controversial.
Secondly, the County did not fully consider ways to reduce the effects of transfer risk—Johnson Controls was given permission to review EMPTA records
only two months before the start of the contract, and the transfer was
performed in the middle of the school year, which allowed Johnson Controls
no adjustment time. Thirdly, the incentive scheme was rendered impotent
because EMPTA had previously identified and removed many inefficiencies in
its operations. Thus, it was difficult for Johnson Controls to receive a substantial bonus by performing under the target cost. This case study highlights the
importance of incentive mechanisms and the pitfalls of getting the incentive
mechanisms wrong.

A historical perspective on contracting

Contracting and outsourcing of goods and services are not new. Those who
dismiss contracting as nothing more than the latest in a series of short-lived
management fashions should take a longer look back in time. In the private
sector, there are well-documented historical accounts of the contracting of
specialist metal manufacturing functions in nineteenth-century England. In
the public sector, Illustration 1.1 highlights the breadth of activities that have
been contracted out in Europe and Australia over the past 150 years.

Illustration 1.1.   A brief history of contracting

Contracting was commonplace, albeit not without its problems, in eighteenth- and
nineteenth-century England. Services provided by the private sector under contract
included prison management, road maintenance, the collection of public revenue, and
refuse collection. Street lamps were made, fixed, cleaned, and lit under contract. Early
convict fleets, excluding the First Fleet (to Australia), which left Portsmouth in 1787, were
also operated by private contractors. Similarly, in early nineteenth-century France, the
rights to build and operate railways and water storage and distribution facilities were
auctioned by competitive tender.

Contracting of mail delivery and postal services in Australia goes back over 150 years. The carriage of mail was entrusted to private operators prior to the formation of Australia's official mail delivery network, as it was in the USA during much of the nineteenth century.

Source: Industry Commission (1996) (with corrections).

Prior to and during the Industrial Revolution, contractual relationships dominated the economic organization of production. But from the mid-nineteenth century, and during most of the twentieth century up until the last twenty years, the internalization of transactions within organizations was the dominant trend. Thus the early contracting experiments faltered, and in many cases they were abandoned in favour of corporate organization. Two reinforcing tendencies played an important part in this reversal. The first was the growth of direct government involvement in economic activity, particularly in continental Europe, the UK, Australia, and New Zealand. The second was the development of production technologies that favoured large, vertically integrated enterprises in both the private and the public sectors.

But those same factors that forced a retreat from contracting led to its resurgence in the 1980s and 1990s. With the coming of the Thatcher era, the frontiers of the state began to be rolled back in earnest, first in Great Britain, then in other Anglo-Saxon countries such as Australia and New Zealand. And on the technological front, recent evidence suggests that, in today's world markets, large integrated enterprises are neither responsive enough nor necessarily more efficient than the more fragmented but cooperative networks of enterprises, specializing in different aspects of manufacturing and service provision. An important feature of these networks is the appearance of 'hybrid' organizations which combine elements of arm's-length market transactions with the close working relationships associated with integrated organizations. These hybrids are usually seen as partnerships or strategic alliances.

Purpose and method

Simply detailing contracting trends and historical precedents, however compelling they may be, does not establish why contracting is evolving the way it is; when it should be gainfully marshalled by public or private sector organizations; nor how it should be applied to yield maximum benefits. The purpose of this book is to develop a framework of analysis which provides a structured, systematic approach to contracting decisions and outsourcing strategies. It should help determine those circumstances in which contracts are sustainable in the long run—where they are likely to be successful, and where internal relationships are likely to work better. Here are some of the questions which will be addressed in this book:

- Why do some contracts succeed when others, superficially similar, fail?
- What are the characteristics of successful contractual solutions? How can client organizations capture the value that can be generated by outsourcing while maintaining control and flexibility over their operations?
- When does it make sense to seek and implement contracts for services? Or put differently, when do the costs of contracting outweigh the benefits?
- How should organizations go about developing a contracting/outsourcing strategy? What factors, such as the competitiveness of the market and the need to retain in-house skills, should be considered when formulating a strategic contracting framework?
- How should contracts be designed to yield an acceptable balance of risks between the transacting parties?
- Are there circumstances in which contractual failure is endemic? Should services prone to 'contract failure' because the required standards are difficult to specify be kept in-house, or can contracts be designed that effectively solve the problem?

A good example of persistent contract failure was the transportation of convicts to the Antipodes by the British government in the eighteenth and nineteenth centuries. The story of the early colonization of Australia does not make cheerful reading, but the role of contracting in getting the job done is not commonly known. Illustration 1.2 highlights the repeated attempts by the government to get the shipping contractors to 'perform'.

Illustration 1.2. Contracting for transportation of convicts

'The First Fleet had been entirely fitted out and provisioned by the commissioners of the navy; it had been a government affair from start to finish, although the vessels had been chartered through a shipbroker at a flat 10 shillings per ton. The results, as we have seen, were muddled and potentially disastrous, but they were better than what might have happened with private contract. Once the guidelines were laid down, every convict transport that sailed from England or Ireland after 1788 was fitted and victualled by private contract. The only people the arrangement did not suit were the convicts themselves, since the contract system guaranteed their miseries and, often, their death.

By the end of the eighteenth century, as experience of the peculiar problems of shipping prisoners halfway around the world grew and was added to Britain's knowledge of sending armies on long voyages and landing them in fighting shape, the private contractor faced an imposing list of government demands. From the number of lifeboats to the size of rations, all was laid down, along with the exact responsibilities to convicts borne by captain, surgeon and officers.

The rules would reduce (but never eliminate) suffering and death on board. People at sea always suffered and died, whether they were prisoners or not. . . . By the standards of the time, then, the convicts did not do so badly once the system of getting them out to Australia was working smoothly.'

Source: Hughes (1987: 144–5).

This book's approach is distinctive in three ways. First, it is not a manual. It does not list a series of steps which help with successful implementation. There is a role for such books, and there are some on the market, but the role is limited because there is no substitute for the application of judgement when making decisions and formulating strategies. Manuals are generally prescriptive—they do not allow for the wide range of circumstances that may be encountered in practical applications and cannot encompass all the nuances of different situations. To some extent only experience can do that, which brings us to the second distinctive feature. The book contains a large number of case studies which are designed to illustrate actual practice and its consequences. The case studies closely accompany the issue or argument that is being illustrated, and they are intended to be both a source of empirical evidence and surrogates for actual experience.

The third distinctive feature of the book is that, although it identifies the costs and benefits of contracting in Chapters 3 and 4, the framework it develops for analysing contracting decisions is not couched in those terms. The problem with decision making based simply on cost–benefit calculations is that the financial outcome depends on how those decisions are implemented. There is no unique set of costs and benefits associated with a particular contracting decision: there are a large number of them depending on which type of approach is taken. For example, the financial savings from contracting may be reduced by choosing to negotiate contracts directly with outside providers rather than inviting competitive bids, but the costs of contract management may also be lower because of the reduced emphasis on price and more cooperative approach that it engenders. There are thus many cost and benefit outcomes associated with different contracting strategies and it is the choice of those strategies that determines the cost–benefit outcomes.

A purely economic accounting approach to contracting is more suited to understanding *ex post* outcomes than as an aid to decision making. A statement such as 'Vertical integration is preferred to arm's-length market exchange when it is less costly to organize activities internally than it is to organize them through arm's-length market exchange' (Besanko et al. 1996: 164), while true, is not particularly helpful. What firms want to know is how much of their value chain should be encompassed internally and what arrangements they should use to link together various value chain activities undertaken by outside firms. These issues are explored in detail in those chapters which examine respectively the role of specialization, value capture, control and flexibility, and organizational change in contracting decisions.

One of the key themes of this book is that market transactions have more detractors than supporters: many organizations have grown accustomed to having their own service providers, perhaps set up at times when a market for those services was not well developed. Their reluctance to contract for services means that it tends to happen when external and internal pressures intensify. While this is changing somewhat, particularly in the USA, concerns remain about non-integrated methods of organizing production. These misgivings, which are deep-seated, stem from an era when power, prestige, and pay within organizations were determined largely by size of revenue and employment, rather than by profitability and added value.

Another theme which will be developed here is that much of the growth of contracting should be viewed in the context of the development of markets for services. Service providers are now large and sophisticated, and can deliver scale and scope that many clients will find hard to match in-house. Many of them have developed the skills required to absorb in-house activities with minimum disruption to the client, and a constructive approach towards the re-employment of former client staff. This development is reflected in structural changes in the economy which are described and interpreted in Chapter 10.

The book invokes both conceptual knowledge and practical case studies in its pursuit of the increasingly complex and sophisticated contractual experiments to be found in the modern marketplace. It attempts to bridge the divide that stands between management theory and economic analysis, at least as far as contracting is concerned. Much has been written recently in the management literature about outsourcing and 'virtual organizations', and in the economics literature about contracting, markets, and firms. Yet the two fields of knowledge rarely intersect. Experts who profess to belong to one or other of the disciplines write for their designated audience, using a specialist lexicon that is largely meaningless to the rival group. Indeed, management academics like to make fun of economists for their propensity to theorize excessively. There is an amusing story about an economist who, seeing something working in practice, immediately asked whether it would work in theory. But despite the mockery, there is more common ground in the two disciplines than most would care to admit.

A note on terminology

This chapter began with a formal definition of contracting and outsourcing. Contracting refers to the design and implementation of contractual relationships between purchasers and suppliers. Outsourcing refers to the process whereby activities traditionally carried out internally are contracted out to external providers. In this book the term contracting will be used in a generic way to describe both the process of outsourcing—the search for and appointment of contractors for the provision of goods and services—and the execution of the contractual relations needed to support such activities.

It should be noted that contracting will also be used to describe an important variant of contracting out, namely the frequently occurring case where public, or private, sector organizations call for tenders and the in-house service provider is permitted to bid. If the competitive tender is won by the in-house team, this is not strictly speaking a case of contracting out, since the activity remains in-house. It is a case of contracting, however, because the relationship between the client and the provider is made explicit through an internal agreement, even though it is not an agreement which has the force of law. An organization cannot legally enforce a contract with itself, even though it can design and implement a set of contract-like agreements with internal producers or service providers. The principal effect of contracting in this instance is the discipline imposed by the introduction of competition and the subsequent management of performance.

The contents of the 'contracting organization' thus encompass the following topics: outsourcing, competitive tendering, and the design of contractual relations between purchasers and providers. They do not address the broader issues which fall under the heading of purchasing management or supply chain logistics and management. The focus is on both private and public sector organizations, drawing out the similarities and differences of approach appropriate to each.

Guide to further reading

For an in-depth discussion of the Fairfax County case study see Reca and Zieg (1995). For a historical perspective on the evolution of firms, as well as additional material on make versus buy decisions, see Milgrom and Roberts (1992). Useful readings on the role of contracts, competition, and cooperation based on recent research are contained in Deakin and Michie (1997) and Buckley and Michie (1996). For a useful discussion of Marks & Spencer's management style see Sieff (1990).

2

The Shifting Boundaries of Organizations

Why is not all production carried on in one big firm?
(Ronald Coase, 1937)

Firms versus markets

Only relatively recently have economists turned their attention from how markets function to the analysis of organizations. The lack of a well-articulated theory of organizations in general, and of the firm in particular, may seem a curious omission. But neglecting the institutions in which the bulk of the market economies' productive activity takes place is, in reality, a serious omission. Not until 1937, when Ronald Coase asked his simple but profound question about the nature of the firm, was this omission partially rectified. It took another forty years before the analysis of organizations became a mainstream activity within the economics profession.

Ever since the rise of the great industrial firms at the turn of the century, it has been recognized that an increasing level of economic activity occurred *within* firms, and not between *different* firms. But the focus of analytical attention remained on the way firms interacted within the market. The structure of markets, whether competitive or monopolistic, was studied much more closely than the size and scope of the firm, which was treated essentially as a 'black box'. The difficult questions regarding the factors which should be considered by the manager or the entrepreneur in choosing between external market transactions and internal production were left unanswered.

Coase's answer was that using the market for economic transactions entails costs. There are costs of searching for the right prices and quality, of negotiating and closing the contracts. These costs can be substantial, particularly when the choice is between pure exchange with a multiplicity of external organizations, and production within a single firm. But if firms are more efficient than markets, why doesn't productive activity become steadily more concentrated in one large firm? Because, as the firm gets larger, it becomes a less effective mechanism for organizing production. According to Coase, 'diseconomies of scale'—inefficiencies associated with large size—will develop as, for example, bureaucratic lethargy creeps in. Thus the optimal size of firm is reached when, on balance, it is equally costly to expand production by using the market as it is to carry it out internally.

This argument was quite general. It did not consider specific market conditions, and how they would alter the conclusion. For example, the costs of transacting may differ between firms because of differences in efficiency and technology. Similarly, diseconomies of scale may occur earlier in some firms than in others. This is consistent with the observation that firms of many different sizes operate successfully in the same market. It is evident that the costs of transacting will differ significantly depending on the level of specialization and development of a particular market. An interesting contemporary example of the changing costs to the customer of transacting in services can be found in facilities management (FM)—the provision of building and ancillary maintenance. A decade ago the provision of these services would have required separate transactions with cleaning, security, fire protection, and other specialist contractors. Today a purchaser can transact with a single provider of FM services which would include all of the above components.

Approximately four decades after the topic was first brought to light, 'transaction costs economics' became a subdiscipline in its own right, led virtually single-handedly by Oliver Williamson. The basic tenet of transaction costs economics is that 'If firms and markets are *alternative* modes of organization, then the boundary of the firm needs to be derived rather than taken as given' (Williamson 1996: 133). Much effort went into the refinement of Coase's original proposition, that market transactions may be inferior to internally organized production. And considerable attention was devoted to understanding the conditions under which one mode would be unequivocally superior to the other.

'Asset specificity' is one such condition. Some transactions require capital assets that are 'specific' and exclusive to them, for example a smelter that needs to be located next to an iron ore mine. Once the two are co-located, the trading opportunities available to the owners of these assets become limited. If the smelter and the mine were separately owned, there would be a potential for a 'hold-up'—one firm refusing to continue to transact with the other unless an exorbitant payment is made, secure in the knowledge that the other party cannot put its asset to an alternative use. This would make contracting between the parties highly problematic. The specific nature of the asset (smelter or mine) and the propensity for opportunistic behaviour may result in one party attempting to extract unreasonable terms from the other. In sum, 'As asset specificity increases, . . . the balance shifts in favour of internal organization' (Williamson 1985: 90).

But these are rather special, even unusual, conditions. In general, it is not obvious why internal organization would be more efficient and effective than using the market. Indeed, some theorists consider that the firms and organizations are themselves 'a nexus of contracts', and that in this respect there may be little to distinguish between transactions within and between firms. Hierarchical relationships within the organization may not look much like a conventional contract, but in reality they are governed by loosely structured transactions which are held together by a series of employment contracts between the organization and its employees. If this argument is accepted, then much closer analysis is required to establish the advantages that firms have over markets.

Recent rethinking suggests that the key may lie in property rights; in particular, the rights which ownership confers upon the owner of the physical assets of the firm. Ownership gives power to direct and control the disposition of assets for productive purposes. According to this theory, which will be explored further in Chapter 4, the benefits of integration of production within the firm arise when physical assets are complementary, as in the mining and smelting example above. In such situations common ownership of the assets is economically superior to separate ownership, and this provides a rationale for both the existence and the differing size of firms.

The 'property rights' approach to the theory of the firm also leads to the conclusion that 'a merger between firms with highly complementary assets is value enhancing, and a merger between firms with independent assets is value reducing' (Hart 1995: 7–8). It has special significance in the context of the present trend towards the fragmentation or de-integration of diversified corporations across a wide spectrum of industries. Vertical integration and conglomerate diversification were recommended, up until the early 1980s, by many academics and management gurus alike. The argument was that they yielded efficiencies in terms of economies of scale and corporate synergies. Today the message is vastly different. 'Stick to the knitting' is the advice proffered by Peters and Waterman (1982), and get back to 'core business'. Companies and organizations everywhere are now outsourcing goods and services they produced for themselves, and divesting peripheral businesses which are unrelated to their core activities.

The movement towards smaller, fragmented organizations demands explanation. The recent developments in the theory of the firm outlined above merely explain which influences make different organizational boundaries more efficient, not what causes those influences to change. To do that one has to look at the external forces—or drivers—of organizational change, but before doing so it is instructive to gauge the magnitude and significance of this transformation.

Bloated corporations or virtual organizations?

After the Second World War, the large, diversified corporation—the 'megacorp'—became the model of organizational prowess and business success. For huge conglomerates such as General Electric of America, Daimler-Benz in Europe, Mitsubishi in Japan, and BHP in Australia there was security in size. And while shareholders remained content, they seemed able to take their existing corporate structure into the next millennium. But research had already shown that big was not necessarily best, and that profitability was not generally higher in larger firms compared to smaller ones. On the contrary, size appeared to be *negatively* related to the rate of return, indicating that larger, diversified firms tended to exhibit *lower* profitability on average. However, larger firms tended to show lower variability of profits, implying a more stable profit stream over time. Since shareholders like other people were assumed to be willing to trade lower risk for lower return, it was generally assumed that there was nothing much wrong with this state of affairs.

This assessment has had to be drastically revised since about the mid-1980s. With the onset of harsher and more volatile trading conditions, the vulnerable nature of the corporate behemoths became highly visible. Daimler-Benz, Europe's largest company, is a leading example of how an ill-matched agglomeration of businesses can result in appalling economic performance (see Case Study 2.1). The lesson of Daimler-Benz is that size does not guarantee profitability, and that often it has the opposite result. The notion that, when put together under common ownership, disparate businesses result in technological superiority and operational synergy is flawed. The recent experience of

---

Case Study 2.1.   Daimler-Benz

Since 1985, acquisitions have lost the shareholders of Daimler-Benz a cool DM 8 billion. One of the largest was the purchase, in 1986, of AEG, itself a large conglomerate with interests in activities ranging from white goods to trains, but with dominance in none. This and later acquisitions led the then chairman of the company, Edzard Reuter, to boast that Daimler had been transformed from a mere automobile manufacturer to an 'integrated technology group'.

But losses continued to accumulate and Daimler's stock price plummeted. In May 1995, Reuter was replaced by Jürgen Schrempp, the head of DASA, Daimler's aerospace subsidiary. Schrempp set about reducing the number of Daimler's businesses, which fell from 38 in 1994 to 25 by August 1996. To be retained by the group, businesses must now achieve a return of 12 per cent on capital employed. Almost 20,000 jobs were lost in 1994 alone as AEG was dismembered and divisions spun off. In January 1996, Daimler let Fokker, its Dutch aviation subsidiary, go into liquidation, and in June of that year it announced plans for the sale of Dornier, an aerospace company based in southern Germany.

Daimler is increasingly concentrating on the things it does best—manufacturing motor vehicles under the Mercedez-Benz and (post-merger) Chrysler names. The car maker's production costs have fallen by 35 per cent, making it allegedly the most profitable luxury car manufacturer in the world. However, more remains to be done in reversing 'the errors of thoughtless conglomerations'.

Sources: The Economist (1995*a*, 1996*a*), *Business Week* (1996).

British Petroleum (BP), an oil and chemicals conglomerate with operations in over seventy countries, also demonstrates the effect on performance of a restructuring strategy which is based on profitability criteria (see *The Economist* 1996*f*: 81).

Conventional management wisdom on what constitutes the ideal type of business organization shifted in the late 1980s, when academics were putting forward their ideas of 'shamrock organizations' and 'virtual corporations'. Charles Handy's shamrock organization is 'a form of organization based around a core of essential executives and workers supported by outside contractors and part-time help' (1989: 22). Its similarity to Davidow and Malone's virtual corporation is discernible: 'the virtual corporation will appear less as a discrete enterprise and more an ever-varying cluster of common activities in the midst of a vast fabric of relationships' (1992: 7). Both represent attempts to describe an organizational form in which a nucleus of 'core' activities is performed permanently in-house by full-time employees, the rest being supplied through contract with other organizations or individuals. Its hallmark is a relatively narrow focus - narrow compared to the degree of diversification of the erstwhile Daimler or BP - concentrating on activities in which it believes it has a distinct advantage, or that are essential to its competitive survival. How to identify such activities is a complex issue which will be discussed in the next two chapters. Benetton, the Italian clothing company, is frequently cited as the classic example of a virtual organization. Illustration 2.1, which briefly describes the structure of its operations, makes it clear why.

Illustration 2.1.   Benetton: the virtual organization

Benetton, which started as a family business in the late 1950s, sees itself neither as a manufacturer nor a retailer, but as a 'clothing services company'. It uses more than 500 subcontractors in the Veneto region, north of Venice. Approximately 80 per cent of production takes place in Italy, and Benetton's own operations are relatively small in terms of in-house staff. It has retained only the design, cutting, dyeing, and packing of garments which it markets under its own label, contracting out the remaining manufacturing operations. Its retail outlets are operated by independent entrepreneurs, enabling it to grow fast and to reduce working capital requirements. But unlike a conventional franchise system, the outlets do not pay royalties, nor does Benetton accept unsold stock from the retailers.

Sources: The Economist (1994*b*, 1996*b*), Lorenzoni and Baden-Fuller (1995).

Strategic networks and alliances have become popular variants of the modern, amorphous organizational structure. The strategic network is claimed to be capable of achieving the efficiency benefits of contracting, while retaining the informational and technological advantages of vertical integration. 'These companies act simultaneously as large integrated companies and as companies that concentrate on only a few things and sub-contract the rest' (Jarillo 1993: 5). The essential difference between ordinary contractors and those that are part of a network is the degree of cooperation and extensive information flows which are encouraged in the latter. Network contractors are made to feel like 'business partners' or members of the same team, working towards a common goal. There is an emphasis on cooperation and a playing down of the competitive threat of suppliers being displaced by potential rivals. In this respect a strategic network is almost indistinguishable from a strategic alliance, which is defined by Lewis (1995: 5) as 'a relationship between firms in which they cooperate to produce more value (or a lower cost) than is possible in a market transaction. To create that value, they must agree on what it is, on their need of each other to achieve it, and on sharing in the benefits.'

Toyota, the Japanese car giant, has its own distinctive way of structuring its relationships with suppliers, but it is often described as the best exemplar of a strategic network. Case Study 2.2 describes how it attempts to capture the efficiency of market transactions without losing the benefits of integration.

International contracting trends

It would be inaccurate to suggest that organizational networks are a new phenomenon. Companies like Marks & Spencer, for example, have had similarly cooperative relationships with their suppliers for nearly half a century. The difference is that while a decade or two ago Marks & Spencer was considered idiosyncratic in its contractual approach, today, it seems, there is no better way to do business. Whether this is actually so is a complex question, and it is inconceivable that a single organizational form will suit every circumstance. It is interesting to note that Marks & Spencer is actually moving away from the network concept and coming closer to the classic type of market transaction, by introducing competitive tendering for some of its bought-in services. But what is beyond doubt is that the vertically integrated, horizontally diversified organizations are not, in general, as competitive in the modern economic environment as they may have been before. Where the boundaries of the organization should now be drawn given its own particular circumstances, and how to structure contractual relationships, are questions which will be considered in later chapters of this book.

While there are many more contemporary examples of contracting, there are few reliable statistics from which to derive accurate trends. Detailing more case studies would serve no purpose other than to reinforce what should already be persuasive evidence: the scope for contracting is wide, and getting wider. And although, as already mentioned, statistical data are very scarce, occasional surveys and other attempts to quantify outsourcing trends suggest unremitting growth. Table 2.1 provides a quantitative and qualitative snapshot of recent contracting trends in the G5 economies, plus Australia. Separate information is given for the public and private sectors, to highlight any major differences.

Case Study 2.2.   Toyota: a strategic network

For a number of cultural and economic reasons, the Japanese system of production in manufacturing is very different from that in the United States. This is more obvious in the automobile industry than in any other manufacturing industry. While car makers in both countries extensively utilize contracting, the framework in which the contractual relationships take place is very different.

In the late 1980s, Toyota produced approximately 4.5 million cars per year with 65,000 employees, which is roughly 70 cars per employee. In contrast, General Motors produced 8 million cars with 750,000 employees, or roughly 10 cars per employee. Much of the difference between the two manufacturers is not attributable to differences in productivity, but to the fact that Toyota contracts almost all of the components needed to assemble its cars. This is only possible because of the cooperative basis with which Toyota enters into its contractual relationships.

Rather than rely on arm's-length relationships with a small number of suppliers, Toyota has a network of some 150 'primary' subcontractors which specialize in complete subsystems (e.g. brakes) required for their cars. A price for the subsystem is usually negotiated rather than achieved through a competitive process. Following specification of the subsystem, the primary contractor turns to a tier of 'secondary' subcontractors, of which there are more than 5,000 for the whole Toyota system, which produce the smaller parts necessary to assemble the specific subsystem. The relationships are often stabilized by financial means: Toyota owns minority stakes in many primary subcontractors, who in turn own minority stakes in the secondary subcontractors.

As a result of this, there is very little intra-system competition in the Toyota model: each primary contractor is a specialist in one area and is not constantly threatened with the possibility of losing its contract with Toyota. Even if the primary subcontractor's quality of work deteriorated, Toyota would not simply replace it, but would reduce the volume of work assigned to that primary subcontractor and attempt to help it iron out its problems. There is a clear sense that all parties are working towards a common objective. As a result, subcontractors are encouraged to contribute to the design and development of the product, learning is supported throughout the system, and any advances in production know-how are shared with others—even if they may be potential competitors. Subcontractors view any improvements to production techniques as advantageous to the whole system because they ensure additional sales and future profits for the entire network to share.

In the Toyota model, competition never occurs at the level of the individual company, rather, it is a competition of Toyota's network against Nissan's network. It is not that competition is not fierce, it is just that it only occurs at the level of the final product. The result of all of this is that Japanese cars are generally built at a higher quality and a lower price than any other car manufacturer is able to do. While American car manufacturers like General Motors have tried to replicate the Japanese production system, their efforts have largely been unsuccessful.

Source: Adapted from Jarillo (1993).

Table 2.1. International contracting trends

Country	Public sector	Private sector
USA	Contracting widespread at local and state level since the 1970s. Extent depends on type of function, local personalities, and varying legislation. Federal National Performance Review reduces regulation of contracting to save on administration. Federal procurement 1995: $202.3bn[a] (approx. 65% defence).	Total market for outsourced services was estimated to be $100bn in 1996. It is particularly widespread in the IT and business services area. Forecasts suggest continued growth.
UK	*Local government*: compulsory competitive tendering replaced by 'best value' programme; total local government procurement 1986: £10.9 bn.[b] *Central government*: increasing emphasis on public–private sector 'partnerships'.	Contracting growth especially since the late 1970s. Widespread use by manufacturing and service industries, possibly some regional differences.
France	Contracting mainly by small, rural authorities, until reform of Paris service delivery in 1980s; tightly regulated by CMP law; central buying of goods available; preference schemes benefit co-ops; total local government procurement 1986: £18.7bn.[c]	French companies have benefited from reform of water distribution system and developed into large multinational contracting specialists.
Germany	*Federal government*: no federal push for contracting. *Local government*: total procurement 1986: £19.6bn[d] at municipal level only; most widespread for essential services; contract awarded not to lowest, but best-value bidder.	Strict labour and co-determination laws for large private companies make it difficult to implement reform which might result in job losses. Contracting pioneered primarily by car industry.
Japan	Decentralized national and local government purchasing, requires inclusion in a list of qualified suppliers before tendering. Contracts mostly awarded on price. 1993 national procurement: £6.6bn.[e] In 1994, procurement laws were reformed after international treaties.	Traditional subcontracting alliance (keiretsu): long-term partnership, trust, information exchange, little competitive pressure. Used by 48% of all Japanese firms. However, keiretsu under threat from economic strains.
Australia	*Federal government*: gradual implementation since the 1980s; federal public sector expenditure in 1994/5 estimated to be $A8bn. *State governments*: mixed; total value estimated to be $A3.3bn in 1993/4.[f] *Local government*: varies; compulsory in Victoria since 1994.	Widespread use of contracting by multinationals and local firms. Growing awareness as a result of 'National Competition Policy' and other government actions

[a] US General Services Administration (1995: 2).
[b] Digings (1991: 173), calculated from Eurostat, *General Government Accounts and Statistics 1970–1986* (1989).
[c] Digings (1991: 173).
[d] Digings (1991: 173).
[e] *Government Procurement Statistics for 1993*, Article VI: 10 (a).
[f] Industry Commission (1996: 59).

It can be seen that in the USA contracting, more commonly referred to as outsourcing in that country, has grown particularly swiftly in the private sector. Unofficial estimates suggest that by the end of 1996 outsourcing by American business will have created 'a nascent industry with annual revenues of US$100 billion' (Byrne, 1996: 28). The same source also suggested that there has been an increase in overall contracting of services of approximately 28 per cent between 1992 and 1996.

By contrast, the growth in contracting in the American public sector has been less spectacular, with defence procurement being the traditional area in which government made significant purchases from private industry. With the ending of the cold war, defence procurement has reached a turning point: in 1996 procurement expenditure reached its lowest level since 1950, and the defence budget has fallen from 27.0 per cent of total federal expenditure in 1980 to 15.5 per cent in 1996.

In Britain, the 1988 Local Government Act made competitive tendering for local authority services compulsory, creating a market for service contracts worth around £2.5 billion annually in 1994, from a paltry £50 million a decade earlier. In central government services, contracts worth £1.8 billion have been awarded in the last few years. There is every indication that the market testing programme is set to continue and that contracting for services by local and central government will continue to grow. Fewer figures are available in the private sector, but all indications are that both manufacturing and service industries are contracting for support services. Johnson Controls supplies IBM UK with facilities management services; BLS, a subsidiary of Federal Express, provides warehousing services to Laura Ashley, and Sainsbury, the food retailing chain, contracts out two-thirds of its distribution services.

In the Antipodes, contracting out has become a major element of the public sector restructuring process. New Zealand has led the way with a complete overhaul of the public sector finances, privatization of public sector enterprises, and corporatization of many publicly owned trading enterprises. Contracting out is particularly widespread in local government, much of it undertaken by or for LATEs—Local Authority Trading Enterprises—which are also encouraged to compete with private sector contractors for the provision of government-funded services elsewhere in the public sector.

Quantitative information has recently become available in Australia as a result of surveys and government inquiries into competitive tendering and contracting in the public sector. The findings are revealing. In New South Wales, the most populous state in Australia, the value of contracts awarded has grown from $A500 million in 1993, to $A1.5 billion in 1995. The most commonly contracted services include information technology, building maintenance, finance and accounting, legal and transport services. It has been estimated by the Industry Commission that the total value of contracts let by the three levels of government in Australia—federal, state, and local—was $A13.3 billion in the financial year 1994–5. When purchases of goods are added, the combined value rises to approximately $A30 billion. Less is known about the scale of contracting in the private sector. However, conventional wisdom suggests that it is becoming widespread: 'every business in Australia is looking at it in some form', according to an article in a popular business magazine.

For the other major industrialized countries for which data are given in Table 2.1—France, Germany, and Japan—the contracting picture is rather blurred. Japan, for example, has had a long-standing and successful subcontracting culture in many manufacturing industries. Whether these 'keiretsu' relationships are likely to change with the pressures now facing the Japanese economy is unclear. In Germany, competitive pressures in the public sector are set to rise, and with them the use of competitive tendering and contracting. And France, which was one of the pioneers of contracting of municipal services in the nineteenth century, has a group of large, multinational suppliers of management services such as Lyonnaise des Eaux and Générale des Eaux, who now bid for contracts not only on their home ground but in markets as far flung as Asia and the Pacific Rim.

Taking stock of the broad sweep of this international evidence, two conclusions stand out. First, contracting out is permeating the public and private sectors with approximately equal force. Neither sector is therefore immune to those forces which are encouraging the use of competitive, market solutions for service provision. Second, although not reported in the table, the evidence, which will be reviewed in detail later in this book, suggests that contractual solutions *can* yield significant economic benefits, both in terms of cost savings and in terms of the effectiveness of service delivery.

A more detailed analysis of the forces propelling organizations towards contractual solutions would be useful. These forces are changing the nature of both the private and public sectors, and they will be considered according to this division.

Factors driving organizational change in the private sector

The forces which are making companies transform themselves are shrouded in speculation and hyperbole. The usual suspects are globalization, competition from low-wage developing countries, and advances in communications and information technology. The sheer magnitude of these forces is given vivid expression in comments like the following: 'Many feel that Adam Smith's invisible hand is trying to push them off a cliff' (*The Economist* 1996c: 3).

It is useful to think of these external forces as emanating from two distinct groups of markets: markets for outputs of goods and services, and capital markets. In output markets, competitive forces have intensified because of rapid changes in demand and supply conditions. Technological change, for example in telecommunications, affects the demand for services, offering a new range of services such as mobile telephony. As demand shifts, expenditure patterns change and firms may find their traditional sources of revenue shrinking.

On the supply side, technological change also affects production methods, requiring implementation of new processes for companies to stay competitive. Just-in-time manufacturing techniques and digitalization of telemarketing services are but two contemporary examples of such innovations. Also on the supply side, new sources of cheap labour, particularly in the Asia-Pacific region, can render manufacturing operations in the high-wage economies unprofitable. Contract manufacturing can be seen as a direct response to this development. GE contracted out the production of microwave ovens to Samsung of South Korea because it could perform the manufacturing operations more cheaply. Another American example, this time from the computer industry, is the manufacturing of parts for laptop computers. Compaq uses Japanese suppliers for the manufacture of LCD screens, power management systems, and other miniaturized parts. Some commentators lament this 'hollowing out' of US manufacturers and warn that it makes them strategically vulnerable. The case that is often cited in this context is GE and Samsung: GE eventually quit the microwave oven business altogether while Samsung became the world's largest producer of the appliances. This case is discussed further in Chapter 6.

However, the economics that underlie these developments are not difficult to understand. Supply side forces are leading to a greater degree of specialization, both geographical and technological, in many production activities. Competition on a global scale means that there is less room for inefficient producers. The search for greater efficiency in turn leads to increased specialization and contracting is a central manifestation of this trend. Not everyone is applauding these developments. Some management commentators are deeply concerned about the social costs imposed by such restructuring. Harrison (1994: 11), for example, claims that 'Although represented as state-of-the-art management, the practice of lean production involves the explicit reinforcement or creation of sectors of low-wage contingent workers, frequently employed by small business.' Nevertheless, small business can develop into big business, and the structural changes on the supply side must be seen as part of a dynamic process which brings longer-term benefits.

The pressures for change in output markets are receiving a substantial boost from capital markets. The capital market is where valuations of a listed company's stock take place. If shareholders are dissatisfied with the returns on investment generated by management, the stock price will move to reflect this and the company will, sooner or later, become a takeover target. Since the mid-1980s, a slow but swelling shareholders' revolt, particularly in the Anglo-Saxon economies, has placed management under intense pressure to increase returns.

The latent tensions between the shareholders and managers of firms have become a matter of considerable debate. Known as the 'corporate governance' issue, it concerns the efficacy of the capital market, whose distinctive feature is the separation of ownership from corporate control, in allocating financial resources so as to maximize shareholders' returns. Doubts over the workings of the corporate governance system have led to tighter supervision of, and larger rewards for, management's efforts to raise corporate profits (see Bishop 1994).

Just when observers of capitalist corporate governance were beginning to view the German-Japanese stakeholder model as a preferred alternative, these same countries have begun moving towards the Anglo-American governance structures. The principal characteristics of the German and Japanese systems are close relationships with the banks, strong stakeholder representation on management and supervisory boards, and a far greater consensus in decision making. Their most striking feature is the relative absence of contested takeovers.

The fate of German conglomerates, such as Daimler-Benz, was examined earlier. It is worth adding that Daimler has recently been listed on the New York stock exchange and has thus signalled its closer allegiance to the traditional shareholder model of corporate control. Wherever capital market discipline has intensified, the result has been a reduction in the internal and external scope of business activity, leading to increased contracting for goods and services. Little wonder that competition is seen to be the driving force behind the virtual corporation. IBM contracts with component manufacturers and facilities management service providers; Sun Microsystems contracts with Fujitsu, Philips, Texas Instruments, and Toshiba; Ford outsources paint finishing to ABB; Motorola contracts with Apple. The list is virtually endless.

Two distinctive features characterize the process of corporate fragmentation. The first is a growing degree of specialization, which has already been noted. The other is the increasingly complex nature of the services being contracted out. This is partly the reason why such transactions require close strategic interaction between purchaser and provider, frequently involving long-term contractual relationships. These transactions appear to have a host of natural enemies: concerns about loss of skills, about loss of expertise in strategically important areas and the adverse consequences of potential 'hold up' of the purchaser by the provider. These troublesome but important questions will be considered in detail when the costs of contracting are identified and evaluated.

Public sector organizations: from bureaucracies to enabling agencies

The public sector has exhibited no lesser penchant for size than its private counterpart. In those countries with a substantial public sector, particularly Australia, France, and the UK, public sector corporations in the transport, communications, and energy sectors grew to be very large indeed. But once again, the accumulated evidence showed that size, and even statutory monopoly in certain markets, was no guarantee of superior performance. Despite that, in the late 1960s, the UK Labour government introduced an explicit policy to encourage conglomerate mergers and acquisitions, both in the private and the public sectors. Larger-scale and vertical integration were expected to lead to the introduction of the 'white heat of technology'. This hope was never realized.

By the 1980s, Britain's Thatcher administration embarked on a wholesale privatization programme which had, as one of its objectives, the break-up of the nationalized industries into smaller entities, allowing greater competition and introducing some capital market discipline. The privatization movement has since gathered momentum in many other countries, and alongside it came the contracting out of publicly funded services from refuse collection to air traffic control services and prison management. Today, the public sector organizations that were formerly producers of services are quaintly referred to as 'enabling authorities'. In practice this means that they are no longer producers but purchasers of goods and services on behalf of the community for whom they act.

The push towards contracting in the public sector has come from several directions. First, the overarching influence has been the post-1970s global attenuation in economic growth, which has brought tighter budgets and pressure on public services worldwide. Nowhere was this pressure felt more keenly than in the Britain of the late 1970s. When Margaret Thatcher's Conservative administration took office in May 1979, the state of public sector finances was parlous. Worse still, the lack of consistency and quality of public services such as transport, communications, and even local council refuse collection services was a national joke. Public sector strikes were frequent and damaging, union power was at its zenith, and the gaping deficits of the public sector corporations were causing concern.

The UK privatization programme, which became the symbol of the Thatcher era, changed all that. Alongside the steady transfer of ownership of the former public enterprises, another, less glamorous revolution was taking hold. It began in 1988, when the Local Government Act made competitive tendering and contracting compulsory for a wide range of municipal services. Research published a few years earlier had shown that considerable financial savings could be realized through competitive tendering, yet very few local authorities (municipalities) in England and Wales had implemented it. Central government felt compelled to introduce legislation forcing local government reforms.

By 1994, the value of municipal services contracted out in England and Wales was approaching £3 billion. Critics have argued that central government control over the programme, through the Department of the Environment, places local government in a straitjacket, that cost savings have been overestimated and quality adversely affected, and that citizens' democratic control rights are being undermined. The UK Labour administration which came into office in 1997 has since repealed the compulsory element of competitive tendering in local government, but remains committed to competition as an important management tool.

The drive by the previous UK government towards competitive service provision has gone well beyond municipal services, to white-collar activities performed within the civil service bureaucracy. A broad collection of services, from facilities management, information technology, accounting and finance, to even the management of the Cabinet Office support and secretarial functions, are now performed by private contractors. The value of services provided under contract to central government, as at June 1995, was estimated to be £2.6 billion.

In the United States, the role of market mechanisms in public sector service provision was given a serious boost with the publication of *Reinventing Government* by Osborne and Gaebler (1992), a polemic on the apparent sclerosis in American government institutions and on ways of combating it. The book emphasized the merits of competition and customer choice as a means of delivering better, more cost-effective services to the community. But the call to use the market for the provision of a whole range of public services was made several years earlier by Savas (1987), in the book entitled *Privatization: The Key to Better Government.*

Despite the widespread influence of the would-be public sector reformers, the US federal administration has not implemented a competitive service programme on the scale seen in the United Kingdom. Defence procurement has been, and continues to be, a joint private–public sector endeavour, although the methods of selecting defence contractors have been subject to frequent criticisms, particularly from academics. At local government level the use of competitive tendering is patchy: the city of Denver has contracted out enthusiastically in recent times, while other municipalities have variously considered and implemented market testing. Budgetary pressures are providing strong incentives to extract greater value from the taxpayer's dollar. But bureaucratic inertia, coupled with political concerns over job losses for public employees, have slowed the process down, in some cases impeding it altogether.

Australia and New Zealand have embarked on a vigorous programme of public sector reform, of which contracting out is a significant component. Between 1984 and 1990, under a Labour administration, New Zealand practically dismantled its public sector, undertaking what is arguably the most radical government restructuring in the Western world. Under a wholesale programme of privatization and corporatization—the latter being a half-way house between public sector ownership and private sector corporate governance—it has transformed its sleepy government departments into commercial enterprises. Many have been sold outright to private sector operators and others, which have been corporatized, operate under public ownership with more or less strict commercial guidelines.

At local government level, New Zealand has adopted a non-prescriptive, mixed model of service delivery. LATEs were explicitly provided for in the 1989 amendments to the Local Government Act. They are business entities, often corporatized under local authority ownership, and ultimately accountable to democratically elected local government. LATEs are the commercial arms of local councils in New Zealand, providing services to local and regional communities by bidding against private sector service providers. However, the central government does not require local council services to be provided only by LATEs; council departments and semi-commercial business units also operate in this market. The cities of Dunedin and Christchurch have reported significant savings in the cost of local services since the introduction of competition.

Australia has proved to be one of the more interesting experiments in public sector contracting. Unlike the UK and New Zealand, where there is a unitary system of government, Australia has a federal structure. The states have considerable discretion over health, transport, education, and community welfare programmes. They also pass local government legislation and thus have the power to determine the extent to which authorities are required to use competitive tendering and contracting. Some states in Australia, in particular New South Wales, Victoria, and Western Australia, have introduced comprehensive policies and programmes in recent years. Victoria, under a reforming Liberal (conservative) administration, passed legislation in 1994 making competitive tendering compulsory for 50 per cent of local council expenditure. Other arms of the state's administration are also encouraged to contract out, and the Department of Treasury and Finance has set up a dedicated 'Outsourcing and Contracting Management Unit', to monitor and advise on effective policy implementation.

During thirteen years of Labor administration, the Commonwealth (federal) government delivered much rhetoric about public sector reform, but relatively few deeds, largely because of opposition from the organized labour movement. This is changing under a fiscally conservative Liberal/National government elected in March 1996. It has pledged to eliminate the public sector deficit during its term of office, and to bring in measures, including contracting out of publicly funded services, which rely more heavily on market mechanisms.

Australia can reasonably be viewed as a unique laboratory in which the effects of independent and diverse policy initiatives can be observed and evaluated. The patchwork of results can be directly linked to the type of policy employed in each state or local government, its duration, and the intensity with which it was policed. It is interesting to note that although the policy stance towards contracting for services differs from state to state, in terms of implementation the trend is uniformly upward. Whether slowly or rapidly, whether opposition is muted or extreme, contracting appears to be taking hold at all levels of Australian government.

Lastly, another significant aspect of the diffusion of contracting is its effect on the boundaries between the private and the public sectors. Sturgess (1993: 1) has suggested that in a couple of decades or so it may become impossible to distinguish between publicly and privately provided services. Most of the service activities which are being put to tender, and which were previously performed within the public sector, will have been transferred to private contractors. But many or most of these services will remain publicly funded.

The nature of the emerging contractual relationships between public sector clients and private sector providers will be the key to determining whether the arrangements will be sustainable. As Sturgess also pointed out, part of the reason why the state became involved in so much economic activity that the market was capable of handling was ostensibly the looming concerns over probity and accountability. Self-interest may be all very well in the context of profit-oriented enterprises, but the public interest demands a clear separation of individual and collective motives. Whether contracting for public services can deliver efficiency and effectiveness as well as probity and accountability is the subject of continuing controversy, and a topic which will be revisited later in this book. What seems beyond doubt is that those same economic pressures that have driven companies to greater specialization and fragmentation have been the underlying cause of the quest for better value from government activities.

Guide to further reading

Coase (1937) is *the* classic treatise on why firms exist and how firms choose between producing goods and services internally and purchasing them in the marketplace. Chesbrough and Teece (1996) provide an excellent critique of the benefits of the virtual organization, focusing in particular on the impact that integrated companies can have on the innovation process.

A futuristic vision of the amorphous corporation of the twenty-first century and the virtual products that these companies produce is given by Davidow and Malone (1992). Drucker (1995) provides an illuminating snapshot of the role that outsourcing and other 'network' phenomena play in the modern, post-industrial society. For an earlier and lengthier variation on the same theme see Handy (1989). A comprehensive review of network forms of organization, including partnerships and strategic alliances, is provided by Powell (1990).

Handy (1995) is a thought-provoking article on the importance of trust and the complexities of managing staff in virtual organizations. Hart (1989) gives a comprehensive summary of the differing theories of the firm, including principal–agent theory and transaction cost theory and Hart's own pioneering work on property rights theory. For a management perspective on changing organizational boundaries, both internal and external, see Ashkenas et al. (1995)

Rappaport and Halevi (1991) is a provocative article which provides a blueprint for the virtual organization through its assertion that the most powerful computer companies are those that define how computers are used rather than how they are manufactured. Bettis et al. (1992) take the view that outsourcing can go too far, leading to industrial decline.

II

BENEFITS AND COSTS

The two chapters in this section outline the benefits and costs of contracting. While there is merit in separating costs from benefits, and that is how managers intuitively think of the issue, the separation is not always easily achieved. As far as costs go, as Milgrom and Roberts (1992: 34) observed: 'The lesson is that although the costs of transacting are real, they are not always easily separated from other kinds of costs.' Similarly, many of the concepts raised under the benefits heading also appear under the guise of costs in Chapter 4. For example, organizational capability is discussed in the benefits chapter in terms of the potential advantages that contracting can bring by allowing firms to focus on their 'core competencies'. But the same concept also appears under costs, when the discussion shifts to the detrimental effects of organizational 'hollowing out'—the result of contracting out too much. Hence costs and benefits become two sides of the same coin, which may not be particularly helpful as a framework for decision making. Therefore, having identified and explored the benefits and costs in the following chapters, there is need to establish which contracting strategies are the most influential in determining cost and benefit outcomes. That is the subject of Part III.

3

The Benefits of Contracting

> Whenever a company produces something internally that others can buy
> or produce more efficiently and effectively, it sacrifices competitive advan-
> tage.
>
> (James Quinn, Thomas Doorley, and Penny Paquette, 1990)

The nature of economic activity

Before discussing the benefits of contracting, it helps to understand the nature
of economic activity. At its most basic level, it can be thought of as two distinct
activities: production and exchange. Production involves transforming raw
materials into finished goods and services, using labour, capital, and other
inputs. Exchange means entering into transactions by which goods or services
are traded for others, sometimes through barter, but more commonly using
money as a medium of exchange.

The extent to which economic activity generates wealth depends on the
efficiency of both production and exchange. Improvements in production
have depended directly on technological advances. The Industrial Revolution,
which first stirred in England in the middle of the eighteenth century, was
propelled by significant innovations in spinning and weaving technology,
followed by major developments in transport (railways) and other industries
which benefited from the application of steam technology. Rapid advances in
information and communications technology over the past two decades are
said to be ushering in a new Industrial Revolution, a knowledge-based society
whose ultimate character is still the subject of much speculation.

But economic development depends in no small measure on the scope for
exchange. The Industrial Revolution was bolstered by the opening up of world
markets for textiles and other manufactured goods. Markets for a wide range of
commodities proliferated, with London claiming the lion's share by virtue of its
status as trading capital of the world. In addition, financial services were
increasing in sophistication, allowing the mobilization of vast amounts of
capital across continents.

Most transactions can be characterized by 'spot contracts', defined as simple bilateral exchange. The good or service is clearly observable, the price is given or struck by agreement, as are the terms of settlement. 'Sharp in by clear agreement; sharp out by clear performance' is a legal scholar's representation of spot contracts (Macneil 1974: 738). The purchase of a book from a bookshop is a good example of a spot contract: the price is posted on the book, the terms are simple, the transaction quickly concluded. In foreign exchange and some commodity and financial markets, forward and future contracts are also entered into. These consist of transactions in which prices are agreed at the time when the contract is drawn up, but settlement of the transaction—the exchange—takes place at some predetermined future date. Since spot prices vary considerably over time, but the contract price is fixed, such transactions transfer risk associated with future price movements from one side of the market to the other. They facilitate the management of price uncertainty by letting those who can more efficiently bear the risk do so. However, in terms of 'clear agreement and clear performance' they are no different from spot contracts.

Most contractual relationships between organizations are not spot contracts. In business-to-business relationships, the nature of the transaction requires a different kind of contract altogether. To see why, we must briefly consider the nature of productive activity.

The structure of production

Modern production of goods and services is characterized by complexity. The typical family car is assembled from 4,500 to 6,000 different parts. The tasks required to complete the finished product include moulding, soldering, wiring, painting, fitting, and upholstering. Managing a retail department store is also a highly complex task, involving not only the merchandising of goods, but also the coordination of a multitude of services, such as lighting, ventilation, cleaning, security, and maintenance. In both cases, it is useful to distinguish intermediate demand from final demand. Intermediate goods and services are demanded not for final consumption, but for use in the production of final output. Steel is a good example of an intermediate input. It is used in the production of motor cars, as are alternators, speedometers, and radiators. In the retail services example, the final output is the retail merchandise; all the support services which are necessary to make retailing possible are intermediate services.

This distinction between intermediate and final production is important to the analysis of industrial structure. It allows government statisticians to measure the extent to which industries are linked to one another through the intermediate transactions chain. In Chapter 8 it will be used to examine, in some detail, the evolution of the services sector in the economy. But the significance of this distinction goes beyond issues of measurement to the heart of organizational strategy.

Every organization that breaks down the production process (also known as the value chain) into a series of intermediate steps leading to a final output faces an important choice: how much intermediate output to produce for its own consumption, and how much to buy in from other organizations? The introductory chapters of this book suggested that there is a general trend to do more purchasing from outside and less in-house production of the requisite intermediate products. But the ratio of intermediate input purchases to final output does vary significantly from firm to firm within particular industries.

Take car manufacturing as an example. Japanese firms such as Toyota and Nissan purchase approximately 80 per cent of the components required for their vehicle assembly from other firms. By contrast, American auto manufacturers such as Ford and General Motors, at around 50 and 30 per cent respectively, buy in substantially smaller proportions of manufactured parts. Among European companies, BMW buys in a high 80 per cent of vehicle components used in assembly, while other German automobile producers, like Mercedez-Benz and Volkswagen, are increasing the number of components made in-house. In the retailing industry, most department-store owners would be expected to manage the support services necessary to keep their retail facilities functioning efficiently. However, Marks & Spencer chose not to do so; instead it took the strategic step of contracting out the entire management of its store maintenance functions.

What is the basis for such choice, and why is it that what appears to suit one company is not necessarily adopted by another? If the contracting trend is merely a fad lacking a sound business case, devotion will quickly turn to disillusion. What, then, drives the decision to contract out, and which goods and services are considered appropriate candidates for contracting in the modern corporation or public sector organization?

Core activities and core competencies

In recent years, the growth of contracting has led to the popularization of the concept of 'core activity'. Conventional wisdom states that core activities stay in-house; non-core activities can be contracted out. Behind the beguiling simplicity of this distinction lies a web of ambiguity. A recent paper by Alexander and Young (1996) suggests that there are four meanings commonly associated with 'core activity'. They are:

- activities traditionally performed in-house;
- activities critical to business performance;
- activities creating current or potential competitive advantage;
- activities that will drive future growth, innovation, or rejuvenation.

The first definition is clearly unsatisfactory since it is tautological: core activities are produced within the organization; everything that is retained is a core activity. Taken to extremes, one could argue that almost all intermediate activities could be essential to business performance. In this context, core business becomes a slogan, one that becomes inappropriately used to justify the organizational status quo. The three remaining definitions are more searching, but difficult to apply in practice. How they might be properly applied has spawned a new branch of management literature known as 'strategic sourcing'.

Like most fashionable management terminology, strategic sourcing means somewhat different things to different people. However, a common-sense interpretation is that it involves making contracting for goods and services part of an organization's overall strategy formulation. That means determining the scope of the organization's internal activities by reference to its overall objectives, in contrast to the view that contracting is something organizations resort to when there is a pressing need to save money or get around a difficult industrial relations problem.

Some management theorists suggest that sound contracting decisions involve identifying and securing core competencies: 'Strategically outsource other activities—including many traditionally considered integral to any company—for which the firm has neither a critical strategic need nor special capabilities' (Quinn and Hilmer 1994: 43). They also maintain that many executives are confused about what core competence actually means. But however imprecisely grasped, the search for core competence has become something of a corporate decision maker's quest for the Holy Grail. Its influence has grown in recent years, and it deserves closer examination.

Core competence burst into managerial consciousness at about the same time as the pressures of globalization and technological change had created a strong demand for new business paradigms. It is defined as 'the collective learning in the organization, especially how to coordinate diverse production skills and integrate multiple streams of technology' (Prahalad and Hamel 1990: 82). According to them, core competence is essentially a bundle of corporate skills that can be put to work in producing different products, both current and future. For that reason they also cautioned companies against thinking that they are simply businesses making products. Instead, they urged companies to cultivate the competencies which will be more enduring than the products they currently produce, will not diminish with use, and will be the platform from which they will launch new and successful products in the future. Examples of core competencies cited by Prahalad and Hamel are Sony's capacity to miniaturize components and audio-visual products, and Philips's optical media expertise and its applications.

As for the benefits of contractual relationships with suppliers, they caution that 'outsourcing can provide a shortcut to a more competitive product, but it typically contributes little to building the people-embodied skills that are needed to sustain product leadership' (1990: 84). In other words, contracting the provision of key parts and components can lose an organization its core competence, or the opportunity to create one. And although Prahalad and

Hamel acknowledge that most companies cannot realistically acquire more than five or six core competencies, the thrust of their argument suggests that organizations must stop to think carefully before they 'surrender' economic activity to an outside supplier. The word surrender is used deliberately here, to highlight the perception that a transaction for an intermediate product or service carries a potential loss as well as a gain. That warning, of itself, does not help determine whether the benefits *exceed* the losses.

Two aspects of the core competence concept need to be noted. First, the concept is most easily applied in the context of technology-intensive economic activities. It is no coincidence that most of the examples cited by the originators of the concept come from high-tech industries including multimedia, telecommunications, electronics, and the like. In these areas technological know-how can be risky and costly to acquire. It often forms the basis upon which whole new product lines and industries are founded. Clearly, protecting that technical knowledge becomes central to keeping ahead of competitors in the race for market leadership. But much business and economic activity does not depend on technological wizardry. The fear of losing technological competence to potential competitors through contracting may, in many cases, be groundless.

The second point is that searching for, and holding on to, core competencies is not helpful in establishing a sound methodology for deciding what should be contracted to outside suppliers. Consider the following example. An organization is able to establish that it has unambiguous core competencies in two complementary activities. The firm is producing both the intermediate and the final product and, compared to outside suppliers, it is more productive in the manufacture of both. But now suppose that it transpires that the firm is actually most efficient at producing the final product, compared to the intermediate one. Should it contract out the provision of the intermediate product and specialize in the manufacture of final output?

The core competence argument would unequivocally say no. Yet it would be demonstrably more efficient, and profitable, if the organization did indeed specialize in final production and contracted for intermediate inputs. To see the benefit of contracting in this perspective it is necessary to invoke a profound, but poorly understood, economic insight: that there are benefits to specialization.

The essence of specialization is based on the principle of *relative* efficiency. This concept was articulated in the nineteenth century by the English economist David Ricardo, who put forward the proposition in a simple but compelling way: 'Two men can both make shoes and hats, and one is superior to the other in both employments; but in making hats he can only exceed his competitor by one fifth or 20 per cent, and in making shoes he can excel him by one third or 33 per cent. Will it not be for the interest of both, that the superior man should employ himself exclusively in making shoes, and the inferior man in making hats?' (Ricardo 1817: 153). What Microsoft did in outsourcing the support function for Windows 95 can be recognized as being essentially a similar step. However, in a business context this proposition is weakened by the fact that skills and capabilities of one firm are purchasable by another, thus reducing the advantages of specialization. But the empirical evidence on mergers and acquisitions suggests that such diversification of business activity by firms does not typically yield the expected benefits (Bishop and Kay 1993).

Of course, to say that there are advantages to be derived from specialization is a far cry from stating where and how such specialization should take place. How do organizations establish where their relative efficiency lies? What type of contractual arrangements should they adopt for the external provision of goods and services? The practical application of these principles is much more demanding in the context of a complex chain of productive processes. Before addressing these issues, the remaining benefits of contracting will be considered.

The force of competition

When an organization first contemplates contracting a good or service previously produced in-house, it effectively considers abandoning vertical integration in favour of a market transaction. Entering into such a transaction involves transacting with other businesses which may not always be privately owned, profit-motivated, organizations. Yet many public sector organizations in, for example, Britain and Australia, when choosing to contract, frequently allow their in-house service provider to bid against outside competitors.

It is useful to digress briefly in order to contrast the discipline of private ownership with that of competition. The discipline of private ownership can be traced to the capital market. Shareholders in companies which are under-performing relative to expectations can express their displeasure simply by disposing of their stock. And they do. In due course, and if the numbers involved are of sufficient magnitude, the share price in such companies will fall to levels which make them attractive takeover targets. A hostile takeover bid which is successful means that the incumbent management is replaced by that of the successful bidder. Hence the threat of takeover is a powerful mechanism by which the endeavours of management in the private sector are aligned with the objectives of shareholders.

Such a mechanism is clearly absent in publicly owned enterprises, which have been known to under-perform for years without any countervailing influences. Without a doubt this has been a significant factor in the worldwide popularity of privatization—the sale of publicly owned enterprises to private investors. And although it is widely acknowledged that privatization has generally improved economic performance, the power of competitive forces to influence performance, irrespective of ownership, continues to surprise.

Much evidence has been accumulated in recent years to suggest that the mere exposure to competition of in-house service providers is sufficient to elicit significant changes in working practices, innovative approaches to work redesign, and, as a consequence, significant cost savings. What is equally interesting is that those savings arise whether the providers in question are privately or publicly owned. It would appear that the force of competition is not only powerful, but independent of the discipline of ownership. This statement should be qualified somewhat by adding that this evidence tends to be confined to situations where competition occurs between privately owned and publicly owned providers: for example, an in-house IT operation is competing against bids for software and hardware maintenance by external, privately owned specialists. The evidence could conceivably be less convincing if competition was confined entirely to the public sector.

Fig. 3.1 depicts the results of an international survey of over 200 studies which examined the effect of introducing competition for service provision. The distribution shows the percentage of studies which reported cost increases within a particular range shown on the horizontal axis, running

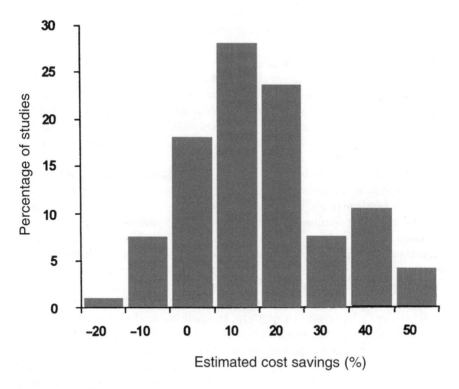

Source: Industry Commission (1996).

Fig. 3.1. Distribution of cost savings: 200 international studies

through to those which reported cost decreases of up to 50 per cent or more. Two features of this distribution should be noted. First, the cases where cost increases were recorded, where *negative* cost savings are shown on the left-hand side of the chart, were very rare: not more than 1 per cent for cost increases of 10 per cent or more, and not more than 5 for increases of 10 per cent or less.

Second, the most frequently recorded contracting experiences indicated cost savings between 10 and 30 per cent of previous expenditures. This range is consistent with the 20 per cent figure most commonly cited for the average savings associated with competitive tendering. That the range of outcomes sometimes shows a cost increase is not entirely surprising. Competition only yields savings where there is scope for greater efficiency to start with, and where competition itself is effective. For example, the in-house service provider may already have been highly efficient, perhaps because of the threat of impending competition, in which case additional savings may be minimal. Also, if the number of potential competitors is small or their expertise is inadequate, the introduction of competition will yield little or no additional savings.

But there is another, equally plausible explanation: that when goods and services that were previously produced internally are exposed to competition for the first time, their qualitative characteristics are often changed. A success-ful transition from vertical integration to market transaction cannot take place without an explicit specification of inputs or outputs. When such a change in mode of supply takes place specifications are typically revised, enhanced, or sometimes even compiled for the very first time. A change in specifications would lead to a change in costs, even if no other changes were implemented. Few of the studies included in the chart were able to control for the changes in specifications and this factor alone could account for some of the variations in costs changes observed.

Over thirty years ago Professor Harvey Leibenstein observed that: 'Clearly there is more to the determination of output than the obviously observable inputs. The nature of the management, the environment in which it operates, and the incentives employed are significant' (Leibenstein 1966: 401). This was the basis for the popular concept which he brought to light and referred to as X-efficiency. Behind this concept lay the empirically incontestable proposition that the level of output of any organization can vary significantly and inde-pendently of the level of inputs. Getting more outputs for a given level of inputs would constitute an improvement in X-efficiency. Motivational factors were seen by Leibenstein as important, and nothing works on motivation quite like competition. In his own words (Leibenstein 1966: 412): 'The level of unit cost depends in some measure on the degree of X-efficiency, which in turn depends on the degree of competitive pressure, as well as other motivational factors.' By introducing such competitive pressures, contracting has the same effect on unit costs. It is interesting to observe that organizations often use contracting as a means of bringing about changes in work practices that they have been unable to introduce themselves. There is therefore an obvious connection between contracting and the concept of X-efficiency.

The power of competition in elevating performance, not just in the business world but also in the realm of sport, art, and literature, is so pervasive that it is taken for granted. But one particularly telling illustration of its positive impact comes from the CEO of an international provider of contract services to government and industry. The company in question is a rapidly growing, UK-based specialist in systems engineering and task and facilities management. It holds over 300 contracts worldwide for services as diverse as operating the ballistic missile early warning system in the UK, and managing operations and maintenance of water treatment and distribution in Australia. Illustration 3.1 comprises the transcript of an interview between the author and the CEO of the company. The key message from this transcript is the role that the company assigns to competition: it uses it as an external management tool. In the presence of recurring competition, the company does not have to engage in costly and cumbersome monitoring of its contractual activities. Contract managers know that the threat of competition is always just around the corner. Since managers and the workforce want to keep their jobs, the net result is an organization whose efficiency is regulated by the market. Senior management can afford to take a light-handed approach secure in the knowledge that the pressure of competition is never far away.

Illustration 3.1. Management by competition

Q. I presume that your organization prefers to bid for long-term contracts, say five to ten years, not only to amortize service-specific investments, but also to generate a steady stream of revenues and profits, bearing in mind that tendering for a large-scale contract is an extremely costly exercise.

A. That is not our approach. Our preferred contract length is between three to five years. We like to recompete for the contracts at these intervals because the competition keeps us sharp, helps us focus on the customer, with an eye to innovation. A contract of ten years would breed complacency and make us uncompetitive at the end of the term.

Q. Does this mean that the performance of each of the company's contracts is assessed separately against other competitors rather than internally within your organization?

A. Each contract operates effectively as a stand-alone business, a profit centre. The managers know that they will be facing external competition within three to five years of winning the contract, and that creates incentives for a continual search for efficiency and effectiveness. We strive very hard to win the contract again on rebidding. We often do. The contract for the management of the ballistic missile early warning system has been rebid several times, and we won it on every occasion.

Case Study 3.1 describes the evolution of a competitively tendered contract to manage a warehousing facility for the New South Wales state government. This case is interesting because of the view taken by the management at the

Case Study 3.1   Q-Stores: savings on the rebid

One of the major reforms undertaken by the New South Wales state government in recent years involved the transformation, through contracting out, of the old Government Supply Warehouse, which is now known as Q-Stores. It supplies government organizations with various items from stationery to dust mats. The Q-Stores operation had approximately 13,000 clients, which includes schools and hospitals, and a turnover of $A54 million in 1990/1. In an effort to improve the efficiency of the Government Supply Warehouse service, a number of reforms were instituted in the 1980s including a major review of its purchasing and inventory management practices and a rationalization of its product lines. As a consequence of these reforms, productivity increases were achieved.

From July 1989, the warehouse was required by the government to become self-funding and operate on a commercial basis. Advice presented to the government by independent consultants indicated that a central government warehouse was important because it provided real economies of scale advantages to government clients. However, it was also apparent that a substantial commercial reorientation of the operation was required in the wake of a deregulated environment where government departments were able to approach other providers. In November 1989, expressions of interest were called for the facilities management of the NSW supply warehouse. Eleven highly specialized firms were then invited to submit tenders and four submitted a formal tender.

The three-year facilities management contract was eventually awarded to the preferred tenderer, AWASCo, which was a joint venture between AWA and Serco UK. The implementation of the contract was smooth and savings were achieved. For example, labour productivity increased by 60 per cent, delivery times were reduced from 40 to approximately 4 days, the number of staff was reduced from 180 to 71, and the purchasing system was converted to an electronic system. As a result, cost savings of $A3 million were achieved.

During the course of the initial three-year contract, Serco bought out AWA's 50 per cent share in AWASCo and created Serco Australia, which subsequently submitted a tender for the new five-year facilities management contract with Q-Stores. Following the apparent success of the initial contract, it was unclear whether additional savings could be made. However, Serco believed that a number of innovations proposed in the new tender could reap additional savings. These innovations included the introduction of two technologically advanced systems of inventory control, bar coding of all stock, reorganization of the warehouse, and the introduction of an electronic data interchange between the warehouse management system and the delivery company. Serco was awarded the new contract in February 1994.

Some problems encountered during the operation of the second contract resulted in a delay in the implementation of some of Serco's proposed innovations. However, effective management of the contract meant that the number of full-time staff was further reduced from 71 to 46 and that additional savings in the order of 10 per cent were achieved.

Sources: NSW Commercial Services Group and Serco Institute.

time, that no further savings were feasible over and above those achieved when the contract was first won from the in-house service provider. Yet, under the pressure of competition, an innovative solution was proposed, using sophisticated new technology. The incumbent, Serco, won the bid against substantial outside competition, adding further cost savings to those already realized by the client. It also serves to underscore the impetus that competition has on the search for innovation.

Whenever integration of production is eschewed in favour of contracting, the door is opened to competition. Competition need not be fierce and destructive: it can be managed and controlled to yield maximum benefits at minimum cost. For example, not all purchasing decisions need be put out to competitive tender. Selective tendering is a viable option when the purchaser approaches a number of known providers and requests proposals from them. That was how Marks & Spencer contracted its store maintenance management functions, and BP selected its IT service providers. However, there are problems in taking this approach in the public sector, an issue which will be considered further in Chapter 5.

Contracts may also be directly negotiated with potential providers, without requesting a formal bid or tender. This would be appropriate whenever the purchaser believes that it has adequate market information with which to negotiate an efficient contractual solution. It should be noted that competition can exist even when a purchaser faces only one alternative to the in-house option. Competition means choice, and choice means comparing alternative options. What makes competition so powerful is that the threat of displacement of existing suppliers is a real one, even if it is veiled, and likely to be exercised only intermittently.

Competition and quality

Few would dispute the power of competition to drive prices down: one need only observe what competition has done for personal computer prices in recent years to acknowledge its force. But the influence of competition on quality is less clear-cut, if only because quality is typically much harder to measure. Indeed, cynics would argue that competition often reduces prices at the expense of quality. That is precisely what critics of competitive tendering for publicly funded services have argued for years. Whether competition reduces prices *and* quality has been a difficult question to answer. The issue is bedevilled by two crucial, but related, problems.

First, one must note that quality is often in the eye of the beholder, particularly in the context of services which are subjectively evaluated. What represents a good level of service to one person may be barely adequate for another. Such differences arise because expectations of what constitute good and bad vary significantly between service recipients.

Secondly, in many situations where a good or service is contracted out there does not exist adequate information about the quality achieved prior to contracting. This makes it impossible to make a reliable assessment about the *change* in quality of service following the introduction of competition. There is simply not enough information to make accurate before-and-after comparisons. One reason for this asymmetry in the availability of information is an asymmetry in expectations. Managers and public administrators become more sensitive to performance issues when an external contractor is engaged to perform the task. This is partly a function of perceived loss of control, but it is also a reflection of an attitude towards risk: contracting is sometimes seen as putting quality at risk, for reasons outlined above, and hence there is greater emphasis on performance monitoring.

The upshot of all this is that reliable studies on the *joint* influence of competition on *both* prices and quality are few and far between. One exception is a recent study which, instead of conducting a before-and-after investigation, looked at the price–performance characteristics of services that had been exposed to competition against those that had not. The study involved sixty-one cleaning services contracts in the metropolitan region of Sydney, Australia. The contracts were essentially of two types: competitively tendered or tied to a monopoly supplier. In this case the supplier was the Government Cleaning Service—a publicly owned provider of cleaning services to government organizations.

Fig. 3.2 shows the distribution of contract prices (per square metre), and cleaning quality measured systematically, over a nine-month period, using a special performance indicator. It can be seen that prices varied widely, while the distribution of performance was less wide-ranging and more bell-shaped. This implies fewer contracts that performed either outstandingly well or exceptionally badly. The question the study sought to answer was whether observed performance was low where prices had been driven down by competition, other things being equal. The answer is provided in Fig. 3.3.

It can be seen that average price per square metre was $A28.0 for contracts that were not awarded competitively, and only $A14.5 when they were. The effect of competition was to reduce prices by 48.2 per cent. As for quality, the performance indicator stood at 0.63 in the presence of competition and 0.56 in its absence, a positive difference in favour of competitive contracts of 12.5 per cent. This study therefore showed that competition reduced prices significantly while simultaneously raising quality, albeit by a modest amount.

Clearly, the findings described above will not convince everybody, and more evidence is required before broad generalizations can be made. But the study shows that empirical analysis of price and quality effects is possible when reliable data are available.

Theoretical analysis of the factors influencing quality suggests that the greatest problem facing vendors occurs when quality is not readily observable by buyers. In a celebrated paper on the 'market for lemons', economist George

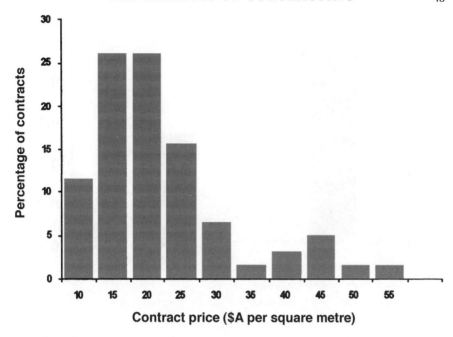

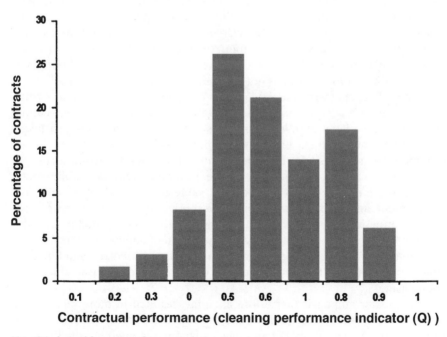

Note: Q is derived from six performance observations per contract.

Source: Domberger et al. (1995).

Fig. 3.2. Distribution of prices and performance (quality): sixty-one cleaning contracts

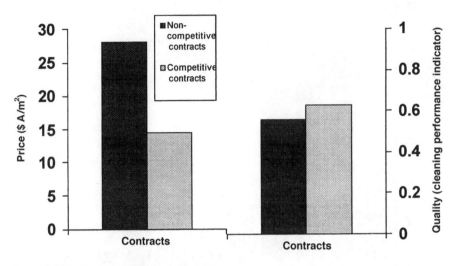

Source: Adapted from Domberger et al. (1995).

Fig. 3.3. Competition, price, and quality

Akerlof showed how the inability of buyers readily to observe the quality of second-hand cars can lead to a situation in which the bad cars drive out the good, literally and metaphorically. In circumstances where quality information is asymmetric—sellers know more about their cars than buyers—only bad cars (lemons) will be offered for sale. The argument can be generalized to any market in which information is not symmetric between buyers and sellers.

The way sellers overcome the 'lemons problem' is by investing in *reputation*. Reputation becomes a useful surrogate for quality when buyers cannot readily observe it. In practical terms this means that vendors which take a long-term view of their business prospects will not sacrifice quality to competitive pressures on prices. Bid evaluations frequently include an assessment of 'reputation for quality' of the different vendors. Public sector purchasers are increasingly following a 'value for money' criterion in bid assessment, instead of the traditional 'lowest price wins'. All this helps prevent price competition from precipitating serious reductions in quality. But ultimately, the most significant positive influence on quality is the availability of information. When meaningful performance data are collected and reported, the characteristics of the services actually delivered become observable by the purchaser.

The greater emphasis on performance has resulted in more reliable and accessible information on quality than was available prior to contracting. This increase in information should, of itself, lead to improvements in quality, since it is now more difficult for vendors to 'shade' quality without being caught out. In sum, it should not be surprising to see in quantitative studies that the introduction of contracting, and the competition that accompanies it, tends to enhance *quality* irrespective of its influence on prices.

The discipline of the market

Besides competition, the transaction framework which accompanies market exchange provides several additional benefits. They may be grouped under three headings:

- separation of client from vendor; the purchaser from the provider;
- purchaser focus on output and outcomes, provider focus on inputs and processes;
- effective, but flexible, interface between the parties, underpinned by a contract.

The separation of purchaser from provider is, by itself, a form of specialization: the party on the demand side concentrates on consumption, the one on the supply side on production. The implications of this straightforward separation of market participants are far-reaching: there are now two organizations where previously there was one; the financial impact of the activities of each becomes transparent through the splitting of the organizational accounts; and the cost of resources used in providing services across organizational boundaries comes into much sharper focus. Many private sector organizations, and most public sector ones, cannot account for their internal costs of service provision on a disaggregated basis, that is, in terms of individual service categories. Traditional accounting systems were not designed to provide information in that manner. While 'activity-based costing' is a theoretically appealing solution, the practical demands it places on management accounting systems have dampened enthusiasm for it, and slowed down its adoption.

But this separation also heightens incentives to perform and to deliver services that meet client needs. Once it is introduced, the prospect of choosing another provider becomes reality. Separation creates a credible threat: the purchaser may now select another contractor if and when it is warranted by performance, or better terms are available elsewhere. Economists refer to these as 'high-powered incentives', a term which is especially apt in this context.

The focus on performance has several aspects to it: its impact on the client and on the provider, and its effect both before and after the contract is let. The client must consider the nature of the service required carefully *before* seeking a supplier capable of producing it, by defining specifications. Experience has shown that, prior to contracting, public sector organizations frequently did not have output specifications for services that were produced in-house. This was true of hotel services in UK hospitals prior to the reforms of the 1980s, and also of most local government services. A study by Walsh (1991) for the UK

Department of the Environment, which was responsible for local government contracting activities, found that the requirement formally to specify and to monitor services had a positive effect on service quality, and a clear emphasis on standards.

Concentrating attention on outputs and outcomes need not mean lengthy and complex specifications: Marks & Spencer allows specifications to evolve over time, starting with a brief statement of requirement from its suppliers, followed by more detailed instructions. The company is continually monitoring and amending its requirements to suit market demand. This information is then transmitted to the contractors. Their focus is no different from that of all service providers to other organizations: find the most efficient current means of production and search for better methods which could be implemented in the future.

The interface between the client and the provider starts with the contract, which defines the terms of the transaction. But service transactions are rarely spot contracts; they are more often relationship contracts. The relationship between the two parties will involve exchange of information, and performance data will be crucial to any evaluation of the contract. This does not mean that the client has a larger stick with which to beat the contractor, but that the assessment of outcomes is based on reliable information. It means that there is a basis for a constructive dialogue between the parties, concerning strengths and weakness both in specific performance and in the nature of the relationship. This provides flexibility, and temporary performance difficulties need not lead to an immediate contract termination. The client and the provider will be acutely aware of the possibility of an 'irreconcilable breakdown' in the relationship. If this occurred, both parties would be free to seek alternative partners. But since this imposes costs on both sides, a termination would normally be treated as a last resort.

Observers of management trends suggest that global competitive pressures have prompted large companies to adopt greater market discipline, reducing their product range and loosening vertical links in the production processes. 'They have divested "peripheral" businesses in order to focus upon their "core" businesses and vertically "de-integrated" by increasingly "outsourcing" their requirements for components and business services' (Grant 1995: 318). Thus the search for improved performance has led organizations to relinquish the production of intermediate output to external suppliers. This has allowed them to reallocate management resources to downstream activities, closer to their markets for products and services.

Many successful companies thrive precisely because they focus on activities in which they have established a special capability. And competitive pressures intensify the search for such capability. Thus, for example, Virgin specializes solely in *selling* products and services as diverse as cola, insurance, and transatlantic air travel to upwardly mobile customers using innovative marketing refinements and a unique brand image. It produces few of the actual products and services itself, specializing instead in the marketing and distribution. On a more modest scale, but no less successfully, Mambo Graphics does essentially the same, focusing on the young surf-set and specializing in design and marketing of niche products.

Flexibility

A surprisingly large number of people believe that markets are not flexible in adjusting to changes in both the scale and scope of production. Flexibility has different meanings in different contexts. Here it refers to the speed and cost of an adjustment to changes in demand or supply conditions. Thus a flexible system is one in which the speed and cost of adjustments to external shocks are lower than that of an alternative system. Friedrich von Hayek, a Nobel laureate in economics, argued that the market mechanism provides the best means yet discovered to cope with the 'rapid adaptation to changes in the particular circumstances of time and place' (Hayek 1945: 524). To put it in a less abstract manner, 'market relations between independent firms may also be preferable to vertical integration in achieving fast-response flexibility to new product opportunities that require new combinations of technical capabilities' (Grant 1995: 322). The problem arises because senior management in both private and public sector organizations do not have access to all the knowledge relevant to resource allocation decisions. As a result, decentralized, market-mediated decision making has benefits which increase the more rapidly circumstances change and new information about them is brought to light.

An interesting example of the lack of flexibility of vertical integration is that of the UK poster and printing firm Athena. Athena was a very successful poster design and stationery producer in the UK which had integrated from upstream production all the way downstream to retailing its merchandise. It had its own design and print shops as well as its retail outlets. In 1995 the parent company Pentos plc went into liquidation. A closer look at the circumstances surrounding its demise suggests it could not respond quickly enough to changes in poster fashions. It could not deliver new designs to its retail outlets quickly enough. By contrast, importers of posters were flooding the market with new designs each time fashions changed. Another example of market responses outpacing the capacity of vertically integrated manufacturers.

The superior flexibility of networks of firms is supported by theoretical research in industrial economics. Analysis of different market structures suggests that, under plausible assumptions, output adjustments are less costly, and therefore more rapid, when they are distributed over numerous small firms rather than over a few large firms. It is common for large, vertically integrated organizations to experience difficulties in making substantial short-run output adjustments, particularly in the downward direction. This often requires the laying off of staff and disrupts long-standing internal relationships within the organization. By contrast, when such an adjustment is widely distributed across a large number of firms, each bears a proportionately smaller burden and the process may be both quicker and easier to execute.

Another way of looking at flexibility is in terms of risk. Having to make large-scale, unexpected adjustments is risky, and organizational design has adapted to minimize such risks. Benetton is a good, and widely cited, example of such adaptation: the company has more than 500 suppliers in the Veneto region north of Venice. Its own operations are relatively small but include design, cutting, dyeing, packaging, and marketing and distribution. The following extract expresses a commonly held view about the source of its flexibility: 'Designer-producers, such as Benetton . . . owe their success not only to a sensitivity to consumer taste . . . but also to the spreading of the risks of their marketing operation over a wide range of sub-contract producers who are small domestically based firms. Risk is reduced by the ability of this production network to adjust rapidly to changes in product design' (Child 1987: 36). Benetton's strategy of spreading output adjustments across its network of suppliers has evidently contributed to its business success, combining market-like flexibility with strong relationships with its contractors.

Recent research on flexibility provides further evidence that neither large-scale production nor technology are the principal determinants of rapid response to changes in market conditions. Instead, 'flexibility . . . depended much more on the people than on any technical factor' (Upton 1995: 75). Other things being equal, smaller organizations tend to breed closer-knit working communities, in which commitment to organizational objectives is easier to elicit. This adds to the ability of small-scale enterprise to respond rapidly to external changes.

The benefits of contracting: a summary

In concluding this chapter, it is helpful to gather the strands of the arguments into a summary table as a reminder of the benefits which contracting makes possible. These benefits can be grouped under four headings: specialization, market discipline, flexibility, and cost savings. Each can bring substantial advantages with it, but may have some drawbacks if not implemented with care. Questions of contract implementation are dealt with in later chapters of this book. Here the discussion is confined to principles and concepts which need to be understood before proceeding to the implementation stage. Table 3.1 identifies the benefits, providing a brief assessment of their significance and some qualifications where appropriate.

The benefits of contracting are essentially the benefits of using markets and market-like processes. But, as was stressed early in this chapter, successful contractual relationships are not simple spot transactions. Contracting appears to yield greatest benefits when it combines market discipline with

Table 3.1. A summary of the benefits of contracting

Title	Definition	Assessment
Specialization	Concentrating on those activities in which the organization has established a distinctive capability, letting others produce supporting goods and services.	Specialization yields demonstrable economic benefits. By concentrating on activities in which an organization is *relatively* more efficient, total value added is maximized. It also facilitates the exploitation of scale economies.
Market discipline	Identifies conditions in which the purchaser is separated from the provider and a formal transaction takes place under contract.	Market discipline provides a range of benefits, namely, focus by the purchaser on outputs not inputs, competition (contestability) between suppliers, choices by purchasers, and innovative work practices.
Flexibility	The ability to adjust the scale and scope of production upwards or downwards at low cost and rapid rate.	Networks of small organizations linked to their clients via contract can adjust more quickly and at lower cost to changing demand conditions compared to integrated organizations.
Cost savings	Lower resource costs of service delivery compared to in-house production.	International studies show that significant cost savings are achieved by contracting, on average of the order of 20%. As a rule efficiency gains need not lead to lower quality.

longer-term, cooperative relationships. Relationship contracting is a fair description of such transactions. But while using the market may well be efficient, it is not free. There are costs—the costs of transacting—and pitfalls, some general and some specific, to entering into contracts of the kind discussed in this chapter. Many commentators are wary of contracting because they believe that besides costs, market mediation creates perverse incentives, increases rivalry, and destroys the trust relationships that are characteristic of integrated production processes. Much of this simply reflects the concerns of those who distrust the functioning of markets. But it remains true that if organizations are to maximize the benefits of contracting they must understand the nature of the costs, and how they might be minimized.

Guide to further reading

Alexander and Young (1996) endeavour to make a distinction between strategic and non-strategic outsourcing and wrestle with the ambiguities of the concept of 'core activities'. Brueck (1995) is a balanced appraisal of the decision-making strategy that firms should consider when deciding whether to produce goods or services in-house, or purchase from the market. A concise breakdown of the crucial cost factors that need to be understood is also presented.

Carlsson (1989) provides a concise summary of the numerous definitions of flexibility in the economics literature, and its relevance to the theory of the firm. Flexibility is also discussed in Harrison and Kelley (1993) and in Harrison (1994). In Child (1987) the implications of IT for modern organizations are considered. Ginsburgh and Michel (1988) provide an economic analysis of the adjustment process of prices and quantities in different market structures.

Chapter 12 in Grant (1995), entitled 'The Scope of the Firm: Vertical Integration', gives a comprehensive analysis of the vertical integration decision from a strategic perspective. It also contains a particularly insightful section on the boundaries of the firm and some possible explanations of the observed trend toward de-integration. Quinn and Hilmer (1994) is a useful article which coined the use of the term 'strategic outsourcing'. It also broke new ground by providing a guide to the functional characteristics of core competencies.

Stigler (1951) continues to be an influential article in economics which challenges Adam Smith's widely accepted axiom that the degree of labour specialization in manufacturing is limited by the size of the market. Akerlof (1970) is the classic reference on the problem of quality in markets where information is not uniformly available to market participants.

4

The Costs of Contracting

Those too numerous people who believe that transactions between firms
are expensive and those within firms are free . . .

(George Stigler, 1951)

The coordination of productive activity

Before industrialization, most of the economically active population was to be
found on the land; hunting, gathering, and cultivating. Land and labour were
the principal inputs of agricultural production; what little capital equipment
there was would be considered rudimentary by contemporary standards:
ploughs and scythes instead of tractors and combine harvesters.

Then, as now, the coordination of economic activity involved aligning
production with consumption, the quantity of output supplied with that
demanded. This is more complicated than it appears at first sight, since both
final and intermediate outputs are involved. Final and intermediate demands
are clearly interrelated: the greater the demand for wine, the greater will be the
demand for grapes. There is a great deal of coordination involved in combining raw inputs into outputs, and agricultural production is no exception.

Prior to the development of modern transport, the bulk of this coordination
was undertaken by local markets. Prices were set by the forces of supply and
demand, whenever buyers and sellers met to trade. As inter-regional trade was
limited, most output was produced for local consumption. Hiring of labour
was also mediated by the market, with local wage rates responding to fluctua-
tions in the availability of employment and the offer of work. Of course, the
role of markets was not all-encompassing, and there were some activities,
primarily those of the state and the military, that were firmly out of bounds.
Coordination of these activities was effected by command-and-control
systems.

Industrialization brought sweeping changes. Technology, in the form of
steam engines and spinning jennies, shifted the limits of what was technically
possible and economically feasible. Advances in transport, both land and sea
based, improved communications and opened up new trading opportunities.

Industrial development, which began in England and later spread to continental Europe, was to bring hitherto undreamed-of riches. The United Kingdom's relative share of world manufacturing output rose from 1.9 per cent in 1750 to 19.9 per cent in 1860. And during Queen Victoria's reign income per head rose 2.5 times. But the price of this new wealth was considerable dislocation, as labour moved from the land to the 'dark satanic mills' and factories of the towns.

The development of manufacturing introduced complexity to the production process by requiring many more intermediate steps of production as raw materials and semi-finished products made their way through to final output. Thus, manufacturing activities required more coordination than traditional agriculture. Even processes that were not capital intensive, but required the application of craftsmanship and specialized skills, were subject to stringent coordination requirements. Take, for example, the manufacturing of small arms in nineteenth-century Birmingham, which became a world centre for such activity. Illustration 4.1, an extract from an economic historian, highlights the complex structure of the manufacturing process.

Illustration 4.1.   Gun-making in nineteenth-century England

'The master gun maker—the entrepreneur—seldom possessed a factory or workshop . . . Usually he owned merely a warehouse in the gun quarter, and his function was to acquire semi-finished parts and to give these out to specialized craftsmen, who undertook the assembly and finishing of the gun. He purchased materials from the barrel-makers, lock-makers, sight-stampers, trigger-makers, ramrod-forgers, gun-furniture makers, and, if he were engaged in the military branch, from bayonet-forgers. All of these were independent manufacturers executing the orders of several master gun-makers . . . Once the parts had been purchased from the "material makers", as they were called, the next task was to hand them out to a long succession of "setters-up", each of whom performed a specific operation in connection with the assembly and finishing of the gun. To name only a few, there were those who performed the front sight and lump end of the barrels; the jiggers, who attended to the breech end; the stockers, who let in the barrel and lock and shaped the stock; the barrel-strippers who prepared the gun for rifling and proof; the hardeners, polishers, borers and riflers, engravers, browners, and finally the lock-freers, who adjusted the working parts.'
Source: Allen (1966: 116–17).

Small-arms manufacturing in nineteenth-century Birmingham was complicated, requiring many different stages of production, varied materials and considerable skills. The market played a significant role in coordinating this activity. The production process was effectively broken down into steps which were undertaken by people who were not members of the same company or organization. To be sure, they worked in close proximity, both geographic and cultural, in the sense of belonging to the same industry and possibly the same guilds of craftsmen. But their relationships were fundamentally economic in nature, based on well-defined transactions for services at agreed prices. In other words, their economic relations were mediated by the market, through contracts, formal or informal, struck between the parties.

One could, however, conceive of such activity being integrated within a single organization. Coordination would then be taken out of the marketplace and into the company. Within it, coordination of economic activity would be undertaken through a hierarchical command system whereby the production manager would instruct various individuals when to conduct their respective task. It is worthwhile to examine the way in which an integrated production system—under common ownership—differs from a market-based, contractual arrangement.

In the former, the craftsmen are employees of the organization. Their contracts of employment would require them to provide services in exchange for an agreed wage. Their employer would then instruct them what to do, and when to do it, as required. Thus in the integrated mode, the transaction is not service specific, but for yet to be determined labour services.

Contrast the integrated mode with the contractual mode: here, the contract is for a specific and specialized service; it looks like a spot contract. One can see intuitively that there may be certain advantages to the market-mediated form of coordination. Payment is strictly for service rendered: no performance—no pay. The incentive to perform is directly related to the consequences of non-performance and therefore stronger under the contractual mode. However, coordinating production and exchange with a myriad external service providers is not without its difficulties.

A particular problem for producers of services arises when performance of the activity necessitates the acquisition of specialized physical assets. This could expose them to significant risks. Going back to the small-arms industry, if contractors need to invest in specialized equipment to perform their tasks, and if they are unsure of the volume of business that their client will be placing with them, they may consider such investment to be too risky. The result may be chronic under-investment in the industry, and contractors' capacity to deliver services on demand, and to specification, may be severely compromised. As an effective coordinating device, the market could fail in these circumstances.

Cooperation and trust

One way to alleviate the coordination problems is by way of cooperation. If participants in an enterprise, joint venture, or contractual exchange work cooperatively towards a common objective, then it follows that coordination will be easier to achieve. It could be argued that wholehearted cooperation is a necessary condition for effective coordination, though it may not always be sufficient. Yet significant obstacles stand in the way of achieving cooperative behaviour. The principal reason is self-interest: it forms the cornerstone of the competitive market economy. The socially beneficial outcomes of such an economy depend on it. The eighteenth-century moral philosopher Adam Smith neatly summed it up thus: 'It is not from the benevolence of the butcher, the brewer or the baker, that we expect our dinner, but from their regard to their own interest' (1880: 15).

Self-interest is tolerated, and even encouraged, in the market economy because the competitive behaviour to which it leads is socially beneficial. Competition between computer manufacturers, and their quest for growing markets, has led to ever more powerful personal computers at astonishingly declining prices. Similarly, competition in telecommunications, transport services, and a myriad other industries continues to yield benefits to consumers. Not surprisingly, most industrial countries have legislation that prohibits cooperative behaviour between firms which could have the effect of restricting competition. Many countries are going even further towards promoting competition, by reducing barriers to entry into existing markets, relaxing government regulations on business activity, and raising penalties for anti-competitive behaviour.

Unlike competition, attitudes towards cooperative behaviour in economic matters have been surprisingly ambivalent. Cooperation in business activity was given a bad press as long ago as 1776 by none other than Adam Smith. In a now famous passage he wrote: 'People of the same trade seldom meet together, even for merriment and deversion, but the conversation ends in a conspiracy against the public, or in some diversion to raise prices' (1880: 135–6). Yet cooperation in business activity is not only desirable, but essential if efficient outcomes are to be achieved.

How does self-interest stand in the way of cooperation, when it is evident to all parties that the overall gain will be that much greater for it? Illustration 4.2 shows how such a situation can arise in a 'contracting game' scenario. For simplicity it will be assumed that client and contractor engage in a transaction for a 'premium-quality' service in a single-period contract. The premium is harder for the client to observe than to specify, as would be the case, for example, in a contract for 'high-quality' prison guards. The higher quality demanded will command a higher price, which will be reflected in the terms of the agreement. But the difficulties in verifying quality will mean that enforcing the special characteristic of the contract—the premium quality—will be prohibitively expensive. Going to court is not a realistic option. Although the pay-offs are not shown in the illustration, it should be clear that the contractor has an incentive to skimp on quality, since this 'renege' strategy will reduce costs and enhance profits. The client has a choice of complying with the agreement or reneging, but is faced with the dilemma that if the contractor complies, then it can profit by withholding the 'premium' payment. If the contractor reneges, then the client would clearly be worse off than if he were to comply. The logic of self-interest makes reneging the 'dominant strategy'.

Illustration 4.2. The 'contracting game'

		Client	
		Renege	Comply
Contractor	Renege	Bad for both	Best for contractor Worst for client
	Comply	Best for client Worst for contractor	Good for both

This contracting illustration is highly stylized, and a more realistic (multi-period) setting would weaken the appeal of the renege option. However, contract failures at the high end of the quality spectrum are not uncommon. It is not unusual to hear of clients complaining that the quality of service delivered by contractors is not as high as they demand and specify. Contractors, on the other hand, often complain that clients are unwilling to pay for high-quality services. Given that too many contractors are selected on the basis that the cheapest bid is good enough, such complaints are not surprising. They are also consistent with the ever-present struggle between client and provider for the achievement of a cooperative solution to the contracting problem.

The way out of the cooperation conundrum is to change the pay-offs or to repeat the game. Take the latter first. Repeating the game has important consequences. Observing non-cooperative behaviour allows the parties to adapt: past performance conditions future behaviour. In the case of the contractor, shading quality will lead to tighter monitoring (costly to the client), declining contractor reputation, possibly a financial penalty, and eventually the loss of the 'premium contract'. Thus, contractual situations are rarely one-period games, and the ultimate implications of non-cooperative behaviour will have dramatic consequences for future transactions. Even though reneging has short-term benefits, in the longer term, non-cooperation will lead to 'tit-for-tat' strategies which will nullify the gains. Some have even suggested that 'selection mechanisms favour actors whose repertoires of behaviour are biased toward co-operation' (Hill 1990: 503). In practical terms this means that market opportunities will be more restricted for non-cooperative clients and contractors.

Alternatively, changing the pay-offs means making non-cooperation less attractive. In the contracting game this means having better methods of detecting quality shading, being able to extract a financial penalty for non-performance (although this raises other problems), or extending the contract duration so that taking a short-term pay-off is no longer an attractive option. The latter has become particularly common in recent years, as contracting parties have sought to move away from short-term contracts, and build longer-term cooperative relationships. In 1993, British Home Stores, a large retailer in the United Kingdom, signed a ten-year contract with IT giant CSC for the provision of data processing and related computer facility management services. Similarly in 1995, the government of the state of South Australia signed a fifteen-year contract with SA Water for the provision of operations and maintenance of water and sewerage systems in its capital city, Adelaide. However, long-term contracts do have some disadvantages which will be considered in Part III.

The ability to make credible commitments to cooperative modes of behaviour represents a form of trust. We are more willing to do business with those whom we trust because of a perception that they will not take the self-interested strategy when we least expect it. The alternative to trust is, of course, legal enforcement. But the costs of litigation are so high that they often outweigh the benefits of legal enforcement. Moreover, the commercial litigation system is typically very slow, which means that contractual disputes remain unresolved for extended periods, while the contract is still in force. This makes the contractual relationship untenable, and often leads to a parting of the ways. Resolution of a disputed contractual issue may take place long after the contract has been prematurely terminated.

Yet it is important to recognize that 'ethical elements enter in some measure into every contract; without them, no market could function. There is an element of trust in every transaction' (Arrow 1973: 24). These remarks are a reminder that narrow, unremitting self-interest is counter-productive. Some commentators have gone even further by suggesting that the role of trust goes beyond individual economic relationships; that it is a pre-condition for successful economic adjustment and prosperity. 'The ability of companies to move from large hierarchies to flexible networks of smaller firms, will depend . . . on the degree of trust and social capital present in the broader society' (Fukuyama 1995: 25–6).

Fukuyama goes so far as to suggest that societies may be classified as high- or low-trust, in terms of their social and ethical habits, and that their prosperity may be directly linked to those levels of trust: 'a nation's well being, as well as its ability to compete, is conditioned by a single, pervasive cultural characteristic: the level of trust inherent in the society' (1995: 7). The argument, in brief, is that since trust is essential to successful economic transactions, where it lies in abundance, business will also flourish.

But it remains true that contractual relationships which have a 'low trust count' are fragile and prone to failure. The importance of trust between contracting parties is highlighted by the modern phenomenon of 'partnering contracts'—contracts in which the parties commit to an open and cooperative management style. The United States Army Corps of Engineers has made extensive use of 'partnering' in construction projects, which had a history of cost overruns, unnecessary delays, and frequent litigation. Partnering is invoked to reduce the adversarial element in contracts and to achieve greater cooperation. It involves creating an atmosphere of trust between the contract-

Case Study 4.1. Ford and Asea Brown Boveri: The importance of cooperation

Antagonistic relationships between buyers and suppliers are a common characteristic of the modern industrial landscape. It seems that in many industries, particularly the automobile industry, the temptation of opportunism is often too great. However, it is widely acknowledged that adversarial relationships create barriers to innovation, hinder the transfer of knowledge from suppliers to buyers, and prevent the reshaping of industry organization—all of which may outweigh the gains associated with lowering purchasing costs. The example of the cooperative relationship between Ford and Asea Brown Boveri (ABB) to build a $300 million paint-finishing plant may help to rekindle optimism for buyer–supplier relationships that are both innovative and cooperative.

As part of its plan to introduce two new models to its range, Ford decided to build a new state of the art paint-finishing facility in Oakville, Canada. By any standards, the facility was very large and technically complex. Despite the difficulties associated with the project, Ford was determined to achieve a 20 to 30 per cent reduction in the cost of its capital investment projects relative to previous similar undertakings. In an unprecedented move, Ford decided to offer managerial responsibility for the entire project to one contractor (a 'turnkey' project), rather than coordinate the project through several specialized contractors.

In early January 1990, Ford approached ABB with an invitation to proceed as a full-service contractor. ABB was given one week to develop a fixed-price proposal that complied with Ford's design specifications. While ABB was able to meet the deadline, Ford was disappointed that no innovative technology was proposed and that the estimated cost of the project ($300 million) did not fulfil its expectations of lowering previous costs by 20 to 30 per cent. Instead of aborting the process, Ford and ABB decided to enter into a 'deferred fixed-price contract'—a three-step process that involved establishing an appropriation price, executing a three-month cooperative engineering contract, and then submitting a final fixed-price bid.

In the end, both parties were able to achieve a mutually beneficial outcome—the final price was 25 per cent lower than the initial bid, the initial design was improved, and ABB was able to make a profit at a lower level of risk than was previously envisaged. The success of the Oakville project can be related primarily to the fact that, during the three-month cooperative engineering contract, the companies created the foundations for a trustful relationship—foundations which might not have been forged if traditional competitive bidding processes had been used.

Source: Frey and Schlosser (1993).

---

ing parties, through open communications, sharing of information, and working together towards a common objective. The partnering relationship is achieved through a charter—an agreement to work cooperatively and in the spirit of trust. Interestingly partnering does not replace the traditional contract which legally binds the parties in the transaction. Rather, it is additional to it and operates as a social conditioning process: if people behave cooperatively there will be no need to invoke the formal contract.

Unfortunately, the precise definition of the partnering concept is elusive. There are as many versions of partnering as there are partnering agreements, the most common of which will be examined in a later chapter. Anecdotal evidence suggests some successes and some dismal failures. But there are few, if any, studies which have tried to measure the impact of partnering, because of serious measurement difficulties. Nevertheless, the importance of trust and cooperation, which form the essence of partnering, will strike a resonant chord in every manager who has been involved either on the buyer's or the vendor's side. Nor is it inappropriate to suggest, as partnering does, that building trust and cooperation is as much a social and ethical process as an economic or managerial one. Indeed, the discussion in this section would lead one to the conclusion that cooperative behaviour, while yielding economic benefits, is essentially a social trait. And if costs must be incurred to induce such socialization among contracting parties, the discussion also suggests that the benefits are likely to exceed the costs.

The costs of transacting

Integration of production activities within a single organization can be justified on the grounds that it reduces 'transaction costs'. Simply stated, transaction costs are the costs of using the market to purchase goods and services. The development of 'transaction costs economics' has highlighted the problems of using the market mechanism for organizing economic activity. As a corollary, it has also highlighted the benefits of integration, and of using hierarchical modes of control, for internal resource allocation. What precisely are those transaction costs?

Using the market is not costless. At a basic level, there are the costs of searching for vendors, or for buyers. In the latter case, these are simply marketing costs, but they are far from trivial. Modern corporations devote substantial resources to marketing and market research, for good reasons. Market participants do not have perfect information and perfect foresight concerning their counterparts on the opposite side of the transaction: information about buyers, their preferences, and their budgets must be acquired. Similarly, knowledge about potential sellers is scarce, and its acquisition entails costs. This is particularly true for services, which must be evaluated on the basis of past performance as judged by clients.

The process of searching for and selecting a contractor can take a variety of forms. A competitive bidding or tendering scheme is often used, particularly in the public sector, to select the contractor which is judged to offer the 'best value for money'. In some cases the bidding scheme is open: any vendor judging him- or herself to be up to the task may submit a bid. In other cases the bidding/tendering may be selective: only those vendors judged to meet certain prescribed criteria are invited to submit their bids. The selection of the pre-qualifying list is based on an earlier round inviting 'expressions of interest' in the contract. Yet a third method is to proceed to direct negotiations with one or more vendors known to the prospective purchaser. Table 3.1 in the previous chapter provides a brief summary of alternative methods of selection, and their respective merits.

Search and selection involve costs. The same is true of writing and negotiating contracts. Specifications of requirements and contract terms are usually determined prior to the selection of the provider. But it would be a very unusual contract that would not require some further amendment and negotiation before it was finalized. And irrespective of the timing of contract completion, writing and negotiation involve costs. Research on these costs is patchy and quantitative information scarce, but what evidence is available suggests they are substantial. The costs involve writing specifications, drafting contracts, consulting relevant end users, advertising invitations to bid/tender, evaluating the bids, and closing the negotiations with the winning bidder. All this is likely to involve considerable senior management time. Estimates of such transaction costs vary, but they can be as high as 5 per cent of the contract values (Industry Commission 1996: 337).

But these are the explicit costs of setting up the transaction. There are also implicit costs. Because it is not possible to foresee all future contingencies *ab initio*, the contract will always be incomplete, to a lesser or greater extent. Depending on the nature of the service or product involved, the need may arise to revise the specification, increase or decrease the quantity stipulated in the contract, adjust quality up or down, or review some other dimension. By definition, such changes could not have been foreseen and therefore will have to be renegotiated. Negotiations of this kind could consume valuable management time and could be difficult to resolve if the parties to the agreement see them as an opportunity to drive a hard bargain. Indeed, some observers argue that contractors often rely on post-contractual negotiations to extract revenue which they have felt unable to in the competitive selection process. Such costly 'variations' are particularly common in the building industry.

The prospect of opportunistic behaviour by the contracting party with greater bargaining power has come to be viewed as a major cost of transacting, even though it is an implicit, rather than an explicit cost. 'Self interest with guile' is how Oliver Williamson describes it; all the more pernicious for being a latent form of self-interest. It raises the prospect of 'contractual hazards' which emerge only once contracts are entered into, and unexpected events unfold. The risks of a 'hold-up' of one of the transacting parties by the other may be highly subjective, but could be judged sufficiently high to act as a deterrent. Potentially beneficial transactions may thus go unconsummated for fear of violation.

Consider, as an example, the contracting by a major UK retailer store chain for a new line of chocolate confectionery from a specialist manufacturer. In view of the retailer's large size, the contract could easily take up the bulk of the supplier's productive capacity. But if such a contract were to be struck, the supplier would be in a highly vulnerable position. Should the client decide to cancel the contract or reduce its scale, the supplier could face bankruptcy if alternative outlets for confectionery output could not be found in time. The problem would be exacerbated if, in order to meet the retailer's special needs, the supplier installed capital equipment designed to produce the speciality product specified by the client. In these circumstances there is a natural risk of loss of demand, but there is a specific risk of opportunistic behaviour.

Transaction costs theory argues forcefully that integration of activities within the organization is a rational response to the problems of contractual hazards. More recently, several management thinkers suggested that the problems of incomplete contracts and opportunism may have been exaggerated. For example 'the US auto industry suggests that in the long run the invisible hand of the market will delete opportunistic actors' (Hill 1990: 508). In other words, opportunistic behaviour can really only be played once, for once it is exercised, the loss of reputation may be catastrophic for the party using its power in this way. Ghoshal and Moran feel the need to 'caution against this growing tendency of applying the transaction cost economics logic for such normative purposes' (1996: 15). In other words, they argue that while transaction costs may help explain the phenomenon of vertical integration, the presence of transaction costs does not imply *ipso facto* that integration is the appropriate normative response.

It could be argued that the problem of opportunism arises in much the same way *within* organizations as between them. What is to stop one division within a multi-divisional organization trying to extract better terms when its contribution becomes critical to a new corporate initiative? And why are threats of strikes so much more common within large private and public sector enterprises as the deadline for completion of a major new project is approaching? Viable solutions to these problems are relatively easily implemented within the market. Marks & Spencer takes great care to avoid placing its suppliers in situations of over-dependence. For example, it encouraged one of its store maintenance contractors, UMS, to bid for other work on the grounds that no supplier should be dependent on Marks & Spencer for more than 30-40 per cent of its revenue. UMS was originally set up as a subsidiary of Marks & Spencer in order to bid for maintenance management services. This arrangement ensures that in the unlikely event that Marks & Spencer and UMS part company, the smaller entity will not be placed in a financially untenable position.

Furthermore, transaction costs economics does not tell an entirely convincing story about the reasons why internal transactions are significantly less costly. Are costs of negotiation always lower within organizations than between them? Is opportunism mitigated by communal *esprit de corps* within the corporation, or is it simply neutralized by the dead hand of internal bureaucratic controls? As one economic theorist suggested, if opportunistic behaviour was always rare inside an organization, it would be optimal to carry out all economic activities within one huge firm. And as management academics put it, it would be wrong to conclude organizations exist 'because they are able to attenuate opportunism' (Ghoshal and Moran 1996: 30). Evidently there must be other costs to contracting which may differ between internal and external transactions.

The costs of monitoring

Do contractors need monitoring? Almost every manager will answer this question in the affirmative. Indeed, many would say that the greatest burden of contracting is the necessity of monitoring. Implicit in this argument is the view, which is not always clearly articulated, that contractors require monitoring with greater vigilance than in-house staff. Superficially, the reason may be attributed to a simple lack of trust. Since the objective of the contractor is to make a profit, whereas the client seeks to obtain the best value for money from the contract, their interests obviously diverge. The contractor stands to benefit from shirking: resources saved mean greater profits. It follows that there will be an incentive to reduce effort, provided such action is not detected by the client. In order to minimize this incentive, the client needs to intensify the monitoring of the contractor's performance.

This, in a nutshell, is the reason why monitoring contractors is assumed to be costlier than supervising in-house operations. The argument merits closer examination. Underlying the notion that monitoring is necessary in such relationships is the principal–agent theory of contracting. A principal hires an agent to perform certain duties on its behalf. A contract is written up which specifies the services to be delivered and the rewards that accompany them.

Now, the principal cannot directly observe the level of effort (or resources) applied by the agent to the task in question. This immediately raises the problem of risk. Consider the case of the manager who is diligent and uses her best endeavours to achieve a profitable outcome for the owner of a firm. If market conditions are such that the outcome is nevertheless a poor one, who should bear the consequences? If the manager is on a pure incentive contract, stipulating a remuneration schedule directly related to profits, she will probably receive little or no pay in that period. She would be bearing a substantial risk for poor performance. Alternatively, if she is on a fixed salary then the owner of the firm bears all of that burden. It can be seen that the structure of the remuneration contract determines the distribution of risks between the parties. There is a classic trade-off between risk and incentives in such situations. The manager will be conscious that any diminution of effort will have an adverse impact on her earnings. But, conversely, there will be a significant exposure to risk, one that most managers will be unwilling to bear.

Standard contracts between employers and employees and between purchaser and service provider embody the same trade-offs between incentives and risks. Although contract terms vary widely with circumstances, risk bearing is usually skewed towards the party best able to support it. Thus, most managers' remuneration schemes involve a base salary, with additional incentive bonuses which are related to performance, since firms can withstand downturns in profitability more than managers can the loss of pay. Similarly, in contracts for services, providers are paid according to a predetermined schedule, with incentives or penalty payments related to actual performance.

In circumstances where the principal bears the bulk of the performance risk associated with the activities of the agent, the need for performance monitoring is self-evident. But why should monitoring be more costly for external transactions? Many observers of contracting trends assume this to be the case, yet the evidence, theoretical or empirical, is both sparse and unsupportive. On the theoretical front, it follows that a principal–agent relationship between employers and employees is not fundamentally different from that between client and contractor. Some believe that, as far as the public sector is concerned, the 'intrinsic motivation on the part of agents' reduces the need for monitoring. This 'sympathy between a civil servant and the goals of his organization and the propensity to advance these goals without compulsion or certainty of material reward' (Donahue 1989: 88) implies that monitoring a public servant's performance is not nearly as demanding as monitoring a profit-seeking agent. Perhaps so, if the public servant's objectives are indistinguishable from those of her employer, and if the profit-seeking contractor is single-mindedly focused on this quarter's profit performance. But the worldwide push towards a 'contract state', in which services are publicly financed but delivered through the market, belies such contention. The move away from public production is consistent with the conviction that public sector workers are, in general, no less responsive to incentives than other people.

On the empirical front, the evidence suggests that contracting does entail monitoring costs. Estimates are hard to come by and they vary depending on the service being contracted. A study by the UK's Audit Commission found that the costs of monitoring varied between 1.1 per cent of turnover in catering, education, and welfare to 9 per cent in building maintenance. The figures are given in Table 4.1.

However, this study fails to show that the monitoring of contractors is inherently more costly than monitoring in-house service providers. The lack of evidence is not hard to explain: prior to the contracting of a service there was very little, if any, performance monitoring. More often than not, the client organizations did not have a clearly defined service specification prior to contracting the function, making effective monitoring infeasible. Of course, one could argue that the optimal level of monitoring under the public sector production mode is effectively zero: one does not need to monitor those whose commitment to organizational goals is total. But this is a proposition which cannot be falsified: if it is believed, then monitoring is clearly unnecessary, but until monitoring

Table 4.1. Monitoring costs as a percentage of turnover

Activity	All authorities (median)	London and metropolitan districts (median)
Building maintenance—response	9.0	5.8
Building maintenance—general	8.4	n.a.
Building maintenance—planned	7.4	8.2
Vehicle maintenance	7.2	5.7
Ground maintenance	5.7	4.2
Cleaning—general	4.5	3.5
Building cleaning	3.7	3.2
Refuse collection	3.6	3.5
Catering—general	2.1	2.5
Catering—education and welfare	1.1	1.2

Note: n.a. = not available.
Source: UK Audit Commission (1995).

actually takes place, the truth of the proposition cannot be established. Scepticism seems the better alternative.

Another reason for stepping up public sector monitoring of private sector contracting is the need for accountability. Public servants can be notoriously risk averse, and given the controversy that often surrounds the contracting of services previously performed by public employees, the desire (and legal obligation) to be accountable is understandable. The natural reaction in this environment is to monitor contractors closely, not because such intensity is necessary, but because it provides the client with additional safeguards. This could account for the perception that private contractors are stringently monitored, but it does not imply that such monitoring is *required* to secure optimum performance. Indeed, this would be an instance of over-monitoring, the additional costs incurred representing an accountability premium but having no value in terms of improving the behaviour of the contractor.

Hard evidence on the costs of performance monitoring is equally elusive in the private sector. But the same issues arise (the exception being the accountability constraints mentioned above). Clients may feel at greater risk with the contractor, because of the absence of direct resource control, and may therefore step up monitoring activities. But this is a response occasioned by an attitude towards risk, and a changing perception of risk. Contracting for a good or a service does not by itself raise the cost of acquiring information about outputs and outcomes. Unless some 'information asymmetries' are invoked— situations in which the contractor has better or less restricted access to performance information than the client—it is difficult to see why monitoring should be significantly different. It is sometimes claimed that the

Case Study 4.2. NSW Government Cleaning Service

In New South Wales, reforms aimed at improving public sector management and increasing productivity and efficiency were initiated by the Liberal-National coalition government in 1988. One of the boldest undertakings in the process of restructuring government business was the reform of the Government Cleaning Service (GCS), which was created in 1915 to clean public schools.

A series of internal restructuring initiatives between 1989 and 1992 and an industrial agreement with the unions resulted in the GCS workforce being cut by 40 per cent and savings of approximately $40 million. Despite the success of these initiatives, the government decided in 1993 that it would sell the GCS's assets and transfer all employees (and their entitlements) to private cleaning contractors. The union attacked the decision—arguing that the previous reforms had been successful and that the standard of cleaning would fall.

The GCS was separated into five independent regional business units, each covering a geographical zone in New South Wales. The average value of work in each zone was approximately $35 million and the number of cleaners in each zone was 1,500. There were two components to the sale: the transfer at predetermined prices of GCS equipment, and a five-year contract for cleaning services in each zone. In order to promote competition, the government stated that no company would be awarded more than two zones and that it was not obliged to award the contract to the cheapest tenderer. Seven tenders were lodged and an evaluation team was established to assess the tenders. Two companies were awarded two zones and a third company was awarded one zone. The estimated saving during the first three years of the contract was $136 million.

A comprehensive performance monitoring system has been initiated to ensure that the various contractors meet the standards specified in the contract. Regular and randomized inspections are conducted by a series of inspectors who are rotated between the different zones. A set of performance indicators is then used to assess contractor performance and a total performance index calculated. An aggregate mark of 80 per cent (of acceptable items) for the site is considered satisfactory. Inspection results are then entered into a central database so that each contractor's performance can be analysed over time and across zones.

A sample data set containing the results of 4,370 inspections over a 22-month period from November 1994 to August 1996 was compiled to assess the performance of the contractors. The results indicate that the mean of the total performance for the entire sample was 84.4 per cent—a figure which is above the satisfactory mark. However, there was considerable variation in the performance of the contractors across the different zones. Using a previous benchmarking study of cleaning performance in schools prior to the introduction of contracting for services in the GCS, it was possible to show that there has been a substantial improvement in cleaning performance since the introduction of contracting.

Source: Jensen and Liebenberg (1995).

principal–agent theory of the firm implies information asymmetries—that it is easier and, therefore, less costly to monitor in-house operations than external contractors. 'The employer, by virtue of monitoring many inputs, acquires special superior information about their productive talents' (Alchian and Demsetz 1972: 793). However, this comment misses the point: performance monitoring is about evaluating outputs or outcomes rather than inputs. And there is nothing in the theory that would help explain why it is easier to monitor the output of an employee than that of an independent contractor.

There may, of course, be circumstances in which monitoring outcomes is not practical, and the client has to fall back on monitoring inputs. Prison services are an example of this, as are welfare and care services for the aged or infirm. In these cases, performance evaluation is dependent on assessment by service recipients, whose judgement is not trusted. This may be because they are incapable of properly assessing the quality of service (the infirm) or because they may be unwilling to do so (prisoners). Given the difficulties of specifying such services, and the monitoring problems they present, it is not surprising to note that contracts with private sector providers in these areas are still few and far between. But they are on the rise, indicating that purchasers are willing to experiment with such contracts in the quest for improved performance.

Control

Another important cost of contracting involves the perceived loss of control. Many managers adhere to the view that ownership means control, as does an employee relationship compared to a contractual one. A contract for services may be considered a contract for specified outputs or defined outcomes. A contract of employment is, to use Donahue's terminology, a 'contract for allegiance'. This expression encapsulates the desiderata of many managers, namely that their employees will be devoted 'agents' on whose best endeavours they will be able to count. However, the wish and the reality typically diverge. Public and private sector experience is replete with examples of employers trying to bring about changes in work practices or to introduce service or product innovations. Such change often stalls, pending negotiations with unions or staff representatives.

Not surprisingly, many managers regard contracting as an ideal tool for introducing changes that were fiercely resisted when they were attempted within the integrated organization. This is true both of the public and the private sectors. And once contracts are in place, changes are not ruled out although they may be restricted by legislation (see the discussion of TUPE in Chapter 8). Generally, such changes can be expected to occur and may be built into the contract design. This does not mean anticipating every variation in scale, scope, or some other contract dimension, but stipulating the terms on which such adjustments will be implemented.

Control of employment is not synonymous with control of outcomes. And controlling the latter does not, in general, require controlling the former, despite claims to the contrary. But what about control of assets? Does loss of control over physical assets impose a cost on the client? This is a highly complex area in which clear-cut answers are not readily available. However, recent advances in the theory of ownership and incomplete contracts suggest some useful insights. The theory suggests that physical assets should be integrated, that is, be brought under single ownership, when they are complementary.

If complementary assets are independently owned, costs will be higher and efficiency lower than if they are held under single ownership. In this sense, therefore, loss of control through fragmented ownership implies higher costs, or losses in efficiency. These costs manifest themselves through inadequate levels, or types, of investments in physical capital. But a high degree of asset complementarity is not particularly common. And it has been noted that as industries expand, specialist suppliers spring up, providing contracting opportunities to erstwhile vertically integrated organizations: 'vertical dis-integration is the typical development in growing industries, vertical integration in declining industries' (Stigler 1951: 189). Or as Hart (1995: 52) puts it: 'When the industry contains a small number of firms (possibly just one), complementarities between the purchaser(s) of input and supplier(s) of input are great, since there are few alternative trading partners. However, when the market is large enough to support many purchasers and suppliers, complementarities between any single purchaser and supplier become smaller and non-integration is then optimal.'

This conclusion is of special significance. When public services and in-house support activities of private sector firms were first produced, well-developed markets for those services did not exist. IT services are a relevant example. As output expanded, markets developed and specialization flourished, the economic justification for keeping a wide range of activities within the integrated organization became ever less compelling. But once those activities had become entrenched, exposing them to market forces and liberating them from the host organization was never going to be easy. Heavy adjustment costs are imposed by the likelihood of severing employment relationships, the perceived loss of control, and the need to develop contract management skills. Overcoming organizational inertia in order to effect changes also presents a problem. These issues will be discussed further in Chapters 7 and 8.

Yet the benefits of de-integration can be large. Consider an unusual example from the mining industry: Argyle Diamonds, which operates the world's largest diamond mine in north-western Australia and has an annual turnover of over $A400 million, contracts out much of its mining operations. Activities including earth-moving, housing, and food services are all sourced from external suppliers. The only remaining activities performed by Argyle are the separation and sorting stages of production. Until recently, distribution of Argyle diamonds was controlled by the De Beers cartel, but Argyle recently decided to terminate its relationship with it (Quinn and Hilmer 1994: 52). This example illustrates the fact that some contractual transactions involve complete separation of the ownership of the physical from the human assets—the separation of the mine from the providers of mining services.

Other costs of contracting

Criticisms of contracting do not end with transaction and monitoring costs and loss of control. There are several others which need to be considered. They are 'hollowing out', loss of in-house skills, loss of corporate memory, and loss of innovative capacity. Table 4.2 provides a brief definition of each with a corresponding assessment of its significance.

Hollowing out essentially means turning the organization into an 'empty box', by performing manufacturing and other operations outside. Together with loss of skills, it is said to afflict contracting organizations both in the public and private sectors with equal force. The potential loss of skills is frequently lamented in the public sector on the grounds that the organization is bereft of the capability to resume its own service activities, should circumstances demand it. But the concern is overstated: what public sector managers fail to realize is that skills are not lost, they are transferred to the marketplace. When contractors take over service provision they bring their own competencies, and, to the extent that they re-employ staff previously employed by the client, they also utilize existing in-house expertise. As a result of this transfer, skills and competencies are often enhanced because contractors are having to serve a wide market, whereas the in-house provider previously had only a single, and captive, client.

The crucial issue is not the loss of skills *per se,* but whether the necessary expertise can be acquired on reasonably competitive terms when it is required. Hence, those who fret over skill transfer should really be watchful that the market for goods and services in which they purchase remains competitive. Private sector monopolies are no better, in general, than public sector ones.

Weakened capacity to innovate is a more problematic question, and one which has been little researched. Returning to the Birmingham small-arms industry described earlier, the academic who used it as an almost extreme example of contracting also noted that the industry eventually went into decline. It was apparently overtaken by revolutionary innovations in production techniques in North America. 'The organization in Birmingham was defective in its provision for technical experimentation' (Stigler 1951: 193 n.). In other words, the contractual arrangements between the myriad specialists apparently left no one with the role of research and development. But it is not clear from this illustration whether the deficiency is generic. It is ever-present in highly fragmented contractual networks which may provide few or no

Table 4.2. Other contracting costs

Title	Definition	Assessment
Hollowing out	Reducing the client organization to a fraction of its former self with the bulk of its production activities contracted out.	Exaggerated concern over hollowing out. Many highly successful organizations are very 'hollow' including Virgin, Benetton, M&S. The same is true of public sector agencies who become contract management organizations.
Loss of skills	By contracting for services traditionally produced in-house the organization loses the skills as both a producer and client of those services.	Skills are lost to the organizations but are retained in the marketplace. The real issue is whether the organization loses the capability of being a smart purchaser.
Loss of corporate memory	Related to loss of skills, corporate memory refers to the collective knowledge within the organization which may be diluted as a result of fragmentation.	Critics suggest that organizations may lose their capacity to build strong relationships with clients as key personnel move around and out to the contractor.
Weakened innovative capacity	Contracting reduces incentives to and capabilities of innovation. Technical progress compromised in the long run.	Contracts based on lowest winning bid are claimed to stifle incentives to innovate because rewards for innovation cannot be captured by the contractor. Market appears to adjust to lack of incentives. Plenty of innovations in contractual solutions.
Transition (switching) costs	Contracting requires organizational restructuring causing dislocation and social costs particularly when associated with loss of employment.	All forms of structural change involving human resources involve costs, financial as well as social. These costs can be mitigated by facilitating the adjustments through re-employment, retraining, and redundancy pay-outs. These costs are transitory.

incentives for innovation by the contractor. More likely the problem was specific to that industry, in that region, at that time.

This conclusion is supported by the fact that there are many examples of successful contracting organizations which have not lost the capacity to bring new products and new processes to market. In high-tech industries, competitors often form joint ventures to collaborate on innovations. The joint development work by Motorola, Apple, and IBM on the new range of PowerPC computers is but one example. Many client organizations encourage and assist their contractors to improve their products and services through innovations, not only between contracts but within the life of an existing contract. To ensure that incentives to innovate are not suppressed, properly structured incentive contracts are required. Many contracts for services allow the provider to come forward with suggestions for improvement at any time. They also build in agreements over the sharing of unexpected benefits through innovation. A fifty–fifty split of any additional efficiency gains realized through process improvement is a commonly found arrangement in service contracts.

It must also be recognized that innovation is the handmaiden of competition. Although economists have for many years debated whether monopoly or competition is the engine of innovation, the evidence favours the competition side. In situations where firms are bidding for contracts, innovation allows them to provide improved solutions at better prices than their competitors. There are numerous examples of this competitive pressure to innovate. The Q-stores case study in Chapter 3 is a clear one; another is the Serco Institute. When the Serco Group plc set up its research and development institute in 1994, whose mission is to research trends in the services market and ensure that Serco products are always at the 'leading edge', its competitors were surprised. Yet the logic is self-evident: the company believes that if it is to stay competitive it must invest in research and development. Note that Serco is exclusively in the contracting business, and has no manufacturing or direct marketing activities. But that does not reduce its incentive to innovate.

Do the costs of contracting outweigh the benefits?

The costs of using the market for anything other than spot contracts are far from trivial. They stem from problems of coordination, cooperation, and trust. There are also costs of searching, of writing contracts, of negotiating (both before and after contracts are let), of monitoring and control, and a host of other costs identified in this chapter.

The crucial question is not whether these costs are significantly higher when exchange of goods and services occurs between separate organizations than when it takes place within them. It is rather whether contracts can be designed and implemented in such a way that the benefits do exceed the costs. The answer increasingly appears to be in the affirmative, for a wide range of activities. For successful contracting to occur organizations need to identify the market conditions which generate potential benefits, and they must be able to appropriate them at reasonable cost. Their contractual arrangements need to combine control with flexibility. Implementing the organizational changes required to switch from external to internal providers is another potentially costly impediment to successful contracting. Part III of this book considers in detail how those elements should be applied to yield the desired outcomes.

Guide to further reading

Boone and Verbeke (1991) use a transaction cost approach to develop a framework which explains the tendency of large, vertically integrated firms to de-integrate. Casson (1995a, 1995b) provides a good overview of the burgeoning literature in the area of the economics of trust.

Hart (1995) is an outstanding summary of the existing theories of the firm, including an extension of the property rights and incomplete contracts approaches, by one of the contemporary pioneers of research into the nature of the firm.

Lewis (1995) delivers a fascinating analysis of four firms that have improved their competitive advantage through enhanced relationships with their suppliers of intermediate goods and services. Putterman (1995) is a valiant attempt to explain the paradoxical observation that firms tend to store information more efficiently, yet the market still remains a more efficient mechanism for allocating resources.

Ring and van de Ven (1992) is an interesting examination of methods of governing transactions between organizations which rely on trust and cooperation, and which have been largely overlooked by transaction costs economics. Williamson (1996) is another in the series of classic Williamsonian treatises on the limits of conventional neoclassical economic theory and how transaction cost economics strives to overcome these limitations.

Other useful references on the structuring of cooperative relationships and the problem of trust are Hill (1990), Barney and Hansen (1994), and in the context of IT outsourcing, Willcocks and Choi (1995).

III

CONTRACTING STRATEGIES

The next four chapters consider the alternative means through which a contracting strategy is devised and implemented. Chapter 5 identifies the sources of added value that is generated through a greater degree of specialization, what the management literature refers to as the focus on the organization's distinctive capabilities. Chapter 6 then explores how this value can be captured by the contracting organization, through either a competitive or negotiated process. In Chapter 7 the design of contracts and performance management systems are discussed, with particular attention being paid to obtaining adequate measures of control while maintaining flexibility. This chapter also considers the important question of risk, and its allocation between the contracting parties. Lastly, Chapter 8 discusses the problems of organizational change associated with the introduction of contracting, problems that are frequently the major obstacles to structural adjustment.

5

Specialization

The main reason for contracting out is functional specialization.

(The Economist, 1994b)

The recessions of the 1980s and early 1990s put pressure on organizations to cut costs and to restructure their operations. American corporate giants such as General Motors, General Electric, and Westinghouse significantly reduced the scope of their internal activities and shed large numbers of permanent staff positions. General Electric is, perhaps, the most notable example. It lost altogether some 300,000 employees by the early 1990s, under the stewardship of its CEO, Jack Welch. His ruthless cost cutting earned him the nickname 'Neutron Jack', after the bomb which eliminates personnel but keeps property intact.

American companies were not alone in undertaking massive restructuring. Many of their European counterparts followed suit. For example, since 1992 BP has reduced the number of employees by over 50 per cent, from 112,000 to around 60,000. This process of headcount reduction, also known as 'downsizing', is coming under increasing criticism for being an unnecessarily drastic solution to a short-term financial problem. The downsizing controversy will be considered in Chapter 11, but in the present context it should be noted that reductions in employment need not represent job losses. More often than not they represent substantial transfers of jobs from one organization to another. Organizations 'have not so much been destroying jobs as handing them over to other people, often with a contract attached' (*The Economist* 1996e).

Much of the restructuring observed in recent times involves the replacement of contracts *of* employment within organizations, with contracts *for* services between purchasers and providers. It is no coincidence, therefore, that services contracting has expanded while companies and public sector organizations have reduced the range of services produced internally. The result is a subtle but important economic transformation which has two distinct elements. First, organizational boundaries are being redrawn as activities previously undertaken internally are handed over to service providers. Secondly, there is a growing trend towards specialization—an increase in the degree to which organizations reduce the scope of their internal functions and concentrate on those they consider their principal or core activities. Consider each of them in turn.

Redefining organizational boundaries

Every organization involved in the production and/or distribution of goods and services, be it in the private or the public sector, has to consider the following question from time to time: could operational effectiveness be raised and unit costs lowered by shifting the boundaries of the organization? Repositioning organizational boundaries thus becomes a management tool: there is always a choice between in-house production and market transactions. To see how this affects the way an organization functions, consider the intermediate chain of production—the value chain—once more.

Fig. 5.1 depicts, in a stylized form, the stages of production for an organization which produces a good or a service. The representation is quite general; it could apply to a broad range of productive activities either in the private or the public sector. It is also highly simplified. The shaded area shows which activities are carried out internally, with inputs that are purchased from outside suppliers. Purchases would also include a variety of support and ancillary services, shown in the figure as advertising and retailing, which are used by the organization to get the product or service to the market. Note that the services explicitly identified in the figure as being provided in-house (production, transport, administration, security, and information technology) have been selected for illustrative purposes only. In reality there may be many others.

Some of the services produced in-house could be acquired from specialist providers through market transactions. Take IT, for example: if the organization decides not to produce the service itself but to contract instead, the IT services entry will disappear from the shaded box which designates 'in-house activities' and reappear outside with the other bought-in services. The organization's boundary will thus have shifted, and the shaded box will have shrunk somewhat. But the result could be a more efficient overall production process.

The impetus to redefine organizational boundaries through contracting need not come from the purchaser. It is often driven by the suppliers: 'Aggressive market specialists, such as EDS and Servicemaster, are increasingly assuming management functions that were done in-house in the large hierarchical firm' (Besanko et al. 1996: 60). As this statement implies, the range of service functions that can be provided through the market is being continually extended, leading to greater specialization in production, particularly in the production of services. Specialization is central to economic efficiency, and the concept of specialization is as old as the dismal science of economics. Its

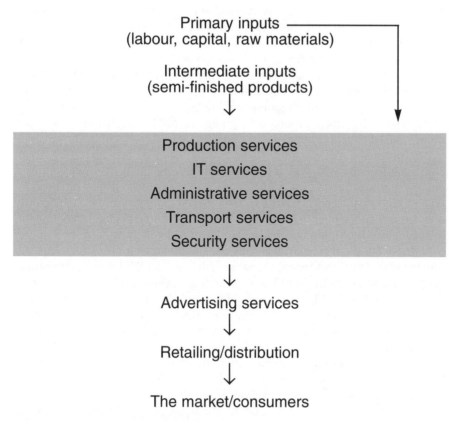

Fig. 5.1. Redefining organizational boundaries

nature and significance to the contracting organizations deserves close scrutiny.

How does specialization add value?

When organizational boundaries are redrawn, functional specialization is enhanced in two main ways. First, the client organization has narrowed the range of its internal production activities. Second, by acquiring an additional client, the external supplier has increased its share of the market, and thus extended the degree of specialization on the supply side of the market.

Writing about university life, the Nobel laureate George Stigler once commented that 'specialization has more foes than friends' (Stigler 1988: 32). Admittedly he was referring to the narrowly constrained range of activities undertaken by a typical university professor, of which he was such a shining example. But his comment does echo a more general sentiment, in that specialization is, by definition, divisive. It erects barriers between those who have acquired complex technical skills necessary for specialist knowledge and those who have not. Specialization by professional groups such as accountants, doctors, and lawyers is seen to confer monopolistic advantages to members of those groups. It was this impression which no doubt led Adam Smith to the view that 'all professions represent a conspiracy against the public' (1880: 134). At the organizational level, specialization is seen to fragment monolithic corporations and public sector behemoths into smaller, more focused constituent parts.

The power of specialization to add value was first articulated by Adam Smith using an example which remains valid despite being over two centuries old: the manufacture of pins. Smith showed, in the context of steel pin production in eighteenth-century Britain, that productivity would be significantly boosted if eighteen people specialized in making one particular part of the pin, instead of each completing the whole range of tasks; if, as he described it, 'one man draws out the wire, another straights it, a third cuts it, a fourth points it, a fifth grinds it at the top for receiving the head . . . and the important business of making a pin is, in this manner, divided into about eighteen distinct operations' (Smith 1880: 6). Their tasks would certainly become exceedingly monotonous, but they would be much more productive. Smith argued that such specialization would result in 240 times as many pins being produced per day as when each worker made entire pins.

This example focuses on specialization by individuals within a single organization, and was typical of its time. But in a contemporary context specialization means something rather different: entire organizations, not merely a group of workers within them, concentrate on particular activities. How does such specialization add value? It does so by allowing an activity to be undertaken on a much greater *scale*. This leads to *economies of scale*, which are cost reductions per unit of output produced resulting from the increase in the volume of production. A specialized service provider, say the firm that took over the supply of IT services from the organization depicted in Fig. 5.1, will most probably be providing similar services to other customers. It follows that its output will be several times greater than that of the organization that is producing the service for its own internal consumption. But where, one might ask, do the scale economies themselves come from?

The answer lies in what Hamel and Prahalad call 'core competencies', Kay calls 'distinctive capabilities', and Besanko et al. refer to as 'organizational capability'. 'The economy of scale arises because the market specialist's investment in the development of its capabilities is, in effect, a fixed set-up cost. The specialist does not have to reinvest in developing the capabilities each time it takes on a new customer' (Besanko et al. 1996: 80). But more importantly, the investment in this capability might never have taken place in the self-supplied organization because such investment would simply not have been warranted for a small IT provider. Once a minimum threshold in the level of activity is crossed, alternative and more efficient methods of production become economically viable. The value that these methods generate is available to, although not necessarily always effectively appropriated by, all potential clients of the specialist goods or service provider.

At this point one may legitimately wonder whether the economies of scale which arise in manufacturing activities are available in equal measure in services. Are the 'fixed set-up costs' of similar significance in services as in manufacturing? Economies of scale arise essentially out of indivisibilities in the application of fixed capital inputs, and the increased productivity of labour through specialization. Modern service activities rely on the application of computer and information technology. Investment in such technology is not linearly related to the volume of activity: typically it is subject to indivisibilities. For example, the cost of a computer network that can process twice as many airline passengers per year is not double the cost of a computer system that can process only half that number. In this way one can see that economies of scale in service industries can arise out of the usage of capital infrastructure.

Economies of scale can also be reaped from higher productivity of human resources in service activities, particularly through training. Training is an activity which can provide significant savings from a larger throughput of students: larger classes need not mean larger buildings; by using distance education methods one can train larger numbers using relatively fixed resources. Other economies common to both services and manufacturing are those that arise in advertising, marketing, and research and development. There are, however, types of scale economies available only in manufacturing industries: those arising from the 'two-thirds rule', for example. This rule of thumb is a simple mathematical representation of the relationship between the volume and the surface area of a vessel. It states that volume of a structure rises with the cube of its linear dimensions, whereas its surface increases with the square. Thus, to double the volume of oil flowing through a pipeline it is necessary to increase its surface area, and therefore its cost, by only a factor of 60 per cent. Such economies typically arise in engineering applications which are more common in manufacturing than in services.

The specialized external provider has a strong incentive to introduce new technologies. This will generally involve raising the capital intensity of production, substituting capital equipment for labour, introducing specialized machinery and hardware, and generally making labour more productive. The extent to which investment in new technology, and specifically IT technology, raises the productivity of the services sector has been the subject of an intensive debate. This question, which will be considered in Chapter 10, is by no means yet resolved. But to make the investment in this capital worthwhile, the volume of services produced must reach or exceed a 'break-even' level. Although it is not possible to be at all precise about what constitutes 'break-even', at low volumes of output labour-intensive technologies are likely to remain economic, even if they are not as cost effective as capital-intensive ones which are run at a higher scale of production.

New technology is typically embedded in replacement capital investment, such as machinery and, increasingly, in computer and telecommunications equipment. The latter have made specialization in services particularly advantageous by, for example, reducing the costs of serving clients who are geographically dispersed in banking, data processing and telemarketing activities. According to Besanko et al. (1996: 67): 'Modern communications and computing technologies have significantly reduced the costs of coordinating complex transactions in the market.' They have also reduced the costs of clients remotely monitoring the performance of external service providers, thus tilting the balance further away from in-house provision towards external specialization.

Investment in more efficient production techniques creates incentives to find new and more productive methods, spurred by competition between specialist service providers. The process is a dynamic one, and is not confined to a one-off improvement associated with a step change in mode of service delivery. It is also self-supporting, a virtuous circle: the expansion of demand makes scale economies possible through capital-intensive methods, which then lead to investment in yet more efficient methods of production, resulting in even lower unit costs.

Another reason why specialization pays handsomely has to do with management. No organizational resource is as scarce as management's time. When intermediate goods and services are produced in-house, management must devote time and effort to this activity. And while it is possible to expand the collective body of managerial resources by hiring, specialization by management in a relatively narrow set of activities is trumpeted in the management literature as a necessary, if not sufficient, condition for corporate success. 'Sticking to the knitting' is another way of saying concentrate, or specialize, in your 'core' business. The greater productivity allegedly stems from the greater focus by management on its principal activities: 'The specialized service firm concentrates all its management attention on a service activity that often represents a peripheral concern of the management of a company performing the service in-house' (Porter 1990: 246).

Specialization and competition

One of Adam Smith's most enduring insights regarding specialization was that 'The division of labour is limited by the extent of the market' (1880: 18). In plain terms it means that specialization, through the division of labour and the fixed investments that yield the economies of large-scale production, will not occur unless it is justified by the size of the market. Demand must reach a minimum level before specialization becomes economically advantageous. But this theorem is ambiguous on the related, yet equally important question: would specialization not yield the same efficiency gains if it occurred *within* the organization as opposed to outside it? As Stigler put it, Smith's proposition is 'less than a complete theory of the division of functions among industries' (1951: 191–2).

If the demand for an input is large enough, could specialization of production take place *within* the organization, much in the same way as Smith described the division of labour in pin making within a single factory? And if the benefits of specialization stem from the joint effects of scale and management focus, would they not be realized just as effectively internally as across organizational boundaries? The answer appears to be that, in general, they would not for two reasons. First, integration has its costs in terms of the 'relationship-specific investments' that the owner would have to make in the internal service provider. These investments create value only if the relationship endures over time; they do not if the parties go their separate ways. Clearly, if the firm invests in its internal service provider and then sources services from the market, there will be no value generated by its investment. With this knowledge, and once such investments have been made, the internal service provider may 'hold up' its captive client, demanding more favourable terms than would be obtained by an external provider.

The second, related weakness of internal specialization is that it lacks competitive pressures. Specialization is like iron: strong, but not strong enough. Combined with competition, the result is an alloy which is far stronger: steel. Competition adds powerful incentives to raise productivity, to improve quality, and to innovate. In a competitive environment, the specialist provider is not alone: there are other specialists in the marketplace vying for the client's business. In order to secure orders the specialists have to try to outdo one another to meet, or exceed, client expectations.

In contrast, a specialized in-house provider will not be operating under the same pressures. Its existence may be less demanding, and therefore more congenial, but this will generally be reflected in its performance. According to Porter: 'The captive in-house service department is a cost centre. It can and should be measured against outside vendors, but replicating the pressures and incentives of competition is difficult in practice' (1990: 246). Indeed, evaluating the performance of the in-house provider is bedevilled not only by its monopoly position, but also by the complexities of internal allocation of costs between different operating divisions or departments. The lack of clear-cut operational data gives it further latitude, a situation which is reflected in the inability of many organizations to assess the true performance of their in-house divisions. Not surprisingly, many CEOs and general managers are willing to make the decision to contract for the provision of services externally without access to precise information about in-house costs.

Competition provides powerful incentives to innovate, in service provision as well as manufacturing. Many of the private sector service firms which have won contracts for services *funded* by the public sector, which were previously *produced* by it, have done so because of the innovative modes of service delivery which they proposed. The Q-Stores case study in Chapter 3 is a particularly good example of a contract won through technology-driven innovation, but there are others.

Competition, and the presence of market opportunities, creates a situation where supply chases demand. As was mentioned earlier in this chapter, a new breed of service providers are scouring the market for new business opportunities. Firms such as EDS and Servicemaster in the USA, Serco and Capita Managed Services in the UK, spend considerable time and resources researching the market, finding out new potential customers and identifying their needs. The intensity of this marketing activity is motivated by self-interest: each provider would like to secure lucrative contracts for new business before one of its competitors. But the scramble for the market is beneficial to potential clients: the services they need are available sooner, and should fit their needs better than would be the case under a more passive supply regime.

With the expansion of the market, new entrants emerge and competition intensifies. The force of competition encourages suppliers to find new niches, those in which they believe they would have a decided advantage over their rivals. This takes specialization a stage further, by leading to ever narrower segments of the market, segments which nevertheless reflect unmet demand. Such *segmented* specialization is unlikely to be feasible, or economical, for an in-house service provider.

In theory, it would be possible to replicate internally the incentive mechanisms provided by the market to encourage innovative and customer-focused behaviour. In practice, such attempts have had mixed results, for reasons that have much to do with difficulties of implementation. There are problems in devising complex reward and remuneration schemes which effectively mimic market incentives. These are compounded by information and measurement problems. According to Milgrom and Roberts (1992: 559): 'When performance is difficult to measure, providing strong incentives is costly, whether they are given to employees or independents.'

Patterns of specialization

Contracting is both a cause and an effect of functional specialization. The first step towards specialization is the recognition that there is a choice between internal production or external provision of a particular function. As the activity becomes more complex and demanding, the capabilities of the in-house service provider may fall short of requirements. This in turn may lead to demands on internal resources which could make contracting seem increasingly attractive. Information technology (IT) services fall into this category. A couple of decades ago most organizations which made use of IT functions tended to provide them in-house. By the mid-1980s the contracting of IT functions was advancing rapidly, whereas by the 1990s it became a veritable flood. Forecasts by industry monitors like International Data Corporation (IDC) suggest that the explosive growth of IT contracting will persist into the new millennium.

Contracting and specialization also lead to a change in the structure of industries. Consider, once again, the case of IT services. When the service is purchased from an outside vendor, the volume of internal activity is reduced. But the gross value of output will not diminish significantly because the organization is now purchasing what it previously produced. What does change is the size of the supplying industry, which will expand with the transfer of activity from in-house to the specialist provider.

Industry growth will also be fuelled by the supply of new services which were not previously produced in-house, but for which suppliers perceive a nascent demand. Global IT specialists such as CSC, EDS, and ISSC are offering a variety of services to potential clients, including hardware and software maintenance, software applications development, database management, and remote data processing, among others. The emergence of the IT services sector epitomizes the evolution of specialization: a new service industry has displaced the countless in-house maintenance operations of yesteryear. This is briefly described in Case Study 5.1. The economy-wide implications of such industrial restructuring will be considered further in Chapter 10.

A good example of the trend towards *segmented specialization* is the way providers of human resource services have evolved into multifaceted professional specialists. The services that firms such as Manpower in the USA and Skilled Engineering in Australia now provide include outplacement assistance, 'career transition management', executive and specialist function contracting, and remuneration and rewards consulting services, among others. These firms no longer just help find people new jobs, they manage the entire employment transition process and often become functional service providers using the former employees of contracting organizations. A summary of this transformation is given in Case Study 5.2.

Another example of segmented specialization comes from the print industry. Printing is a highly fragmented industry, with large numbers of firms of varying size and capabilities employing a variety of print technologies. This can pose problems for customers who may need to devote substantial resources to search amongst suppliers for the appropriate level of service at reasonable terms. Some large organizations do their printing in-house, which undoubtedly reduces their transaction costs, but does not mean they receive the best service at the most competitive price. Printing technology has been advancing rapidly in recent years, with the introduction of computer-supported, digital printing. This adds further complexity to the buyer's task.

A solution to the buyer's problem is a print broker. Print brokers emerged in response to the need to match supply to demand. Their role is to act as

Case Study 5.1.   The international IT industry

Many companies are choosing to outsource the set-up, operation, and maintenance of their computer systems and networks, accessing the equipment and expertise of a specialist provider. A recent survey of 162 European companies found that almost 50 per cent outsourced all or part of their information technology (IT) functions. These contracts represented, on average, 24 per cent of IT budgets, and this figure is expected to rise to 36 per cent by 1998. In the UK in 1994, the software and IT services industry grew by 14 per cent to £7.75 billion ($US12.38 billion).

One reason for this rapid outsourcing growth is uncertainty about IT value: while a unit of processing power which cost $US1 million in 1965 costs less than $30,000 today, many senior executives feel that their expensive computer solutions have failed to deliver the competitive advantage promised in the 1980s. The CEO of a US conglomerate of petroleum, natural gas, and chemicals was reported to have had the following exchange with his internal IT service provider:

CEO. All I see is this amount of money I have to write a cheque for each year. Where is the benefit?

Internal IT provider. Well, we process data faster than we did last year.

CEO. So what? Where have you increased revenue? All you do is increase costs, year after year, and I am sick of it. All I get are these esoteric benefits and a bunch of baloney on how much technology has advanced. Show me where you put one more dollar on the income statement.

The use of outsourcing is often as much an attempt to regain some sense of corporate focus as it is to reduce costs. But computer companies themselves also outsource a great deal. The market is so large that specialists have arisen at all stages of computer design, manufacture, operation, and maintenance: Intel makes the processors for all IBM-compatible PCs; Motorola makes them for Macintoshes; Microsoft produces software; Novell specializes in networks; Syquest and Iomega make removal storage systems. Beyond basic technical support and short-term warranties, few hardware manufacturers offer extended assistance programmes, leaving a niche to be filled by specialist maintenance companies like EDS. The nature of the IT industry is such that each company supplies many others; in this respect, the high degree of specialization necessitates outsourcing.

Sources: Willcocks et al. (1995) and Lacity et al. (1995).

intermediaries between buyers and sellers. Brokers collect print orders from clients, solicit competitive bids from a variety of printers, select the printer on the basis of price, coordinate and supervise the printing process, and charge the client a brokerage fee, usually based on the cost of the printing job. The function of the broker is to advise the client on the type of printing required and to find the printer offering the best price for the job.

But there is more to the management of printing services than print brokerage, including document and graphic design, warehousing of the printed material, distribution, and fulfilment, which refers to the mailing of the

Case Study 5.2. Specialization in human resource services

One ramification of the growth of outsourcing around the world has been the expansion of human resource firms that provide both blue- and white-collar labour for temporary hire. While temporary employment agencies have existed for a long time, the industry has evolved over the last decade. No longer does the industry simply provide a temporary secretary when the permanent employee is sick. It has now developed to the point where it has become a specialist human resource service provider.

And the provision of human resource services has proven itself to be big business. Manpower, which is the world's largest temporary employment agency, has revenues of $US7 billion and acts as an agent for approximately 1.5 million workers a day in the United States. In fact, Manpower is the largest single private employer in the United States, employing more than twice as many people as General Motors. In order to stay on top, Manpower's business has adapted to the evolution of the industry. In May 1996, Manpower formed an exclusive alliance with Drake Beam Morin, which is the world's largest executive outplacement company. Drake Beam Morin's business revolves around training executives that have been retrenched. The benefit of the alliance from Manpower's perspective is that it provides a continuous flow of highly skilled executives who are looking to re-enter the workplace. And this obviously complements Drake Beam Morin's objectives.

Despite the presence of multinational firms such as Manpower in Australia, there is one Australian firm which dominates the supply of temporary blue-collar labour: Skilled Engineering. Although there are no adequate estimates of industry market shares, it is estimated that Skilled Engineering has a 60 per cent share of the temporary blue-collar labour market.

After commencing business in 1964, Skilled Engineering has now grown to a size where it has 34 offices around Australia, employs approximately 5,400 staff, and is a publicly listed company. Approximately 50 per cent of its staff are full-time employees. The company is divided into a number of different divisions including supplementary labour hire, contract maintenance, communications, and mechanical workshops. One interesting facet of Skilled's operations is the way it treats its staff. Contrary to the popular belief that contract blue-collar labour is subject to poor terms and conditions of employment, Skilled's workforce is 99 per cent unionized and is paid above award wages. Skilled's reputation for resolving staff and union issues is a strong factor in its ability to continue to win new contracts.

The deregulation of the Australian telecommunications industry has turned out to be a boon for Skilled Engineering—its communications division is the fastest growing division in the firm and has undertaken tasks as varied as the roll-out of coaxial pay television cable, and the construction of mobile telephone networks and cabling communication networks. In early 1997, Skilled Engineering signed a $A45 million contract with Telstra for the connection of households to Telstra-Foxtel's expanding pay television network. Skilled has also won a $A20 million contract to manage and construct a large part of Telecom NZ's cable television network in Auckland and Wellington.

Sources: First Pacific Stockbrokers (1997), Melcher (1996), and *The Economist* (1996d).

printed copy to designated addressees. Thus employing a print broker would still leave the client with a number of print-related tasks to perform. 'Print management' specialists have sprung up to fulfil the need for the multiplicity of services associated with the provision of printing solutions. One such company in Australia is Print Concepts.

Headquartered in Sydney, with an additional office in Melbourne, Print Concepts has grown steadily since 1988 to an annual turnover of $A15 million in 1996. Its corporate clients can pick and choose among the variety of services offered: from a complete company printing service to a straightforward print brokerage or graphic design function. Once again, the major driving force behind the development of this service industry is technological change, in the form of digital printing technology. It allows customization of documents which, once designed, can be reprinted in small batches incorporating some changes to the standard document without incurring the cost penalties traditionally associated with small print runs.

Providers of print management services require at least two distinctive capabilities to be successful: up-to-date knowledge of fast changing printing technology, and well-honed coordination skills supported by sophisticated computer systems. The investment required in this computer infrastructure is substantial, which reinforces the point made earlier in this chapter: effective functional specialization is conditional on a minimum operating size being attained. This threshold is much more likely to be reached whenever service providers are in the marketplace serving multiple clients, than when they have a single, captive, in-house client.

In the United Kingdom, Australia, and New Zealand, an altogether different type of specialization has made its mark in recent years. A group of private sector service providers have been winning competitive tenders for the delivery of government-funded services. These providers are not really functional specialists of the kind described earlier: they do not have core competencies in, say IT services, or in human resource management or in print management. Their expertise lies in delivering, to governments and public sector organizations, the same services they themselves previously funded *and* produced. What is unusual about their activities is that they take over public sector operations as diverse as rail track maintenance, leisure centre operations, facilities management, military installation management and support, operations and maintenance of municipal water and sewerage facilities, public transport operations, managing the administration and provision of welfare services, and many others. What is equally remarkable about them is that they utilize public sector assets to deliver services at significantly lower cost than was previously possible.

With such a wide and functionally unrelated set of activities, specialization hardly seems a term applicable to these service providers. But their operations do have common characteristics which define the firms' distinctive capabilities. These capabilities stem from their ability to completely redesign—re-engineer—the service delivery mechanism. The scope for redesigning public sector delivery mechanisms is considerable because of restrictions which are imposed on work practices and the deployment of human resources; restrictions which can often be traced back to restrictive agreements between unions and management.

When bidding for government contracts, the service providers are hampered neither by custom and practice nor by these historical restrictions. They redesign the service delivery mechanism from scratch, using alternative technologies where these can lead to efficiency gains. Private sector service providers also have the freedom to introduce staff incentive and bonus schemes to boost productivity and encourage innovation and reform in the workplace.

Ironically, when it comes to bidding for public sector contracts, the lack of a distinct functional specialization can turn out to be a strength, rather than a weakness. Not having a set of in-house, function-specific skills or technologies means that the service delivery solution can be considered afresh, free from 'supplier bias'. If the service provider happens to be an IT specialist there will inevitably be an incentive to figure out ways of tailoring the solution around the company's IT capability. By contrast, the generalist contractor can acquire those functional skills by building the necessary alliances or subcontracting arrangements. The important characteristic of this process is that, in searching for the most efficient and effective solution, the provider is not unduly influenced by proprietary technologies or sunk investments. Many contracts that have been awarded to 'generalist', task-management contractors have required them to link up with functional specialists. The specific arrangements entered into sometimes include strategic alliances between generalists and specialists, and sometimes consortia of two or more firms with differing capabilities.

This feature of the market for public sector services has caused surprise and some consternation among bidders who believe they have the required functional skills, yet lose out to the generalists in competitive bidding contests. A good example of this phenomenon is the successful bid by Capita Managed Services, a large UK contractor to local and central government, for the administration of teachers' pensions in England and Wales. Capita won the bid in the face of competition from many large and respected insurance and fund management companies who, by virtue of their expertise in their respective industry, would have expected to be favourites to win the contract. Instead, they lost out to Capita because, in the final analysis, an efficient *administrative* solution was judged to be the critical element of contract. Functional expertise, while useful, was far from essential.

This is not the only contract won by Capita that was based on a 'total service solution', integrating a variety of skills and technologies necessary for service delivery. Case Study 5.3 outlines some of Capita's activities: the contract for the management of the UK's Driving Theory Centres, and the IT management contract with a county council. The lesson painfully learnt by some of the

Case Study 5.3.   Capita Managed Services

Amidst the boom of the professional services organizations in the UK, the Capita Group plc has been one of the star performers. Having severed itself from the public sector professional accounting body CIPFA in 1984, Capita sees its core business as the provision of general outsourced services. While initially helping local councils run their computers, Capita's contracts now span fields as diverse as assisting council departments in their own buy-outs, selling personalized number plates, distributing welfare payments, and property tax collection. Well positioned for the rapid growth in outsourcing that has occurred in the UK over the last five years, Capita's pre-tax profits for 1996 rose 31 per cent over 1995 to £12.3 million. Its contract base in managed services covers 60 contracts within the UK, employing approximately 3,500 people and dealing with £7 billion worth of public funds.

One of the most interesting of Capita's recent contracts is the administration of the written driving theory test, which was awarded to DriveSafe (a Capita subsidiary) in December 1995. The successful tenderer was to be responsible for booking, scheduling, invigilating, collecting, and marking the written driving theory test. Among contractual requirements were the establishment of 150 test centres across the country, servicing an estimated 1.5 million driving theory tests per year. The contract also involved taking responsibility for the handling and processing of postal and credit card payments. By awarding the contract to DriveSafe, the government made it clear that the important aspect of the contract was administration and logistics, rather than examinations or driving theory-related expertise.

According to Capita, outsourcing provides real benefits to an organization because it introduces clearer definitions of customer requirements and heightens focus on service delivery standards. This tendency is particularly pronounced within the public sector, with which Capita has had many positive experiences. The five-year contract for IT facilities management and finance services with Mendip County Council in Somerset is a good example: the £2.8 million per year contract is the widest-ranging local government facilities management contract let in the UK to date, and covers services such as revenue collection, housing benefit administration, IT support, accountancy, treasury management, printing, and electoral registration. After almost four years of contract operation, Capita has been able significantly to improve service performance, including lower cost of support services, higher revenue collection rates, and a coordinated and planned approach to reinvestment in IT for support services.

Sources: Capita Managed Services annual reports and interviews with management.

functional specialists is that, in some circumstances, their technical capabilities become a constraint, when their functional strength turns out to be a weakness. Identifying such situations prior to bidding, and seeking appropriate partners who can provide a total service solution, is the key to success in this increasingly sophisticated market.

Generalist service providers such as Capita and Serco tend to specialize in the type of client they serve—principally public sector clients seeking to achieve greater efficiency by bundling a range of services into a single contract. By far the largest client base of both companies lies in the various corners of the government sector, at local and central government level, in the UK and New Zealand, and including state governments in Australia. Public sector clients understand that these providers know how to do business with government. For contracts in which functional expertise is required, the generalist contractors can enlist the cooperation of functional specialists either through subcontracting or the formation of alliances.

Serco has developed a strong track record in winning defence contracts in the UK. It is clear that it understands the defence department's culture and can operate within it. It is not surprising to find, therefore, that Serco has won several other military support contracts around the world. But perhaps the most striking illustration of its special capability in the public sector is attested by the award, in 1996, of the contract to manage the UK's National Physical Laboratory. This is an unusual contract in that it essentially involves the operation and management of a scientific/academic unit, where the scope for service redesign is limited and where cultural factors are critical to its successful management. As shown by Case Study 5.4, Serco's contract with the Department of Trade and Industry for the management of NPL reinforces the view that the company's distinctive capability lies in the way it is able to manage contracts for public sector clients.

The continuing reforms in the public sector create a cornucopia of opportunities for service providers who have a demonstrable capacity to establish and sustain stable contractual relationships with government clients. The public sector manager is typically risk averse: for him, awarding contracts to a service provider with a history of successful contractual relationships is a good bet. It means that contracts are unlikely to be awarded to operators who take a short-term view of the market. The other side of the coin is that entry by new firms into this market may be made more difficult precisely because of the propensity for risk aversion by public sector managers. But there is sufficient expansion in the market to create room in it for functional specialists as well as the task management generalists discussed above. And contractual opportunities come in many guises and sizes: reputations for reliable and efficient service provision can be gained on small contracts, and later transferred to larger, more complex ones.

It is unlikely, however, that the generalists will eventually drive the specialists out of the market. Instead, new forms of specialization will develop, as the market for services grows in breadth and depth.

Who benefits from specialization?

This chapter argued that specialization has the potential to generate economic benefits, to create value by increasing productivity and reducing costs. The

Case Study 5.4.   National Physical Laboratory

The National Physical Laboratory (NPL) was set up in Britain in 1900 in order to maintain standards for measurement scales such as mass, length, time, and radiation. As such, it is regarded as one of the world's great metrology (science of measurement) laboratories. Around 85 per cent of the work performed by NPL is commissioned by the Department of Trade and Industry (DTI), which acts as a proxy customer on behalf of industry and the community at large. NPL's annual turnover is approximately £40 million.

As part of the UK government's initiative to evaluate the effectiveness and efficiency of its service provision, the five laboratories—including the NPL—under the auspices of the DTI were transformed into executive agencies in 1990. In a 1993 review of the options available to the government, KPMG Peat Marwick recommended that the NPL be contracted out—that the government should maintain ownership of the facility but that its operation should be outsourced. However, certain difficulties presented themselves: for example, it is impractical, if not impossible, to implement a user-pays system for the use of a metre rule. Despite these problems, the government was keen to enhance NPL's commercial viability. The then-head of the DTI, the Hon. Michael Heseltine MP, stated in 1994 that 'Commercial progress under the management contractors will be carefully reviewed, and might in due course result in NPL becoming ready to move into private-sector ownership.'

In December 1994, five bidding consortia were invited to submit a tender for the operation of NPL. The government was to maintain ownership of the main NPL site at Teddington and all major scientific equipment, which would then be leased to the successful contractor. Any necessary minor equipment would be purchased outright by the contractor. Under the conditions stipulated in the TUPE legislation, all 540 NPL staff were to be transferred to the successful contractor with their terms and conditions of employment unchanged. The contractor would also be responsible for the day-to-day management of the facility—that is, functions such as heating and security. The government guaranteed that a specified volume of research contracts (totalling £145 million over the five-year agreement) would be provided to the NPL.

The contract was eventually awarded to NPL Management Limited, a wholly owned subsidiary of Serco, and commenced on 1 October 1995. Since Serco's expertise lies in administration rather than specialist technical knowledge, the requisite technical expertise was subcontracted by NPL Management Ltd. to AEA Technology and Loughborough University. Serco's impressive international network of business operations certainly helped its bid, allowing it to make a strong case for attracting additional commercial work

After the first year of operation, costs had been cut by around 10 per cent, although on the whole the Serco proposal outlined an evolutionary rather than a revolutionary approach: the majority of the senior management team at NPL has been maintained and, although a steady stream of changes has been implemented, none has been particularly radical.

Sources: Serco plc, UK Department of Trade and Industry.

benefits of specialization come from the economies of scale and the invest-ment intensity of functional specialists. Quinn and Hilmer (1994: 51) express it as follows: 'In certain specialized niches, outside companies have grown to such size and sophistication that they have developed economies of scale, scope and knowledge intensity so formidable that neither smaller nor more integrated producers can effectively compete with them.' The combination of specialization and market competition is particularly powerful: it ensures that every latent opportunity for efficiency gain is vigorously pursued.

Specialization can take a variety of forms, and, as discussed, it need not always be based on specific activities or technical functions. Competitive pres-sures are forcing organizations to become more efficient, to add more value through their operations. The search for efficiency is leading them down the path of specialization. However, chief executive officers are unlikely to think of raising the operational efficiency of the organization in terms of adjusting the 'degree of specialization'. They probably do not even think of the problem in terms of altered organizational boundaries, of changing the balance of activi-ties carried out internally and externally. Most probably, they will frame the question in the following way: what are the distinctive capabilities—the core competencies—of this organization, and what 'business' should it therefore be in? Despite sounding like an entirely different question from the one on specialization, it is essentially the same. Of the myriad activities the organiza-tion can undertake, which are those it should perform itself, and which ones should be 'contracted out'?

The answer will require a systematic analysis of internal activities of the kind outlined in Fig. 5.1. It will necessitate a review of distinctive capabilities by reference to what others are capable of. The most profound lesson learned by Mambo Graphics, the designer and marketer of sportswear introduced in Chapter 1, was that its distinctive capability did *not* lie in the production of apparel. Once it recognized this and made the strategic decision to quit production and concentrate on design and marketing, its fortunes changed virtually overnight. The problem was not entirely solved until it discovered a suitable 'partner'—Gazal Apparel—who would undertake all manufacturing activities on its behalf.

Analysis of effective specialization also requires identification of those activities whose outputs can be specified with sufficient precision to frame a contract. Another factor requiring consideration is whether the industry from which the service may potentially be sourced is sufficiently developed and competitive to offer a suitable choice among service providers. A negative answer to this question is often seen as sufficient reason for retaining activities in-house, particularly if it concerns the public sector. But experience indicates that even if a market does not currently exist it can be developed quickly and effectively. When Marks & Spencer searched for providers of store mainte-nance management services for its UK stores, there was no market of such a specialized service. But in response to the client's needs, three firms that were operating in related fields acquired the necessary resources to serve the new client and a new industry was formed. Marks & Spencer thus created a small supply base for the specialized services it required. This supply base may grow if other clients come forward and demand similar services. But the lesson from this example is that even when supply is not currently available, *potential* supply may be there, just below the surface, waiting for the right demand.

Once it is established that there are tangible benefits to be had from specialization, two other questions remain to be addressed. The first is: how is the value created from greater specialization to be distributed between the client and the provider? The second is: will the creation of a market interface between purchaser and vendor create problems of control, flexibility, and organizational change, problems that could dissipate the benefits, perhaps even eliminating them altogether?

These are important questions because the benefits to be had from greater specialization are of little value if they cannot be appropriated by the contracting organization. The crucial issues concerning the appropriation of the benefits from contracting—how value is captured—are discussed in the next chapter.

Guide to further reading

For theory and evidence on specialization and the organization of firms see Abraham and Taylor (1996), Alchian and Demsetz (1972), and Hoekman and Karsenty (1994). Useful references on flexible specialization, not specifically discussed in this chapter but an interesting development nevertheless, include Sabel (1989), and Storper (1989).

On the development of specialized networks of firms in the age of flexibility see Harrison (1994), and for a specific discussion of specialization in IT contracts see Lacity and Hirschheim (1993). Another useful contribution on the role of information technology is Brynjolfsson (1994). For a stimulating discussion of 'core competencies' or 'distinctive capabilities' in the context of dynamic competition between firms see Hamel and Prahalad (1994).

6

Value Capture

In any vertical relationship, whether with suppliers or distributors, the first, and central, issue is the contract price.

(John Kay, 1993)

Contract prices determine how the value generated by a transaction is distributed between vendor and purchaser. There is a straightforward transfer between buyer and seller: the higher the price, the more value is captured by the latter at the expense of the former. But this transfer is not generally a zero-sum game: 'the more value I capture the less you are left with' does not mean that one side's gain is the other's actual loss. Both parties to a transaction gain from the transfer when a larger 'cake' is made available by it—when there is more value available for distribution because of innovation, specialization, or cost-cutting measures by the vendor. However, the actual distribution of the gains varies with the type of market in which the sale takes place, and the respective bargaining skills of the transacting parties.

In 'perfectly' competitive markets—that is markets where commodities are undifferentiated, where numerous buyers and sellers come to trade, and prices are openly announced to actual and prospective traders—the distribution of value between buyer and seller is the result of the impersonal forces of supply and demand. There are no bilateral negotiations in such markets: the competitive price satisfies all willing traders. No-one who wishes to purchase or sell at the prevailing price is turned away.

Such markets generate prices which reflect *value at the margin*: the price at which some buyers are just willing to buy, rather than forgo the good or service in question. If the price were any higher, they would not buy. For these *marginal* purchasers, the price exactly reflects their willingness to pay; it is the *maximum* value they place on the good or service. But other buyers pay less than that value. They obtain what economists call 'consumers' surplus', and thus capture value whose magnitude will depend on the difference between what they would have been prepared to pay and the asking price.

In the context of contracting, there are several other factors which influence how much value can be captured by the purchaser. First, these transactions typically involve goods or services that are specific to the buyer, and are usually differentiated in some way from similar purchases made by other buyers: automobile assemblers source many vehicle components from outside suppliers, many of which are customized to particular models. This will introduce some price differences between buyers.

Second, contracting transactions are not spot transactions: they involve the flow of goods or services over extended periods. This creates opportunities for variations in performance and/or requirements, which in turn means that contracts need to be structured in a manner that will accommodate corresponding variations in prices. Third, the number of suppliers capable of complying with purchaser requirements will often be unknown at the outset. The purchaser is likely to need to search for vendors who not only provide value, but who are able and willing to meet the terms and conditions stipulated in the contract.

It is clear that contracting for goods or services does not fit the economist's stylized description of perfectly competitive markets. In most contracting situations, purchasers and vendors operate in a vastly different environment: products or services are differentiated, information about prices and quality may not be as easily obtainable, and bargaining strength can make a significant impact on the terms of the transaction. But for those very reasons, using market-type mechanisms is an important way in which buyers can increase value, and capture a good measure of it.

Competitive tendering: bidding for contracts

Competitive tendering is not a new phenomenon. As was discussed in Chapter 1, contracting for transport and other public services was common in eighteenth- and nineteenth-century England. Prospective contractors responded to advertisements inviting them to submit sealed bids for the provision of such services. Their bid constituted the price at which they were prepared to perform the required service over the life of the contract. The lowest bid usually won, this being the price that was perceived to maximize the value obtained by the purchaser.

Setting up a competitive tendering process involves the following steps:

- compiling a detailed specification of requirements;
- publicizing an invitation to tender that will be accessible to potential providers;
- selecting the preferred contractor on the basis of predetermined criteria.

The third step is possibly the most difficult. Although price is often the overriding consideration, it should not always be at the forefront of decision making. The reasons for this will be considered later in this chapter.

When stripped down to its bare essentials, a competitive tendering process resembles an auction. In an auction, a seller invites buyers to submit bids so as to maximize the value of the item offered for sale. Auctions were used as long ago as Roman times, and there are different types. The most common are the English and the sealed-bid auctions. In English auctions, the bids are communicated orally to the auctioneer, and the highest bid wins; this is the way works of art are commonly sold. Participants can readily observe the intensity of competition which is reflected in the rate at which the price is bid up. Bids can be continuously revised upward. Clearly, the seller stands a good chance of getting a price which reflects the highest valuation amongst the buyers at the auction.

In sealed-bid auctions, participants cannot observe their rivals' bids. Consequently they have to make an informed guess about the intensity of competition. One would expect that, in general, English auctions would generate higher prices for the seller than sealed bids. Yet, it has been shown that, on average, the two auctions yield results which do not differ significantly.

Although tendering for contracts is similar to an auction process, there are a number of complexities which necessitate significant procedural changes. First, a competitive tendering process conducted in the style of an English auction would be utterly impractical. Contracts for goods and services cannot be awarded simply on the basis of price. There are many other conditions and requirements that must be met: for example, financial standing, past performance record, and ability to meet changes in requirements and costs. If the contract were to be awarded in an English auction, subsequent negotiations with the winner might reveal that one or several of the contractual conditions could not be met. The end result could well be having to repeat the auction several times until a winner was found that could fulfil the necessary conditions.

The complexity of modern contracts favours the sealed-bid method of tendering. With sealed bids, tenderers do not only submit their bid price, but respond in writing to all other terms and conditions sought by the seller. The result is often a voluminous document, covering in considerable detail every aspect of the client's requirement and how it will be met. Each vendor would put the best possible case forward as to why the contract should be awarded to him, emphasizing such aspects as the range of existing clients, experience, and reputation.

The sealed-bid method of tendering, whilst providing volumes of information to the client, does not remove the need for face-to-face negotiations. Once the client has identified the preferred tenderer, there may still be some discrepancy between what is offered and what is required. In addition, there may be several aspects of the future contractual relationship which, while intangible, are central to the smooth operation of the contract; for example, the nature of performance monitoring and purchaser–provider interfaces. After all, the parties will be tied by the contract for a considerable period of time. Consequently, the purchaser will wish to be satisfied about those intangible aspects which cannot readily be documented, but which can be discussed and evaluated as part of an overall contract negotiation.

Open tendering, which means that any vendor who considers himself suitably qualified can submit a bid, has the advantage that it maximizes competition. Surprising as it may seem, however, there may be such a thing as too much competition! Having to process a large number of bids is costly for the purchaser, since each bid has to be individually assessed. Comparisons have to be made not only on price, which is relatively easy, but on the other criteria, which involve complex and often subjective judgements. Assessments of quality of service are particularly troublesome, since quality cannot be observed at the time of bidding. Evaluation is therefore generally based on reputation, derived from references and testimonials from existing and former purchasers.

Open tendering also imposes significant bidding costs to the industry, for there can only be one winner, even if there are dozens of bidders. Indeed, contractors are often wary of open tenders, and may decide not to bid on the grounds that, relative to the cost of submitting a bid, the probability of winning is simply too low.

Pre-selection: calling for expressions of interest

One way to reduce the number of bidders at the tendering stage is through pre-selection. Under this arrangement, the purchaser posts a request for 'expressions of interest' from suitably qualified vendors. The advertisement usually contains information about the type of service required, its quantity and quality, the likely duration of the contract, and other relevant facts. Information requested from vendors typically includes their financial standing, number of years in operation, the nature of services supplied and their client list. The amount of information solicited at the expression of interest stage is much lower than at the bidding stage. Importantly, vendors are not asked to submit a price: the purpose of the pre-selection stage is merely to narrow the field of potential bidders to those who are considered to have the necessary capabilities and experience. Fig. 6.1 shows a typical form of advertisement for expressions of interest in the supply of prisoner escort and courtroom custodial services by the New Zealand Department of Corrections.

The advantage of pre-selection is not simply the reduction in the number of bids. It also allows the purchaser more readily to identify and select the provider that best suits its needs. The purchaser is asking the following question: which are the vendors in the market with whom we could do business? Those that have been pre-selected therefore satisfy the 'could do business' criteria. This means that, at the tendering stage, the purchaser will not find himself selecting a contractor who is likely to fail on non-price criteria.

This problem is particularly acute in the public sector, where the tendered price has traditionally carried the greatest weight in the assessment process.

DEPARTMENT OF CORRECTIONS

The New Zealand Department of Corrections seeks expressions of interest in contracting for the provision of prisoner escort and courtroom custodial services in the Auckland and Northland regions.

Prisoner Escort and
Courtroom Custodial Services

The services will primarily involve:

- prisoner transport from police cells to courts
- prisoner transport between courts and prisons
- prisoner custody and security at court facilities.

The services will be provided in accordance with the Penal Institutions Act 1954.

Expressions of interest must be addressed to:

John Carnegie, Contracts Group, Department of Corrections, Private Box 1206, Wellington, New Zealand. Telephone **64-4-460 3171,** fax 64-4-460 3212.

Expressions of interest must be received by the closing date, Friday 14 November 1997.

After the closing date, all interested parties will be invited to submit a brief setting out details of their corporate structure, financial strength and relevant experience. This information will be used by the Department to pre-qualify and short-list interested parties. Those parties who are successful in the pre-qualification process will then be eligible to participate in the formal tender process.

Expressions of Interest

Fig. 6.1. Request for expressions of interest

Going through the expression of interest stage reduces the chances of appointing a low-price contractor whose performance characteristics are questionable. The contracting out of the New South Wales Government Cleaning Service (GCS) provides a useful illustration of the way expressions of interest can be used to narrow down the set of prospective tenderers. The GCS was the largest cleaning business in the state, with a turnover of approximately $A180 million in 1992. Most of its activities were in the state sector: cleaning schools, police stations, and other publicly owned buildings. When the government decided to contract out its cleaning operations, the enterprise was split geographically into five zones, each zone covering a different area of the state. The reason for doing so was twofold. First, to contract out the activity in its entirety would be risky because of doubts that any of the existing contractors could undertake the necessary expansion in the volume of business activity. The public sector operation was several times larger than the largest private enterprise. Secondly, the zoning strategy meant that the business could be distributed amongst several contractors, promoting competition and rivalry, allowing performance comparisons to be made between the different contractors. No contractor would be awarded more than two zones.

Only companies with an annual turnover of over $A15 million, more than 500 employees, and with a line of credit of over $A5 million were allowed through to the tendering stage. Twelve companies submitted expressions of interest, seven were invited to bid, and three emerged as winners. The final distribution of contracts was as follows: two companies won two zones each and another won a single zone.

While competition was reduced in terms of the *number* of bidders, their bidding behaviour and the final outcome was intensely competitive. The contract costs came in at around 30 per cent less than the previous GCS operating expenditures—a saving of over $A50 million per annum to the Treasury of New South Wales. This result confirms what has been observed in similar circumstances: restricting the field of bidders through a pre-selection process does not mean that savings, and therefore value, have to be sacrificed by the buyer. For this reason, pre-selection of contractors is becoming commonplace in the public sector, particularly for large and/or complex projects. It has always been widespread in the private sector, which is generally freer to adopt more flexible procurement policies. While pre-selection is an undoubted improvement on open tendering, it is not the end of the story when it comes to sourcing goods and services from the market.

Alternative sourcing methods

Some buyers can search efficiently among potential suppliers without engaging in a formal bidding process. A notable private sector example is Marks & Spencer. It has the lowest ratio of net output to total revenue amongst Britain's major retailers (Kay 1993: 213). To put it another way, the value of bought-in goods and services is three times the turnover generated from its own retailing activities. Several years ago Marks & Spencer made the strategic decision to contract out the *management* of its store maintenance functions. Store maintenance requires a large number of specialist service providers including electricians, air conditioning experts, security and cleaning staff, and other personnel. In the past, Marks & Spencer had managed the coordination of the store maintenance function in-house, until the decision was made to free its own managerial staff to concentrate on its principal activity—retail merchandise trade.

Instead of inviting expressions of interest, Marks & Spencer held discussions with a handful of suppliers who it believed could quickly develop the capability to deliver the services required. Initially it struck an agreement with three suppliers, each taking over the store maintenance management function of about a third of its 300 UK stores, grouped by region. After the contract had operated for a few years, Marks & Spencer invited the three firms to bid formally for a contract renewal, awarding contracts to two of the three former service providers. The interesting aspect of this example is that the buyer did not consider it necessary to go through a formal tendering process at the initial stage in order to secure a contract that generated value. What then could be the reason for going to tender at the rebid stage? It seems reasonable to suppose that, having decided two suppliers was a more efficient solution than three—because it reduced the costs of monitoring and coordination—a formal selection process was considered a fairer and more transparent way of reducing the number of existing suppliers than arbitrarily terminating the contract with one of the contractors.

Another example of alternative sourcing strategies can be found in the Japanese automotive industry. Instead of utilizing formal competitive tendering processes, assemblers of vehicles enter into long-term contractual relationships with carefully chosen subcontractors. The relationships emphasize performance, long-term investments by one party in the other, and product innovation. Also, the relationships typically involve more than one subcontractor; the entire system of contracts is generally referred to as 'multiple sourcing' or more specifically as 'parallel sourcing'. With parallel sourcing two or more subcontractors are used to supply similar components in a way that their performance can be directly compared. Such arrangements offer some protection to the purchaser, in that if performance problems emerge with one subcontractor, there are other(s) to whom switching can take place at relatively low cost. 'Parallel sourcing works to provide competitive incentives for supplier performance while at the same time providing the benefits of sole sourcing, principally reduced costs for communication and coordination' (Richardson 1993: 348).

The Toyota case study discussed in Chapter 2 describes a variant of this parallel sourcing model. In the Toyota 'network' there are some 150 prime subcontractors who specialize in the manufacture of complete subsystems such as headlight assemblies or brake systems. Toyota negotiates prices with these contractors, who turn to another tier of secondary subcontractors—some 5,000 in total—who supply basic components. At the secondary tier level there is likely to be ample scope for parallel sourcing, even though such practice may be restricted at the prime subcontractor level (see Chapter 2, Case Study 2.2).

Despite the absence of formal competitive processes, Toyota obtains good value in terms of price and quality of parts delivered. And although competition is attenuated at the prime subcontracting level, suppliers are well aware that in the final product market—the market for completed vehicles—the force of competition is very keenly felt. Evidently that force can be transmitted to the entire supplier network.

An unusual illustration of 'parallel sourcing' can be found in the case of BP Exploration's contracting out of its IT functions to three service providers, discussed in Case Study 6.1. Not only were they required to supply the specified service, but they were also expected to cooperate fully with one another in providing the client with IT services which were integrated. In other words, the three contractors, who would normally be competitors in the marketplace, had to collaborate to satisfy the needs of this buyer.

The lesson from the BP IT case is that competition exerts a potent force even when there is no formal contest for a particular contract. A purchaser may search among as many potential providers as considered appropriate, but each one of them will know they are being assessed against their rivals. In this environment, when the supply side of the market is well developed, direct negotiations with service providers can yield value gains to the buyer as effectively as more formal competitive processes. Furthermore, the range of contractor capabilities that are tested in the selection process can be both wide and evolve over time.

Table 6.1 summarizes the alternative processes for contractor selection, together with their principal advantages and disadvantages.

The contract price

When new contracts for services are announced, the contract price is frequently trumpeted as a measure of contracting's conquest over vertical integration. Generally the bigger the deal, the bigger the victory. In June 1994 the Xerox corporation awarded EDS a $3.2 billion, ten-year contract, for IT services. Caldwell (1995: 36) referred to it as 'the largest megadeal so far'. But such proclamations are misleading. The arrangements are made to appear as if they involve fixed-price contracts: the provider commits to supply the specified services over the life of the contract at the price struck at the bargaining table. Some contracts may, however, last an entire decade, and sticking to any price schedule may prove impossible.

Although most contracts for services are fixed-price in principle, the variations in volume and type of services required over the contract term mean that revenue flows from purchaser to provider are bound to vary over time. A good contract is therefore not necessarily the one that stipulates the toughest terms,

Case Study 6.1. BP IT

In 1993, the $13 billion British Petroleum (BP) Exploration Operating Company outsourced all of its information technology operations. Rather than outsource the work in one large contract to a single supplier, BP decided to buy IT services from three separate suppliers, but required them to work together to provide a seamless service to BP's network of forty-two businesses around the world. According to BP's head of IT, this outcome enabled BP to 'combine the flexibility and control of selective outsourcing with the comprehensive service offered by a single provider'. How this was achieved is an interesting story about how cooperation and competition can coexist and provide a mutually beneficial outcome.

Like many other companies, BP was aware of some of the benefits of outsourcing IT functions—cost cutting, increased flexibility, specialization, and higher-quality services. When BP was first considering outsourcing its own IT capabilities, it visited other companies that had outsourced IT and soon concluded that outsourcing to a single supplier was not suitable. BP believed that to do so was a mistake because the firm became too dependent on the supplier's skills, management, technology, and service know-how. In other words, the threat of 'hold-up' was too great. BP also realized that it did not want to fall into the trap of signing long-term contracts with IT service providers.

After experimenting with small contracts for a number of years, BP was able to acquire some experience with managing outsourcing contracts. After dedicating some time to ensure that the entire organization understood the upcoming outsourcing process, BP turned to the market. Since it had already been decided that the contract would be awarded to a number of suppliers, 100 companies were sent requests for information in late 1991. The information package outlined the firm's commitment to refocus its IT department and summarized the scope of work to be outsourced.

Following extensive analysis of the information provided, BP decided to conduct interviews with 16 US and European companies, from which a shortlist of 6 was chosen. Rather than simply outline a detailed description of the specifications, BP decided that it might be better to determine how the suppliers would operate with each other—after all, such cooperation would be an essential characteristic if the new contract was to be a success. All six suppliers were subsequently invited to a workshop where they were able to test each other's capabilities and form alliances in order to meet BP's objectives. At the end of the week-long workshop, the six suppliers submitted five proposals covering an array of alliances, dividing responsibility among them and containing detailed solutions for all of BP's needs.

The contract was awarded to a group of three suppliers—Sema Group, Science Applications International Corporation (SAIC), and Syncordia—because its members were able to complement one another's services and expertise, create detailed responsibility allocations, and ensure seamless integration and operations. European 'antitrust' laws prevented the three forming a formal alliance, so BP signed a separate agreement with each supplier. By testing the market and asking suppliers to create solutions to its needs, BP was able to get the best of both worlds—competitive prices and services, and cooperation between suppliers—without the significant hold-up threat which outsourcing often entails.

Source: Cross (1995).

Table 6.1. Contractor selection processes

Type	Process	Advantages	Disadvantages
Open tender or single-stage tender	Invitation to tender widely advertised. Tender is open to all. Tenderers required to provide a large amount of information, addressing all selection criteria and requirements.	No restrictions on competition. Maximum number of potential contractors to choose from. Maximum transparency in terms of 'openness' of the process.	Highest contractor selection costs. Time-consuming process. Maximum total tendering costs. Low perceived probability of success may reduce number of bids. Under-bidding may occur in response to strong competition.
Selective tender or multiple-stage tender	Invitation to submit 'expressions of interest', is followed by shortlisting of those who meet the pre-qualification criteria. In the second stage, those who are shortlisted are invited to submit bids.	Lower costs of contractor selection. Lower total tendering costs for contractors. Restricted dissemination of contract information. Greater certainty about suitability of contractor.	Some restriction on the degree of competition, possibly higher prices. Limited transparency, application of pre-qualification criteria may be challenged. Possible barriers to new competition.
Negotiated contracts	One or more contractor(s) / supplier(s) contacted to specify requirements and negotiate terms.	Economizes on resources and time if restricted number of contractors have required expertise. Greater flexibility through negotiations.	Very limited competition. Lack of transparency. Depends on purchaser having accurate information about suppliers.

but the one which makes provision for the possibility, indeed likelihood, that some variations in service levels and prices will arise. An efficient contract should contain a formula, mechanism, or blueprint for dealing with such occurrences, and for negotiating changes that are difficult to foresee at the outset. The most common provision for such variation is known as the 'schedule of rates' clause, whereby the contract allows for additional services to be purchased at predetermined rates.

When organizations first began seriously to consider contracting as a management tool, they appeared satisfied with the average 20 per cent savings which had been widely reported as the norm. In general, they expected to have to wait until a subsequent contracting round to be able to capture additional value from the supplier. Indeed, doubts have been expressed in some quarters, particularly by those who were sceptical of the merits of contracting, as to whether *any* savings would be achieved after the first round of competitive tendering. Some even suggested that bid prices would go up, once contractors felt they had obtained a strong enough position *vis-à-vis* the buyer. These 'incumbent advantages', as they are known, arise from the fact that, after some time, the existing contractor has acquired valuable knowledge about the demands of the buyer, knowledge which will not typically be available to outsiders. This would appear to confer some kind of monopolistic advantages on the incumbent contractor.

But the evidence indicates otherwise. Competition is present whenever a contract is retendered, and, as demonstrated by the Q-Stores case described in Chapter 3, additional savings can emerge from the most unexpected quarters. The Q-Stores experience is not unique, and, in general, additional value is generated and passed on to the client at the rebid stage. The level of savings may not be of the same magnitude as on the first round, which often produces substantial efficiency gains as the entire service delivery process is restructured, but it is there nevertheless (see Case Study 3.1).

However, in the 1990s, purchasers in the public and private sectors have realized that the gains can be brought forward. An increasing number are expecting to reap additional savings during the life of the contract, as the contractor makes those much sought-after productivity improvements. Consequently, many contracts now contain a provision which says that the purchaser shall share with the contractor any realized productivity gains. This form of contract, known as a 'gainsharing contract', creates incentives for the contractor not only to achieve continuous improvement in efficiency, but to communicate it to the purchaser. This type of contract might be awarded to the supplier promising the largest continuous reduction in cost, as well as a competitive initial contract price. The sharing formula can vary, but a fifty–fifty division is common, and has the advantage of parity and the appeal of fairness.

To implement the sharing mechanism, the contract would stipulate that at regular intervals, usually yearly, the contractor shall disclose to the purchaser full information regarding all costs incurred in the performance of the contract. If the costs (including an agreed profit margin) are less than the annual contract price, the difference is shared between purchaser and provider. If they are higher, the contract price stands. This scheme places heavy demands on mutual trust and cooperation between the parties. It may also appear to blunt the contractor's incentives to generate greater value for the client, since it can retain only half of any realized gains. But the expectation of further savings would be built into the selection process, and would be only one criterion on which the contractor's bid would be assessed. The contractor's reputation would be damaged if, having generated expectations of additional savings at the end of every year, it were to fail to deliver them. Such performance would certainly count against it at the rebid stage.

An interesting example of how a final contract price can converge on the purchaser's expectations of value capture is provided by the Ford-ABB case study discussed in Chapter 4. Ford was seeking to build and operate a new paint-finishing facility in Oakville, Canada. It invited ABB to submit a hastily compiled bid, which was duly rejected. Instead of going to the market the two parties spent three months on a cooperative engineering phase, determining ways of designing the facility so that costs would be between 20 and 30 per cent lower than ABB's original bid. At the end of this process, Ford solicited a second fixed-price bid from ABB, which turned out to be approximately 25 per cent lower than the original. The bid was accepted. It is interesting to note that Ford's target level of savings from the second round of bidding lay within the range that the international evidence suggests is most frequently achievable in competitive situations.

Winners and losers

Competition for contracts can become very intense, resulting in bid prices which may seem like good value for the purchaser but can put financial pressure on the provider. A widely discussed phenomenon which affects auction participants is the 'winner's curse'. The term was first coined in the context of bidding for offshore oil exploration leases. When oil companies bid for exploration licences of blocks of underwater terrain, they must arrive at an assessment of the reserves available for extraction. These assessments will differ between the companies, and the bidding will reflect the variations in these estimates. The winner's curse occurs when the highest bidder, having won the lease, discovers that the price paid exceeds the value of the oil eventually discovered—the estimate turned out to be too optimistic.

According to Kay (1993: 273), 'The winner's curse is a particularly serious problem for the rather mechanical tendering procedures often carried out by public authorities.' The problem arises because contractors' bids are based on a multitude of factors, assessments, and expectations. For example, a particularly attractive bid from a service provider may reflect the fact that the company has underestimated the complexity of the task to be performed. If this contractor won the tender, the winner's curse would afflict the provider and would also have serious implications for the purchaser. In the event of contract termination, a replacement would have to be found at considerable cost and inconvenience, not to mention embarrassment, to the buyer.

At the other extreme, a highly competitive bid may represent a provider who has not underestimated the capabilities required for the task and has the requisite resources, but wishes to enter a new market segment. In these circumstances the bid, which is deliberately set to maximize the probability of winning the contract, does not represent the winner's curse but a calculated commercial decision reflecting the supplier's willingness to take a loss as the price of market entry. Such a contract would be known as 'loss-leading'.

These hypothetical cases highlight the important principle that, in seeking to capture value from the contracting process, the principle should be *caveat emptor*—buyer beware. Sometimes what seems to be exceptional value will turn out to be illusory, and sometimes it will be a genuine 'bargain'. The latter are relatively rare, and buyers need to be conscious of the range of possibilities behind outlying prices. Loss-leading bids are particularly problematic as it is often difficult to distinguish them from genuine bidding errors or situations in which the contract losses could place the supplier's viability at risk.

Recent innovations in value capture from selling spectrum rights—licences to use scarce spectrum frequencies for services such as mobile phones, paging, and broadcasting—demonstrate how difficult it can be to design efficient bidding systems. In 1994 the US Federal Communications Commission (FCC) began auctioning spectrum rights using highly complex and sophisticated 'simultaneous multiple-round auctions', designed by auction theorists. Under this scheme, each sale of a set of frequencies involves multiple bidding rounds. On each round, the bids, which are recorded via computer, are effectively sealed so that no contestant knows what another is bidding. The rules forbid contestants from cooperating, collaborating, or discussing their bidding strategies. After each round, all bids are revealed to the contestants so that they can observe the range of bids submitted. This step-wise process is designed to overcome the effect of the winner's curse, the risk of which might otherwise induce participants to bid cautiously.

In an ordinary sealed-bid auction, bidders will be aware that the highest, winning bid may be the one that eventually loses the firm money. To reduce the risk of being caught out and paying too much, firms will be inclined to revise their bids downward, discounting them for the winner's curse factor. As a result of this restrained bidding, the seller will capture less value. However, by allowing firms to observe their rivals' bids on each sealed-bid round, the FCC offers firms information on what value their rivals are placing on the licences. Just as in an English auction, the price goes up as new bids come in, except that in the multiple-round spectrum auctions the bidders do not know who is bidding any given price—the bids are anonymous. The net effect is that firms become less cautious in their bidding, less risk-averse, and more value is thereby generated and transferred to the seller.

Since they were introduced in 1994 by the FCC, spectrum auctions of this type have been judged an outstanding success. In fourteen separate auctions the FCC has raised $23 billion, much more than could have been realized under the traditional system of licence allocation, which relied less on prices paid and more on rather nebulous merit criteria.

But in April 1997 things started to go wrong, and questions were asked about the multiple-round auction system. In an auction for wireless data transmission frequencies which was expected to raise $1.8 billion, only $13.6 million was realized. At the time of writing the matter was being investigated by the US Department of Justice, but bid rigging—collusion amongst bidders—has emerged as the leading suspect. The multiple-round auction system was designed to minimize the incidence of collusion by relying on sealed bids: even when the bids were revealed, firms would not be able to match prices to bidders.

However, it appears that firms have learned to signal rivals and warn them off bidding for particular frequencies in spectrum rights auctions. 'In one early auction, a bidder apparently signalled its aggressive intent by entering two bids for a particular region's licences in the first round. Its competitors got the message, and it won the licences without much of a battle' (*The Economist* 1997*a*: 96). The multiple-round auction system may have overcome the winner's curse, but it does not appear to have effectively dealt with collusion.

Collusion can always occur in competitive tendering situations, and the conditions which promote it are varied. In general, the fewer the bidders the more likely is collusion to take place. A well-established or standardized product or service also makes agreement between bidders easier to establish and sustain. Collusion is less likely to occur in negotiated contracts, when the buyer enters into detailed discussions with supplier(s) and becomes well informed about relevant costs and prices. Although collusion is illegal in virtually all industrialized economies, informal agreements to restrain or prevent competition are uncovered by the regulatory authorities from time to time. The effect of collusion is to reduce the value captured by the buyer to the benefit of the seller. In the final analysis there is no substitute for vigilance on the part of the buyer, who must look behind the observed differences in prices to determine whether the 'best offer' is one which represents genuine value or not.

Value migration

Contracting for goods and services often begins with an analysis of internal costs. An organization would normally expect to contract out an activity if it can be done more cheaply by an external provider. But simple accounting comparisons can be misleading. Costing internal activities involves not only direct and indirect costs such as labour, materials, and overheads, but also implicit costs—'opportunity costs' in the language of the economist—which are seldom taken into account in these calculations. Such costs include the management time devoted to the internal activity, and the cost of capital and other resources which could be released to alternative activities. Indeed, the principle of specialization discussed in the previous chapter rests on the notion that certain resources are scarce within the organization, and that value can be maximized by concentrating these resources on fewer principal or 'core' activities. Organizations increasingly recognize that there are implicit as well as explicit costs to internal activities. For this reason some private sector firms would contract out an internal activity even if on a strict accounting basis going 'out' would appear to be cost neutral. The only constraint would then be the availability of external supply.

The public sector is often very reluctant to acknowledge the significance of implicit costs, probably because it is particularly difficult to cost activities within governmental organizations. Capital costs, too, are rarely factored in, since 'capital' is provided by the taxpayer. The cost of management time is even more elusive in such an environment. It should therefore come as no surprise that advocates of the public sector production model often bemoan the introduction of contracting, arguing that the taxpayer is actually worse off, in monetary terms, as a result. They see value which was previously created and retained within their sector migrating to the private sector. However, this criticism is based on faulty economic logic because it does not account for the true costs of producing public services.

Nevertheless, there are situations in which value literally migrates from purchaser to provider. Whether this is a good or bad thing depends on the circumstances of the case. One way it can happen is through the transformation of a supplier from a benign service provider into the dominant party in the transaction. Initially the client saves money, capturing value from the contract. In time, the vendor acquires more of the specialist expertise associated with the activity, while the client loses that distinctive capability. The purchaser may then be vulnerable, since the provider is in a position to demand higher prices for its services thus reducing the value going to the buyer. Whether the situation becomes critical depends on how client specific is the provider's expertise, for if it is not, the client may simply turn around and seek another service provider.

In certain cases, the purchaser may choose to exit from the entire line of business which is dependent on the provider. A good example of this situation is provided by the General Electric-Samsung case study of microwave oven production (Case Study 6.2). This case study illustrates two things. First, once GE had lost its distinctive capability in producing microwave ovens, the only way in which it could profit from bringing the product to the market was if the value of the GE brand was a significant factor in the retail microwave market.

Case Study 6.2. GE-Samsung

Although the technology for the microwave oven was developed in the United States, the first companies to commercialize it were the large Japanese electrical manufacturers Matsushita, Sanyo, and Sharp. The US company General Electric also entered the burgeoning new market and by 1980, GE had a 16 per cent share of the market and a factory in Maryland dedicated to the production of microwave ovens.

Despite continued growth of the market, GE's market share had dropped to 14 per cent by 1983 as consumers became more price-conscious and GE found it difficult to compete with the high-quality, low-price products offered by its Japanese competitors. GE decided to investigate the possibility of outsourcing microwave production. Discussions were held with Matsushita, the world leader in terms of both volume and technology, but GE management decided that it was too risky to outsource production to one of its main competitors. GE began to look for alternative sources.

GE decided to outsource production to Samsung, a small Korean company with limited experience in microwave production. GE decided to outsource the production of the cheaper models to Samsung while producing more advanced models at home, and to send American engineers to Korea to ensure that GE's reputation would not be tarnished by the production of low-quality goods. This strategy worked well, and the quantity of microwaves produced by Samsung gradually increased as the quality of the final product improved. GE's margin on Korean-built ovens was significantly higher than that on those built in the USA.

However, as price competition intensified with the maturing of the market, GE found that it was becoming harder to produce microwaves in the USA at a competitive price. GE had reached a flashpoint—should it outsource all microwave production to the cheaper alternative in Korea, or should it consider radically restructuring its US production facility? In May 1985, a decision was made to shut down GE's Maryland plant, and all microwave production was outsourced to Samsung. Shortly afterwards, GE quit the domestic appliance market altogether, while Samsung went on to become the world's largest manufacturer of microwave ovens.

Samsung has grown to a position of great market strength, a mere ten years after first entering the business with no technology, no expertise, no production lines, no marketing or distribution lines, and no brand reputation. Samsung learned about quality control and production techniques from GE and was guaranteed continued sales because of GE's reputation. Once Samsung had acquired the technological know-how, it was easier for it to branch out on its own and develop its own brand name, a feat which they have now successfully achieved.

Source: Jarillo (1993).

If it was not, then clearly GE could not make money by having the ovens produced by Samsung and marketing them under its own label.

Secondly, it is not clear that GE suffered from quitting the microwave oven business altogether. It is quite possible that its strategic analysis suggested that its technical capability and brand power could add much more value in different markets, for example refrigerators and washing machines, where GE remains a leading brand. GE may not have embraced the policy of other 'white goods' manufacturers of supplying the entire range of kitchen appliances. In fact, it is well known that company policy requires its different divisions to make high returns on capital, or else quit the business (see the *General Electric Annual Report*, 1993). It may have taken a narrower, more focused view of its markets, in which case the Samsung episode represents a step-by-step withdrawal from that market.

If GE's policy towards the microwave oven business had been more protective, it would have proceeded along a different contractual path. It could, for example, have instituted special provisions in the contract which gave it part or whole ownership of the production technology used by the contractor. It could have split production among two or more producers, along Japanese automotive lines, to give more leverage against each individual supplier. In other words, it could have designed a contract or set of contracts which gave it the degree of control, and attenuation of risk, that it required. How contracts should be designed to provide purchasers and producers with a fair measure of control and flexibility in contractual relationships is the topic of the next chapter.

Guide to further reading

Useful surveys of auctions and bidding are to be found in McAfee and McMillan (1987) and in Engelbrecht-Wiggins et al. (1983). A highly theoretical treatment is given by Milgrom and Weber (1982), and a more accessible discussion is provided by Milgrom (1989). Another important contribution is Bulow and Roberts (1989), and an interesting account of the airwaves auctions in America is to be found in McAfee and McMillan (1996).

For a theoretical discussion of government contracting and procurement see Laffont and Tirole (1993), McAfee and McMillan (1989), and Globerman and Vining (1996).

Bulow and Klemperer (1996) demonstrate the superiority of auctions, in terms of prices, over direct negotiations. Thaler (1992) provides a wide-ranging discussion of the winner's curse and its consequences.

On alternative sourcing methods as developed by the Japanese, see Dyer and Ouchi (1993) and Richardson and Roumasset (1995). For a discussion of benefit-sharing contracts see Goel (1995). See also Venkatesan (1992) and *The Economist* and Arthur Andersen (1995) report on outsourcing of financial services.

7

Control and Flexibility

Power is a scarce resource that should never be wasted.
(Oliver Hart, 1995)

Two fundamental problems are routinely perceived to stand in the way of successful contractual relationships. The first is trust, an issue discussed in Chapter 3. The problem of trust arises because, to the extent that the *objectives* of the contracting parties differ, the fear of opportunistic behaviour or downright non-cooperation may seem justified. It may also appear sufficiently risky to make in-house provision the only safe option.

The second problem is control. When a contractor undertakes an activity which is part of the purchasing organization's value chain, control over the human and physical resources rests with the provider and not with the purchaser. Control over performance can be exercised through the provisions of the contract, monitoring, and levying of penalties, but that generally precludes having direct access to, and influence over, the contractor's resources. It is this latter aspect that creates concerns over potential loss of control: many client organizations, particularly in the public sector, believe that unless they have direct control over the *inputs* required for the production, they have little if any control over the *outputs*. Much of this chapter is concerned with the validity and implications of this belief.

Control

The *Oxford English Dictionary* defines control as 'the power of directing'. When asked what confers this power in ordinary commercial settings most people would reply: ownership. The power to control the deployment and disposition of resources is vested in the owner of the enterprise, a view which is consistent with the following standard legal definition of ownership. 'But what are the rights of ownership? They are substantially the same as those incident to possession. Within the limits prescribed by policy, the owner is allowed to exercise his natural powers over the subject-matter uninterfered with, and is more or less protected in excluding other people from such interference' (Holmes 1963: 193).

Owners of productive assets therefore have considerably more control over their use than those who simply contract for the services of those assets. Organizations that believe they ought to have maximum control over activities and assets along much of the value chain will therefore opt for the integrated, in-house production model. Although there seems to be little scope for doubt over this proposition, the reality is more complex and the conclusions ambiguous. At least two practical illustrations suggest that ownership of assets which are used as *inputs* in the production of goods and services does not always confer an acceptable measure of control over *outputs*.

Shareholders are the official owners of publicly listed corporations. In the eyes of the law they should be allowed to 'exercise natural powers' of control over the way the corporations' assets are used to create value for its owners. But ever since Adolf Berle and Gardiner Means published *The Modern Corporation and Private Property* in 1932, it has been recognized that direct control of a corporation rests with management rather than with shareholders. Because ownership is dispersed among many and because information about the best use of company assets is difficult and costly for shareholders to obtain, the senior management has considerable latitude in its actions. How much latitude it actually has, and what disciplinary mechanisms are available to shareholders for corrective or preventive action, has been hotly debated in recent years. According to Bishop (1994: 3), 'Everywhere shareholders are re-examining their relationships with company bosses—what is known as their system of "corporate governance".'

This is not the place to delve deeply into issues of corporate governance. The reason for bringing up the subject is to highlight situations in which ownership does not confer control (in the sense defined above). Indeed, some leading protagonists in the debate have argued that the relationship between owners and managers is best viewed as a contractual one: the owners hire the managers to maximize the value of their assets, but problems arise in aligning the objectives of the managers with those of the owners. Designing and enforcing the appropriate form of contracts is therefore at the heart of the corporate governance problem.

Another situation where ownership does not confer control arises in large bureaucratic organizations, whether in the private or public sector. There are circumstances in which internal service providers become resistant to demands from corporate management. It can become difficult or impossible for managers to elicit performance improvement without extensive negotiations and concessions. Many a manager has commented that the benefit of contracting for services is that, faced with a competitive market, contractors will revise working practices and introduce new technologies at a pace that is rarely achievable by the more sheltered in-house providers.

Such problems are essentially ones of *incentives*. Ownership of the physical assets does not confer similar rights of control over the human assets—the people—without whom the services required could not be produced. Ownership of physical assets is not sufficient for generating cooperative and productive behaviour from the relevant staff. Financial incentives, bonuses, and other perks may provide a way of inducing changes in behaviour that improve performance. But this begins to look suspiciously like the relationship between a contractor and a client, in the sense that a bargain is struck and payment is related to performance. However, the overwhelming weight of evidence suggests that nothing works on incentives as powerfully as the force of competition. Several examples have already been cited in this book concerning its impact, and its boost to performance can often be far greater than that achieved through restructuring and informal contracting with internal service providers.

Does this mean that it is always preferable to break down the value chain so as to introduce competitive supply at every stage but the final one? The answer is almost certainly no. There are circumstances in which ownership of assets matters and matters very much. In these situations, a vertically integrated mode of production is to be preferred over the contractual mode. To see how this comes about, consider the classic illustration of General Motors and Fisher Body. For many years Fisher Body supplied General Motors with pressed steel car bodies under a long-term contract. In the 1920s, when demand for cars in the USA soared, General Motors turned to Fisher in order to revise the quantity of bodies required and the formula for the prices at which they would be supplied. Fisher Body refused to revise the formula and eventually General Motors bought out Fisher Body.

This illustration is used in the economics and management literature to highlight cases where ownership—and the integration of production—is desirable. In this case, Fisher Body had the power to disrupt General Motors' production activities because it could not easily and costlessly turn to another supplier for such car bodies. The productive assets of the two companies were so complementary to one another that it was more efficient that they be under common than separate ownership. Complementary assets are assets that are highly specific to the economic activities in question: for example, Fisher Body cannot use the moulds used for pressing GM car bodies to supply any other vehicle assembler and, likewise, GM cannot employ other manufacturers' moulds to produce its own cars.

In contrast, a set of computer terminals used to conduct routine office functions would be classified as independent assets. They could be transferred from one organization to another and be equally productive because they are not specific to the activities of any particular one. Such assets as non-specialized IT hardware and software are non-complementary and therefore should be independently owned. However, Hart (1995: 7n.) does recognize that even when complementarity of physical assets leads to vertical integration, the resulting benefits through enhanced control may be mitigated by the blunting of incentives: 'There has been some debate about whether GM did in fact increase its power over Fisher Body by buying Fisher Body out.'

Controlling outcomes

It may be something of a cliché, but the notion that 'If you want something done well, do it yourself' exerts a powerful hold over people in all walks of life. Management is no exception. The notion is intuitively appealing because of the belief that control leads to direct influence over performance. Within an organization, the degree of control is influenced by its structure and level of decentralization. In a typical functionally structured organization, groups of employees responsible for specific functions report to their superiors who in turn have a reporting line going higher up the management of the organization. Senior management may set performance targets and time frames within which they should be achieved, but there are reasons why such internal control mechanisms may fail to deliver the desired outcomes. Two of them stand out: information and incentives.

Information about appropriate and realistic performance standards for an internal service provider can be difficult to obtain. Consider Case Study 5.1 in which the CEO of a large US conglomerate reported that he could not evaluate the benefits provided by his internal IT department despite spending more money on it each year: 'All I get are these esoteric benefits and a bunch of baloney on how much technology has advanced.' IT may be a special case because of its technological complexity, but the information problem can permeate a range of other internally provided services.

Incentive problems arise because responding to management's demands for enhanced performance will typically require a review of existing production methods and working practices. The changes that are recommended by management could be disruptive and discomforting to staff. In environments where they are represented by unions, such changes are likely to be delayed while protracted negotiations are entered into. Information and incentives interact here: management will be given reasons why its demands are unrealistic and need to be scaled down. The internal service provider can always claim that it operates in a special, indeed unique environment which makes comparisons with outside organizations rather misleading.

The nature of the contracts between employees and the organization can also become an obstacle to change. They are typically long-run or undated arrangements in which the terms of the relationship are not specified too precisely, relying on the parties involved to respond cooperatively to events affecting the organization. Once a particular work pattern is established within the organization, it may be difficult to dislodge: it becomes enshrined as 'custom and practice'. And workers are bound to feel that management are effectively changing the terms of their contracts, demanding greater performance for much the same pay. In short, there may be little or no incentive for the internal service provider to adjust rapidly to external demands, unless external pressure is brought to bear—for example, the threat of competition.

This does not mean that every organization will have to threaten its internal service provider with contracting in order to ensure that performance is kept up. Some tightly managed companies set overall financial performance targets for their businesses which have the effect of forcing all internal functions to operate efficiently and cooperatively. General Electric is a good example. It sets high financial performance targets for its twelve global operating businesses, and reviews them regularly. There is an expectation, fostered by GE's CEO Jack Welch, that each business should be number one or number two in their industry. Such financial discipline, coupled with a competitive ethos, tends to engender a continual search for additional efficiency gains that can be captured either by internal streamlining or by harnessing the capability of an external service provider.

But structured employment relationships do not by themselves guarantee effective control over outcomes. The notion that an organization can exercise control over the activities of its employees can be rudely contradicted by the facts. Before Rupert Murdoch transformed British newspaper publishing in 1986, the highly restrictive, almost archaic working practices in the industry stifled productivity and held back innovation. Murdoch's strategy was to sack existing employees, recontract with an entirely different group of workers and service providers, and move operations to a high-tech facility on a greenfield site. It was a highly controversial and politically charged break-up and reconstruction of a newspaper production plant, with implications for the entire industry. Such drastic action was born of years of powerlessness. Jack Welch (1994: 2) expressed the tendency towards internal sclerosis in terms that are universally recognizable: 'Simply put, people seem compelled to build layers and walls between themselves and others. . . These walls cramp people, inhibit creativity, waste time . . . and, above all, slow things down.'

The question that faces organizations at some time or another is: what is the most effective way of achieving the desired control over outcomes? There is a choice. General Electric used a mix of contracting and internal restructuring, most recently attempting to create 'boundaryless behaviour' which allows the capabilities of the different businesses to be shared towards the common corporate goal. Others may choose to buttress and enforce internal performance standards, while there are those that may turn to outside suppliers. What all three cases have in common is the need to obtain and interpret information about performance outcomes. Monitoring these outcomes becomes an important element in the management of contractual relationships.

Monitoring performance

As suggested earlier, contracting is often perceived to lead to a loss of control compared to the 'command and control' of in-house operations. Whether such perceptions are justified is hardly the point; what matters is that they have practical consequences. In general, the externalization of production leads to a much more intensive focus on performance monitoring. Organizations that contract out elements of their value added chain want to be sure that any deviations from prescribed standards are quickly and effectively rectified. To do that they need timely and relevant information: compiling and interpreting it is the core of every performance management system.

Much more effort appears to go into performance management when external contractors are enlisted than when in-house production is involved. Yet in principle, the same type of performance information is required for management purposes irrespective of whether production is internal or external. What creates this discrepancy is the *perceived* difference in control: with internal operations the presence of direct and informal channels of communication creates the impression that swift intervention is always possible; with external production such channels are limited. The client organization must turn to the contractor to put things right, which it cannot do unless it has credible and up-to-the minute performance information.

This asymmetry in the application of performance management systems became disturbingly evident with the contracting out of publicly funded services in the UK. In most cases, specifications of the services to be put out to tender did not exist prior to the introduction of competition. Without proper specifications, performance monitoring would become highly subjective and imprecise. Indeed, that is the reason why it is virtually impossible to find examples where performance can be adequately compared before and after contracting.

Which performance measures are actually used matters less than how they are deployed. Frequently, and particularly in public sector contracts, performance measurement is used in an adversarial fashion. This means the parties are engaged in a cat-and-mouse game: the client in pursuit, the contractor trying to avoid being caught. Besides poisoning relations between the parties, such use of performance monitoring is not particularly effective, providing no help for dealing with the cause of the problem, but focusing only on the symptom.

Another problem with performance monitoring is excessive reliance on KPIs—Key Performance Indicators. They are measures considered essential to the performance of the contract and on which assessment of performance becomes based. However, too narrow a focus on KPIs can lead to perverse results. The operator may give so much weight to meeting a particular performance target that the cost, in terms of a deterioration of other activities, can become significant. A good example of this phenomenon is the behaviour of City Rail, Sydney's metropolitan railway system. It had been set a 90 per cent target of on-time arrivals and departures, which is defined as being no more than three minutes late. Due to operational difficulties, performance was slipping below target when it was reported that trains were not stopping at all their designated stations. 'At worst, up to 44 per cent of peak-hour City Rail trains were running late, forcing them to skip stations' (Morris 1997: 2).

Examples of innovative and effective performance management systems can be found in the private sector. One such example is Sun Microsystems, described in Case Study 7.1. In the public sector, some of the more interesting applications of performance assessment emerged in activities considered potentially difficult to contract out. Management of state prisons is a good example. Prisons raise all sorts of problems for an authority wishing to bring in private management. Public concerns over the treatment of prisoners, the level of training and skill of the contracted prison officers, and the potential incompatibility of the profit motive with the ethical requirements of prison management are all issues that need addressing. Some economists have also added weight to the argument that there is a class of activities which must remain in the hands of government, within which they place prisons (see Hart et al. 1997).

Yet despite the theoretical difficulties, experiments with private prison management around the globe suggest that on average results have been positive, and are actually getting better with the benefit of experience. The UK Home Office has recently let a prison contract in Doncaster to Premier Prison Services, a joint venture company between Serco and Wackenhut Corrections Corporation of Florida. In the USA private prisons have been in operation for some considerable time, and in Australia several states have contracted out prison management since 1990.

A recent report by the Australian Committee for the Review of Commonwealth-State Service Provision (Steering Committee 1997) concluded that some improvement could and should be made to the tendering process, the separation of the purchaser from the provider, and the performance monitoring system. But overall, the experiments in contracting of prison services have been judged successful. One factor emphasized by the committee is the need to implement independent performance assessment, which can provide unbiased information about achievements and shortcomings in the contractual relationship. The independence of performance monitoring is particularly important in the public sector context where the policy is controversial. There is clearly a world of difference between Sun Microsystems' performance assessment of its suppliers, and the evaluation by the publicly accountable prison authority of the provider of correctional services. Case Study 7.2 describes how the Junee correctional facility, the first privately operated prison in the state of New South Wales, has implemented monitoring and evaluation systems of the contractor.

In the public sector, there is greater emphasis on monitoring and assessment of standards once external contractors are hired. In the preliminary report on the impact of compulsory competitive tendering on local authority services in England, Walsh (1991: 5) concluded that: 'Competition has led to major changes in the monitoring of service, with explicit inspection processes

Case Study 7.1.   Sun Microsystems and supplier relations

A good example of an efficient and effective supplier relationship within the computer industry is provided by Sun Microsystems. Sun produces a range of personal computers and file servers, and has become well known for its extensive use of suppliers, and the 'symbiotic' relationship with them. Known as the computer company that does not make microchips, Sun purchases between 75 and 80 per cent of components from other companies.

Sun itself does not produce computer chips, disk drives, monitors, keyboards, or computer chassis. It concentrates on the manufacture of CPU (central processing unit) boards and the efficient assembly of parts. Company managers explain: 'We try to do internally those parts that provide us with a competitive advantage . . . we take our talent to address the most critical value-added areas and partner the rest. The goal is to eliminate non-value-added and to simplify.'

Given its high level of dependence on suppliers, Sun must closely monitor their effectiveness over a wide range of criteria, and a rigorous appraisal system has been developed to this end. Sun looks at the total cost of dealing with a particular supplier, including ongoing technological development and back-up support. Supplier performance is reviewed quarterly in joint meetings and analysed with a scorecard developed by Sun, which details factors like price, quality, and delivery reliability, as well as flexibility and communications. The targets for suppliers are continuously made tougher; for example, previously a supplier would pass the delivery performance test if delivery was made up to three days early or one day late. Now up to two days early, but no days late, is the acceptable standard. None the less, the delivery scores of suppliers have continued to rise. Improvements have also been made in inventory and cycle times, allowing new products to reach customers faster than those of its competitors.

Sun's assessment system has also prevented the company from thinking it could have a single supplier as a global partner, an idea it views as the biggest delusion in the industry. The use of scorecards has even been extended to its relationships with other companies, such as airlines and rental car operators, and between its headquarters and subsidiaries. Annual awards are presented to the best suppliers.

The benefits of this system can be seen in improvements in supplier performance, and on the balance sheet: in the fiscal period to 29 December 1996, Sun's revenue climbed 19 per cent, to $US2.08 billion, while fiscal second-quarter earnings in 1997 soared 41 per cent, to $US178.3 million. Sun's share of the market also continues to rise: from 38 per cent of Unix workstations shipped in 1995, to 41 per cent in 1996. Sun's operating margins are around 9.5 per cent. In a market as competitive as international IT, these figures speak for themselves.

Sources: Vasilash and Bergstrom (1995), Wheatley (1994), Hayes (1997), Schaff (1996).

being introduced, and a clear emphasis on standards.' This view is echoed in the city halls of a handful of American cities that have recently adopted competitive tendering for municipal services, cities such as Indianapolis, Cleveland, Philadelphia, and Milwaukee. These contracting initiatives will be discussed further in Chapter 9 on the public sector.

Case Study 7.2. Prison management at Junee

There has been much debate recently about the efficacy of using private companies either to own or manage correctional facilities. Most of the objections to 'private prisons' revolve around difficulties in ensuring and monitoring the quality of services provided, particularly with regard to intangible areas such as levels of health care, violence towards inmates, and rehabilitative services. For example, how can a contract specify the level of force that a prison guard can or should use during a prison riot? And how can this level of force be measured, both during and after a riot? Although it is difficult to incorporate such factors within a contractual framework, a rigorous system of performance monitoring can be used to overcome these problems.

While the United States has been at the forefront of the movement to introduce privately managed prisons, Australia has not been far behind. Both New South Wales and Queensland have privately managed prisons, and Victoria is in the midst of an ambitious programme which will see approximately half of its incarcerated personnel being detained in prisons run by private firms during the term of its present administration.

New South Wales has only one privately operated prison, at Junee, in the south-west of the state, 500 kilometres from Sydney. The contract for the design, construction, and management of the facility was awarded in 1991 to Australasian Correctional Services (ACS), a consortium of Thiess Construction, Wackenhut Corrections, and ADT Security. The construction of the 600-bed minimum/medium-security facility cost the Department of Corrective Services (DCS) $A60 million. The management of the facility was subcontracted to Australasian Correctional Management (ACM), a subsidiary of ACS, for five years, with an option to extend the contract for a further three years in 1998. The Junee correctional facility became operational in March 1993, and at present accommodates around 10 per cent of the NSW inmate population.

Since only the management of the facility was outsourced, the ownership of the complex remains with the Department of Corrective Services. Similarly, the state retains responsibility for the health and well-being of Junee's inmates. Various contractual provisions are used to ensure that the contractor meets this responsibility. To this end, the Department defined certain 'minimum standards' covering operations management, security control, inmate care services, and inmate management.

Due to the intangible nature of the services provided, and the difficulty of accurately and adequately measuring and quantifying them, an important provision within the contract is for a comprehensive, multi-layered performance monitoring system. As part of this system, the NSW Prisons Act was amended in 1990 to provide for a liaison officer to monitor privately run facilities. The Junee liaison officer assesses contractor compliance with the 'minimum standards', and undertakes compliance audits, which entail regular visits to Junee. The officer reports directly to the commissioner of the DCS, and the audit findings are published in the Department's Annual Reports. Medical services at Junee are monitored by the Correctional Health Service, which provides the medical care at Department-run facilities.

Other aspects of the services provided by ACM are monitored by the DCS to ensure standardization of service through two official 'visitors', a specially constituted Community Advisory Council, and the potential intervention of the NSW ombudsman. It is important that the various practices at Junee are compatible with those provided in other NSW prisons. Thus, performance monitoring at Junee plays an important role which not only ensures adequate compatibility between the public and private prisons, but also provides the DCS with a benchmark for its own facilities.

Source: NSW Department of Corrective Services.

Controlling risks

For obvious reasons, the principal risk in a contract is non-performance. If the contractor does not deliver the goods or services according to the requirements stipulated in the contract, the client organization could suffer a loss. That is what risk means: the possibility of an adverse consequence causing loss, damage, or injury. Contracting has been perceived to be risky because control of inputs associated with the activity is effectively ceded to the provider. Although there is risk associated with any activity, the subjective 'distance' that contracting places between the client and producer creates a heightened perception of risk.

Purchasers go to great lengths to ensure that the provider performs in line with contract specifications. The selection process, with its emphasis on previous experience and company reputation, is the first line of defence against the risk of poor performance. Then there are contractual instruments which are used to keep performance within the acceptable bounds: incentives for superior performance and penalties for poor performance. These, coupled with elaborate performance monitoring systems designed to detect every deviation, minimize the risk to the client organization. But it is a mistake to suppose that performance risk stems entirely from the supply side. The behaviour of the client can have a decisive effect on whether the contractor will perform or not. There are numerous examples, of which the Fairfax County example discussed in Chapter 1 is one, where the stance of the client made it almost impossible for the contractor successfully to take over an internal activity.

In the Fairfax County case there was latent political opposition to the contracting of maintenance services for school buses. As a consequence, the weekly service requirement of buses requiring maintenance was understated by the client, and the general condition of the bus fleet worse than expected, stretching the contractor's resources to the limit. In addition, the transfer of service delivery occurred at the busiest time, the middle of the school year, putting further pressure on performance. Lastly, the client's former maintenance supervisors were made responsible for monitoring performance. In the contractor's opinion this resulted in overly critical assessments of outcomes (Reca and Zieg 1995: 51–64). Using displaced and potentially resentful staff as contract monitors certainly places at risk the integrity of the performance evaluation process.

It is up to the client to incorporate appropriate risk-minimizing safeguards in contracts, through the use of incentives and penalties. But there has been a debate among practitioners as to whether incentives are more effective than penalties, or vice versa. In economic terms, there should be no difference between the effect of incentives or penalties on behaviour, unless the contractor is unusually risk averse. To see this consider the following simplified example: a client considers alternative contract structures to safeguard performance: one with a penalty and one with an incentive. The incentive or penalty is of equivalent monetary value in any currency, and Table 7.1 describes the payments to the contractor under alternative performance regimes.

As Table 7.1 shows, the effect of the financial incentive or penalty on the payouts is exactly the same. What differs is that, in the incentive contract, the initial contract sum is smaller, the full payment being conditional on performance. In the penalty model, the initial sum is the full payment the contractor can expect to receive if performance meets the standard. If it does not, the financial penalty brings the contract sum back down.

However, there are reasons for real contracts not working quite so simply. First, contractors (and their clients) tend to be risk averse, or more precisely loss averse. The prospect of losing a sum of money appears to be more daunting than the opposite, satisfying effect of winning an equivalent sum. One of the pioneers of decision analysis summed up this behavioural characteristic in the following words: 'The major driving force is loss aversion. It is not so much that people hate uncertainty—but rather, they hate losing . . . People are much more sensitive to negative than to positive stimuli' (Tversky 1990: 75). That would suggest that penalties, in general, are likely to be more effective than incentives.

But penalties can create an adversarial climate between the contracting parties, one in which there is a presumption that performance standards are permanently under threat. In practice, this is often overcome by requiring the contractor to supply a performance bond or guarantee. This is a facility provided by a bank or financial institution, usually valued at between 5 and 10 per cent of the annual turnover of the contract. Having a guarantee means that, should performance be deemed to have slipped persistently below the required standard, the client organization can draw upon it and recover the funds. Ostensibly, this facility indemnifies the client for the additional costs of securing alternative service provision at short notice. But in theory, it also acts as powerful incentive for the contractor, who would not only be facing a financial loss if the guarantee was drawn upon, but also damage to its reputation.

Performance guarantees cost money, a cost which will tend to vary with the financial standing of the contractor. Such a cost will find its way onto the contract price, although industry sources suggest that it is typically insignificant

Table 7.1. Incentives or penalties in contracts

Alternative performance regimes	Payment schedule: incentive-based contract	Payment schedule: penalty-based contract
Baseline contract sum	900	1,000
Satisfactory performance	900 + 100 = 1,000	1,000
Unsatisfactory performance	900	1,000 − 100 = 900

Note: Values in the table could be in any currency.

relative to the annual contract sum. It is also interesting to note that the requirement to provide performance guarantees tends to vary widely between clients. In general, public sector clients demand guarantees more frequently than private sector ones. But perhaps what is most interesting is that such guarantees are rarely, if ever, drawn upon. According to an industry source, a review of the use of performance bonds in the USA showed that not one had been called upon from among the contracts in the study. However, this raises the question: if bonds are not drawn upon, it may be precisely because they are effective in safeguarding performance. The only way to be certain whether they are worth their price to the client is to study groups of contracts with and without such bonds. No such study has yet been carried out.

It is a major advantage of performance guarantees that they are rarely invoked. This means that day-to-day performance management by the contractor and monitoring by the client is effectively decoupled from the 'penalty system'. Performance issues can be discussed without the threatening presence of financial penalties for every default or fall in standards. A contract incorporating such a penalty system would quickly become unworkable. It should also be noted that in service contracts payments are usually made in arrears, typically 4–6 weeks after delivery. This gives the client an automatic leverage, as payment can be further withheld if there are serious performance difficulties that need resolving.

Simplicity also works best for incentives. Complex incentive mechanisms, where additional payments are linked to key performance indicators, are problematic for two reasons. First, they require detailed measurement of selected and agreed dimensions of performance which is more difficult than it sounds. Secondly, once such a system is implemented, the contractor is inclined to devote too much attention to keeping those indicators up, rather than maintaining overall performance. 'A weakness of such complex schemes is that increasingly effort goes into influencing the parameters of the scheme, rather than in performing well within it' (Kay 1993: 277) . For this reason the incentive schemes that work best are the simple ones. The clearest example discussed in Chapter 6 was the fifty–fifty cost saving split of any productivity improvement achieved by the contractor during the contract term.

Besides performance, other contractual risks depend on the type of service being provided. Environmental risks loom large in water and sewerage operations and management contracts, while commercial and financial risks are important whenever the service is 'mission-critical' to the contracting organization. In contracts involving large manpower requirements there may be industrial relations risks, while in IT contracts there are confidentiality and intellectual property risks. Continental Bank, which was taken over by Bank America in 1995, contracted its IT operations in 1993, despite concerns about losing control over its 'crown jewels' and exposing the bank to greater risks (see Case Study 7.3). Continental was the first bank to go down the outsourcing path, contracting its entire IT operation. Today, a large bank that does not

Case Study 7.3. Continental Bank

Continental Bank had struggled though the late 1980s in a state of financial turmoil, after a liquidity crisis. By 1990, Continental had turned to outsourcing in an effort to alleviate its fiscal troubles. Its cafeteria, security services, legal department, and property management had all been outsourced, but the unprecedented step of outsourcing almost all IT services was viewed with much scepticism by managers and financial markets. Information, and IT, are commonly regarded by banks and bankers as essential to their business. Surrendering them to an outsider is often perceived as endangering core competency; banks, it was thought, must retain complete and secure internal control over their IT functions.

But no bank's technology has ever led to a truly dominant position, or locked its rivals out of the market. Managers at Continental slowly came to the conclusion that information was a tool used by clever bankers to their customers' advantage, but *managing* that information was not a banker's core competency; access to IT is important, but owning it is not. More important were intimate knowledge of customer desires and requirements, and building solid long-term relationships with clients.

Market analysts expressed doubts about the wisdom of opening up proprietary technology—for example, cash management products, derivative instruments, and accounting systems—to an outsider. These technologies can take years and huge investments to create; wouldn't outsourcing control over them be handing over the 'crown jewels', endangering the bank's security? In fact, this fear was exaggerated. Certainly, in the past, proprietary technology could produce large profits, but today it can be cloned in months or even weeks. Competitive advantages no longer naturally accrue to those institutions with the most internal IT 'resources', but to those with the flexibility to tap the source of the best available technology at an acceptable price.

Continental's in-house IT department was unable to respond quickly and flexibly to customer needs, lacked overall strategy, required large investments, and had too many staff members for routine operations. Everything it did cost too much and took too long.

Therefore, in September 1991, Continental Bank chose ISSC (Integrated Systems Solutions Corporation, an IBM subsidiary) to manage its IT functions. Over the following three months, precise contract conditions were negotiated, covering issues such as the need for tight management and monitoring, confidentiality, penalties and pricing. The multi-million-dollar deal, spanning ten years, was signed in December 1991, and the contract commenced in January 1992.

Sources: Huber (1993).

consider transferring IT functions to an outside specialist would be thought of as the exception.

Whatever the source of the risk, the purchaser will typically demand a risk assessment/management plan which spells out and quantifies both the probability of adverse events and the magnitude of their impact on the organization.

This plan would normally also outline various risk mitigation strategies. Risk management plans are then evaluated as an element of the overall bid assessment process. The weight attached to the plan depends on the type of service being contracted and the attitude towards risk by the purchaser. For example, in large complex IT contracts the risk management plans provided by the bidders will typically be very substantial documents, spelling out dozens of different risk scenarios and how the contractor proposes to deal with them. Nevertheless, such plans will not cover all risks to the purchaser or the provider, for example, the risks associated with premature contract termination. Both parties will therefore need to assess their respective risks arising from the contract and reach a mutually acceptable allocation. A good example of such arrangements is provided by the contracting of treasury operations (Case Study 7.4).

Allocating risks in contracts

An important distinction must be made between the risks that arise from the contracting process—the separation of the purchaser from the provider—and the risks that are inherent to the activity being contracted. An IT contract ostensibly exposes the purchaser to the potential loss of competitive advantage which springs from exclusive technical and operational know-how. The Continental Bank case suggests that these risks may be overestimated, but it remains true that such concerns arise only as a result of the contracting decision. By contrast, one type of risk in a catering contract arises from the variability in the demand for meals, a variability which will be present whether the activity is managed in-house or contracted out. Catering contracts with public sector clients often have a pricing structure based on a schedule of rates for different types of meals, but with no guaranteed volumes attached. Given the relatively high fixed costs of maintaining a fully staffed kitchen, the contractor is facing a risk that the volume of food consumption will be insufficient to make the contract viable.

In this situation the contractor is being asked to bear a risk which is entirely outside its control, and research has shown that contractors often refrain from bidding for such contracts. Whether the client has complete or partial control over the demand for catering services, it is clear that it is in a better position to predict and manage this type of risk than the contractor. One solution would be to design the contract so that it has a fixed and a variable component. A minimum volume of catering work is paid for whether the demand is realized or not. The variable component is based on actual demand, over and above the minimum, and payment to the contractor would depend on the number of meals consumed. This would be a risk-sharing strategy. Its advantage is twofold: it tilts some of the risk towards the party that has more control over it, and it means that a mutually beneficial transaction, which might otherwise have been abandoned, goes ahead.

Case Study 7.4. Oakvale Capital Ltd.: contracting out treasury functions

From a control point of view, outsourcing a corporate treasury may seem risky: letting someone else hold the purse strings. When one considers the diverse range of investments that must be successfully juggled—including cash in various currencies, securities, gold, and shares—this risk and the consequences of error could be tremendous. The natural desire to retain control makes this seem a strange activity to entrust to an outsider. However, if basic checks and balances are in place to mitigate the risks, and if the contractor possesses the necessary expertise, treasury functions become a good candidate for outsourcing.

Oakvale Capital Ltd. has found a niche providing outsourced treasury services to over ninety small and mid-sized companies across Australia. Formed three and a half years ago in Western Australia from the merger of FinCorp and Campbell Capital, it has since grown rapidly, doubling its staff, and became the largest independent treasury operation in Australia—managing over $A8 billion in funds, debt, foreign currency, gold, and commodity exposures. To mitigate some of the risks associated with any financial transaction, Oakvale uses two main strategic tools. The first is an analysis of the 'value at risk', identifying and quantifying likely risks associated with a given decision, based on historical volatility and market behaviour. The second is the creation of risk frameworks, which are used to establish a maximum level of risk with which the client is comfortable, and around which a hedging framework is then built.

Far from simply taking control of all treasury functions within a company, Oakvale often prefers an advisory role. John Meacock, managing director, sees Oakvale's function as linking treasury activities to corporate strategies and board policies. 'Our best relationships are [those] where we work with an existing corporate treasury function' (Treadgold 1996). Oakvale therefore always recommends that its clients keep at least one treasury executive in-house; Oakvale will propose a course of action, but it is up to the client to accept or reject the suggestions. 'We have invested heavily in financial and pricing models and we sell that expertise to our clients . . . We provide them with all the advice, all the information to allow them to make an informed decision,' says Meacock; each client fully controls the management of their treasury. This advisory relationship encourages Oakvale to see itself as a partner to each client, rather than as a separate contractor. Meacock maintains that 'the relationship has got to be allowed to develop', and suggests that it can take anywhere from six months to a year to build it.

Oakvale is not affiliated with any bank or other financial institution. It does not earn transaction fees, nor does it sell or promote financial products; it is paid a flat fee for its services. All transactions are conducted in the client's name, rather than Oakvale's; corporations can therefore feel confident that the advice they are receiving is objective, and focused on achieving maximum returns within agreed risk parameters. L.E. Chrystal, chairman of the Hospital Benefit Fund of Western Australia, said: 'their independence gives us confidence.'

Sources: Company and industry reports.

There are two important principles of risk allocation in contracts: first, more risk should be borne by the party that has greater control over it. Second, if both have the same or no level of control, then more of the risk should be allocated to the party that has the greater capacity to bear it. Application of these principles means that the price of risk, which is reflected in the premium that is added to the contract price, is minimized. This principle is identical to that of insurance: insurable risks can be eliminated altogether, but at a price. Some risks in contracts are insurable, which makes their pricing straightforward and their allocation irrelevant. For example, workers' compensation and accident insurance is easily obtainable, because insurance companies have statistical information on the incidence of such hazards, making precise calculations of expected pay-outs possible. But many risks are uninsurable because the data required are not available. In these situations the parties to the contract have to negotiate an appropriate pricing and allocation of risk.

Some purchasers have been unaware of the financial burden associated with risk because in essence they have been self-insured. This means that financial losses or claims from adverse events are met through the organization's own resources. It does not imply that the risk is not present, only that it has not been explicitly accounted for. In many situations it may indeed be more efficient for the client to self-insure against a risk for which commercial insurance is too costly or unavailable. Examples include environmental hazards and natural disasters. Public sector organizations have often been self-insured by default, but they are generally well placed to do so. They have the public purse behind them. To expect the contractor to accept unlimited liability for such risks is unrealistic. Relatively few firms worldwide, perhaps only giant corporations, can effectively deal with events of this kind and come through financially unscathed. Table 7.2 contains some examples of different contracts/activities and a particular risk associated with them, the source of the risk, and which party has better control over it. The table does not describe how risks are actually allocated in such contracts, but rather how they should be according to the criteria outlined above. In fact, the allocation of risks in contracts does not always follow these principles: purchasers seem to be inclined to transfer more and more risk onto contractors who complain that this is unreasonable and uneconomic.

But this trend is not entirely surprising. Clients have discovered that the risks *inherent* in the contracting decision are not as formidable as was once thought. This has raised their confidence in contractors' ability to discharge their responsibilities, take on a wider range of tasks, and accept more risk. The Shawbury Helicopter Training School contract in the UK, where the contractor was asked to take ownership of and finance the purchase of almost forty training helicopters, is a good illustration . The risk of damage, loss, or depreciation of the physical assets now rests entirely with the contractor. For the contract to be economically viable the price must reflect the additional risk. But from the public purchaser's point of view there is another advantage: the need to obtain public finance to purchase capital equipment has been eliminated. Clients

Table 7.2. Risks in contracts

Contracted activity	Type of risk	Source of risk	Who bears and controls
Catering	Volume or type of food required may be variable and unpredictable.	Number of personnel using the catering location is subject to change.	If the client is responsible for the variability in use (e.g. a defence force catering facility) the burden of risk should be on the client.
IT support: database management	Corruption or loss of data.	Technical or operational deficiency; unauthorized access to IT system.	Contractor is in best position to build in safeguards and back-up system and should bear the risk. Liability may have to be limited.
Water and sewerage systems: operations and management	Water pollution.	Operational failure or act-of-God (e.g. a major flood).	Contractor bears risks for operational failures but does not accept unlimited liability.
Pilot training for the defence force organization	Damage to equipment: aircraft and helicopters.	Negligence or accidental damage.	Contractor controls equipment used. Risk (insurable) may be transferred to contractor by requiring ownership of equipment.

should make the assessment and desired allocation of risk explicit in the bidding process. And if there are benefits to altering the initial allocation, prospective contractors should be allowed to demonstrate that it is so. In general, if the client requires an investment in contract-specific physical assets, this will substantially augment the risk borne by the contractor.

Flexibility in contracts

Changing the course of a supertanker is a slow business: it can take several hours to complete a 90- or 180-degree turn. There is no question that the supertanker cannot be controlled; on board computers allow very precise calculations of the duration of every change of speed or direction. But as for flexibility, there is virtually none, because there is no way of speeding up those manœuvres.

Flexibility is defined as the ability to make changes in an activity at a fast rate and low cost. But there is always a trade-off between the rate of adjustment and its cost. For example, an increase in output following a rise in demand can be achieved if additional resources are diverted to this activity from elsewhere. That is true whether the activity is conducted in-house or by a contractor. In both cases there is a cost to speeding up the adjustment process. However, contracting can enhance flexibility by effectively reducing these costs of adjustment.

How does this come about? From the way resources are distributed among specialist contractors in the marketplace. There are two types of scenarios: first, where the client sources from a single specialist contractor, and second, where there is a network of multiple providers. In the first case, if the client demands additional output at short notice, the contractor should be capable of responding by reallocating resources from other contracts where demand may be relatively slack.

Consider the provision of security services on a university campus. Even in large universities of say 30,000 students, normal security requirements would be modest: one would not expect the university to employ more than a dozen security officers. Suppose that a series of annual campus events take place which require extra security, the university would not be able to respond using its own resources. It would have to resort to body hire: bringing in temporary security officers from outside. How successful this is depends on the market for temporary security back-up services. The less developed it is, the greater the cost of searching for appropriate personnel and the larger the hire fee. The alternative, which is to hire and train additional in-house security staff, is prohibitively expensive and may result in substantial campus security capability lying idle for much of the time.

A large security contractor providing services to the university is likely to employ several hundred or even thousands of specialized personnel scattered across dozens of contracts. To shift a handful of additional security guards to the university contract is not difficult because the burden is spread over a large number of other security contracts. A general principle operates here: the costs of adjusting output upward or downward within a single production unit tend to rise disproportionately with the absolute size of that adjustment. This is a well-established proposition in economics. When the adjustment is distributed over several production units the costs fall disproportionately also. Contracting provides this *distributed adjustment* effect: the contractor is able to spread the burden of adjustment, something which could not be achieved by the in-house production unit.

In the network-of-suppliers case the effect is the same but the contractual structure is different. Here the client sources similar services and goods from a group of suppliers: any upward or downward adjustments of scale or scope of output are distributed among them according to predetermined criteria. Such arrangements tend to be more common in manufacturing than in the services sector. The sports shoes manufacturer Nike has developed one of the most sophisticated supplier networks in the business (Case Study 7.5).

Flexibility can thus be obtained at lower cost through contractual arrangements than in-house production could achieve. In times of low turbulence, when demand and technology are relatively static, the premium on flexibility may be small. But in times of rapid and unpredictable changes across a wide range of industries, greater flexibility takes on a special significance.

Although contracting can deliver greater flexibility at lower cost to the purchaser, it does not mean that flexibility will be costless. All adjustments that involve resource shifts will incur costs. The magnitude of the costs depends on the initial disposition of resources, and the time available for the adjustment. In general, the longer the lead-up time to the adjustment, the easier it will be to execute and the lower will be the costs. Unfortunately, such adjustments can rarely be fully and accurately predicted in advance. The client organization would therefore wish to build flexibility into the contract, specifying the likely range of adjustment but neither its exact magnitude nor timing.

This raises the following question: how should the contract be structured to provide for that flexibility without sacrificing control or expected cost savings?

Which contract: classical or relational?

Nowhere is the potential trade-off between control and flexibility more apparent than when it comes to designing the contract. Since spot contracts are not appropriate to the type of transactions considered here, that leaves essentially two types of contracts: classical and 'relational'. Classical contracts are formal, legally binding, and can be of short or long duration. They are precisely framed, specifying as fully as practicable the terms and conditions of the contract, the obligations of the parties to one another, and the courses of action to be taken in case certain foreseeable contingencies arise. Classical legal contracts remove flexibility by building in as much legally enforceable control as possible. They protect both parties against short-term opportunistic behaviour, but provide little incentive for the parties to share information in a way which could ultimately benefit them both. Another problem with a classical contract is that the more comprehensive it is the more unwieldy it becomes: to specify responses to all foreseeable contingencies is virtually impossible, and makes the contract excessively cumbersome—it becomes a supertanker.

What legal theorists call 'relational' contracts, and economists refer to as 'implicit contracts', are more commonly known in commercial circles as

Case Study 7.5. Nike: the search for flexibility and partnerships

Nike is famous for two things: the 40 million pairs of running shoes it sells each year, and the fact that it does not manufacture any of them. How does it do it? With the aid of an advanced worldwide network of subcontractors, developed over the last twenty-five years. The fluid and dynamic footwear industry is not technologically intensive, but rather characterized by large-scale vertical de-integration and a high level of subcontracting. It is therefore the management of Nike's subcontracting system, rather than any technological superiority, which is usually credited as the source of Nike's competitive advantage. The two most distinctive characteristics of Nike's production network are the flexibility it provides and the partnership relations it creates.

The major competitive advantage provided by the Nike production system is flexibility. The entire footwear industry is focused on the rapid introduction of new shoe styles. As markets become increasingly difficult to control, the time taken to react to variations in fashion and competitor strategy become correspondingly more important. Nike manages to produce an entire range of new shoe designs semi-annually.

Like all of its major competitors, Nike relies exclusively on Asian sources for its manufacturing. One production executive said: 'personally I would say . . . the biggest reason for being there [Asia] is flexibility. We can turn our product around there very quickly—even more quickly than we could ever do in our own plants.' Nike has around thirty-two footwear production plants across Asia, which are separated into two basic tiers. In the first tier, Nike has what it terms 'developed partners' and 'developing sources'; in the second are 'volume producers' and general low-level suppliers.

'Developed partners' are long-term suppliers, usually located in Taiwan or South Korea, which possess sufficient technology and expertise to be entrusted with the production of Nike's more expensive products; in other words, they are closer to the core of the company. 'Developing sources' are the low-wage, semi-skilled production facilities, located in countries such as Malaysia, Thailand, and China, which are gradually being upgraded by Nike: experienced technicians from the USA, Taiwan, and South Korea are often assigned to these facilities on a rotating basis. Most of the 'developing sources' produce exclusively for Nike.

Those that produce for Nike's competitors as well, termed 'volume producers', make up less than half of the company's suppliers, but are used to undertake the bulk of Nike's low-level production, and are usually kept at arm's length from the company—in the second tier. The rest of this tier of the production system consists of the numerous materials, components, and subassembly sources.

The flexibility that this partnership tier system offers is based upon variation in the number of factories and workers. Nike's production network is not static—head office is constantly refining its supplier system, so the company frequently shifts its production from one factory to another, and from one country to another. It has been known to open plants and begin contracts with suppliers, only to end them and move on within one or two years.

Source: Donaghu and Barff (1990).

'partnering' or 'alliance' contracts. They are softer forms of contracts, characterized by an agreement between the contracting parties to cooperate in the achievement of mutually agreed goals. The agreement may be written down, but it is neither highly specific with respect to terms, nor legally binding. Its major advantage over classical contracts is that it creates an environment where trust can be built up and information shared. Information is an important element of contractual relationships: flexibility of response depends not only on cooperation, but on frank and rapid exchange of information. A relational contract is a response to the problems of inflexibility and non-cooperation that often plague classical contracts. If the parties can respond to events as they unfold without invoking the small print in the contract, the solution to the problem is likely to be more effective and achieved more quickly. It may involve some post-contractual bargaining, but that should not be a problem in the partnering or alliance environment.

Relational contracts are not legally enforceable, they are self-enforcing: cooperation and frank exchange of information cannot be enforced, only mutually solicited. While they make for a much more flexible response, they appear to reduce the level of direct control available to the client. That does not mean that performance monitoring is no longer relevant. Rather, it is used constructively to identify problems and rectify them rather than impose fines and penalties in an adversarial fashion. But what if the contractor chooses to behave opportunistically? What measures of control are available?

One possibility is to fall back on the classical contract. The existence of a relational contract does not preclude having a classical contract as a last resort, a contract that is kept in the bottom drawer and with luck and cooperation will remain unused. Whether such a strategy is successful is difficult to say; there is to date insufficient evidence on the success rate of such arrangements. Some purchasers, for example Marks & Spencer, do not feel they need to rely on the dual-contract structure: the prospect of a long-term relationship with a purchaser of high reputation turns out to be a sufficiently effective enforcement mechanism.

Another mechanism used to secure the relationship is to require substantial investments by the provider that are specific to the relationship, such as the purchase of some fixed assets. These investments give the contractor a long-term stake in the relationship, reducing the incentives to engage in short-term opportunism. As was mentioned earlier, clients are increasingly expecting contractors to take a long-term financial stake in the relationship, one which would impose costs if the relationship were to be terminated.

The other dilemma facing clients is the following: medium-term classical contracts have the advantage of impending competition: the contract may be rebid every few years and this keeps contractors on their toes. But 'relational contracts work best when all parties recognize that they are bound into a repeated game' (Kay 1993: 57). Effectively this means the contract should be long enough to make termination an unlikely or very distant prospect. Such developments have been observed in recent IT services contracts, for which a ten-year term is common. There are clear advantages to such relationships, but they need to be balanced against the advantages of shorter, classical contracts. Using such contracts, the purchaser can appropriate a greater slice of the cake; but by using a relational contract the size of the cake may be increased.

Table 7.3. The characteristics of classical and relational contracts

Contract type/characteristic	Classical	Relational/partnering/alliance
Contract duration	Variable depending on activity, but generally between 3 and 7 years.	Variable, but generally longer than classical contracts. Durations of 10 to 15 years are not uncommon.
Contract document/ specification	Detailed, formal (legally binding), and highly specific. Documentation may be very lengthy in cases of complex services.	Agreement between the parties spells out general purpose and objectives of the relationship. Documentation will be parsimonious and not formal.
Control	Contract contains detailed performance provisions including monitoring systems, penalties, and guarantees.	Control is achieved through a high level of cooperation which may include monitoring. Penalties generally omitted but provision is made for sharing of benefits.
Flexibility	Limited, but contract may specify that additional services may be required based on agreed schedule of rates.	Flexibility is the hallmark of the relationship, based on rapid and full sharing of information. Adjustments in scale or scope of activities are negotiated in this spirit.
Dispute resolution	Mechanisms spelled out in contract document, including the provision of special arbitrators.	Expectation is that potential disputes are resolved before they reach adversarial level. No formal mechanisms specified.
Others		Joint venturing: the client takes an equity stake in the contractor to align objectives further (Commonwealth Bank/EDS 1997).

Table 7.3 contains the main characteristics of classical and relational contracts, with a few examples of where they are typically used. The table shows how the choice of contract will affect control, flexibility, and other contractual elements. These are generic contract types. In practice there are many variants within each which cater for differing circumstances and preferences of purchasers and providers. The table illustrates the differences between the two types of contracts, rather than their similarities. It is not uncommon for classical contracts to take on many of the positive elements of relational contracts without sacrificing their inherent properties. A contract can be partly implicit and partly explicit. The optimal combination of contract features is a matter of careful design, where management needs to exercise judgement and appeal to those criteria that have been highlighted in this chapter.

Guide to further reading

On the issue of control through ownership see Grossman and Hart (1986) and Hart and Moore (1990). The question of control in an incomplete contracting framework is explored in Bolton and Whinston (1993), Hart (1991), and Spier (1992). Other useful references on this topic are Waterson (1993) and Macleod and Malcomson (1993).

On performance monitoring, particularly in a public sector context, see Hall and Rimmer (1994) and Domberger and Rimmer (1994). See also the UK Audit Commission (1995), and the United States General Accounting Office (1997) on the practical problems of performance evaluation in public sector contracts.

An entertaining and comprehensive discussion of risk and the evolution of risk management strategies is given in Bernstein (1996). A useful analysis of risks in contracts is to be found in Kay (1993), but see also Chiles and McMackin (1996).

The flexibility question is considered in Carlsson (1989), Del Monte and Esposito (1992), Denton (1994), Harrison and Kelley (1993), and Suarez et al. (1995). For a general overview of the new age of flexibility through business networks see Harrison (1994).

8

Organizational Change

Change is not without inconvenience, even from worse to better.
(Samuel Johnson, 1755)

Much of the writing of modern management experts has been devoted to one major issue: change. The difficulties of accepting, adapting to, and accommodating change are not new: Samuel Johnson, English lexicographer, was writing about them in the eighteenth century, and he was not the first. What has made writing about change so ubiquitous in recent times is an insatiable demand for knowledge on this topic. Deregulation, globalization, and technological innovation are the alleged culprits—they create upheavals resulting in dislocation and 'reinvention' of productive activity. In the former case activities which were previously viable domestically are 'exported' to more competitive locations in newly industrializing countries. In the latter, whole industries are destroyed as new ones emerge based on the technology. Witness the disappearance of the typewriter caused by the invention of the PC.

Joseph Schumpeter referred to this process of industrial decline and renewal as the 'perennial gale of creative destruction' (1943: 84). A more modern interpretation of this phenomenon, by Pam Woodall, economics editor at *The Economist*, is that 'change is simply economic growth by a different name' (Woodall 1996). It is relatively easy to quip about economic change, but another matter to survive it. And although contracting does not quite create such upheaval, it does involve internal organizational change which is typically feared and often resisted.

This chapter is concerned with organizational change brought about by contracting. Keeping one's sights on the benefits of such change without recognizing the organizational challenge involved is a recipe for failure. Many contracting exercises have not yielded the desired results because organizational and staff issues were neglected. Several lessons concerning change in the contracting organization can be learnt from past experience—about the treatment of staff, the interfaces with customers and suppliers, and the additional demands that must be shouldered by the management prior to, and during, implementation.

Contracting and organizational change

The impact of contracting on the organization differs according to whether existing goods and services are affected, and the sector to which the organization belongs. If contracting involves activities not previously undertaken internally, the adjustment required is modest. Similarly, the constraints on organizational change affecting staff are generally less severe in the private than in the public sector. Employees in the public sector often have security of tenure over their jobs in excess of that provided by employment legislation applicable to all workers. While this may be a reasonable trade-off against the typically lower levels of remuneration in the public sector, these differences can slow down or even stand in the way of corporate restructuring.

To the affected employees, the prospect of contracting out may seem like the threat of a hostile takeover bid. The activity with which they have been associated is about to fall under 'new management', and their own job may be on the line. The employment relationship—broader than a narrow interpretation of an employment contract—is about to be broken, betrayed to the principle of economic efficiency. The level of anxiety tends to be proportional to the uncertainty that surrounds the impending changes. With it can grow feelings of resentment and anger at the prospect of 'unfair' treatment of staff.

Organizations tend to evolve into communities, with strong social interactions between members which foster feelings of fellowship and solidarity. This is true even for private sector organizations that are focused on commercial objectives. When a member group from such a community is perceived to be threatened by potentially adverse changes, its fellow employees may rally to the cause, fomenting opposition to the proposed change. And once trade unions enter the fray, the stage can be quickly set for industrial confrontation.

Understanding the sources of conflict caused by contracting can help the development of countermeasures. There are some remarkable examples of organizational change associated with contracting which, despite their radical nature, have steered change through without industrial disputation. One such example of a radical shake-up of organizational boundaries is Semco S/A, a Brazilian company specializing in marine and food-service equipment. During a time of immense economic upheaval, Semco found an innovative way to survive while many other businesses were going bankrupt: it contracted its work out to its own employees. The case stands out for the audacity of the owner-manager of the enterprise.

Semco's experience is as innovative as it is rare. It may be argued that such fundamental restructuring would stall in countries with more restrictive employment protection legislation, or more belligerent unions. Nevertheless, the case is instructive inasmuch as it shows how far contracting can go when economic conditions demand organizational change. In more stable circumstances, such change may be unacceptable because it is seen to produce losers as well as winners.

Case Study 8.1. Semco

In 1990, the Brazilian Minister of Finance came to the conclusion that Brazil's high level of inflation was the result of too much money being used for too much speculation. He therefore seized 80 per cent of the country's cash, and introduced what Ricardo Semler, majority owner of Semco S/A, called 'an extended period of economic bedlam'.

To weather this economic storm, Semco encouraged its existing workforce to leave the payroll and start their own 'satellite' companies who would work, initially at least, for Semco. These satellites were allowed to stay under Semco's larger umbrella—leasing machinery, working in the plant—but would be free to work for other companies as well, again on Semco machinery in Semco factories. Each company was guaranteed a certain amount of initial contract work, and lease payments on equipment and space were deferred for two years. Seed capital was provided by the layoff payments and severance pay and other legally required benefits. Workers were given courses in cost control, pricing, and inventory management. Workers' compensation changed from simple wages to contract payment, royalties, profit-sharing, commissions, piece-work, or any combination of these—whatever they could think up that management could live with.

White-collar workers—Semco's accountants, human resource staffers, computer programmers—were the first to take advantage of these opportunities. The blue-collar workers in food service and refrigeration followed suit. The benefits of this system proved to be substantial: Semco was able to cut inventory and payroll costs, and was ensured a supply of subcontractors who knew the business and the way it worked. Former employees had the chance to increase their incomes and to build themselves a secure future.

'When I describe Semco to other business people, they laugh,' says Semler (Fierman 1995). ' "What do you do?" they ask. "Make beads?" And I say, "No, among other things we make rocket-fuel-propellant mixers." ' Today, around half of Semco's former in-house manufacturing is done by the satellite companies. In 1990, Semco employed 500 people; today the figure is closer to 200, plus at least that many again in satellite companies, and around 50 people who work for satellites and work for Semco part-time. In the seven years since the satellites were set up, only one has failed.

Sources: Fierman (1995), Semler (1994).

Impact on staff

Contracting will typically have an impact on employment within the organization, on wages, and on working conditions. The effect will vary from case to case, and from the short to the long run. The general effect on employment is the most clear-cut: in the vast majority of cases, contracting leads to a reduction in manpower requirements for the performance of a function or delivery of a service. Often this reduction in labour utilization results from the substitution of capital for labour, for example, where greater use is made of information technology so as to reduce the need for manual document processing. In other cases, staff economies are achieved simply by utilizing labour more efficiently across several functions, relying on what has become known as 'multi-skilling'. In submitting a bid to manage fire-fighting facilities, one contractor's proposal was for the deployment of firemen to carry out selected maintenance, reprographics, and site security functions during 'down-time', thereby raising labour productivity. This example illustrates one among the many possibilities for more efficient deployment of staff when competitive pressures spur the search for imaginative solutions.

At the organizational level, the effect on employment depends largely on what proportion of the staff is transferred to the contractor, or to the winning in-house tenderer in the case of public sector contracting. This in turn depends on the policies towards staff transfer adopted by the client organization. In some cases, particularly in the public sector, the purchaser requires the contractor to take on the entire workforce as a condition of the contract. The advantage to the client is that it avoids redundancy payments to staff who otherwise may lose their jobs. It also attenuates the concern over job losses, easing the transition to contracting. For the contractor, this restriction means a short-term constraint on efficiency gains, implying a higher contract price because of the costs of carrying surplus labour. In the long run, however, contractors rely on natural attrition and redeployment to other activities as a means of aligning manpower requirements with the demands of the contract.

As a general rule, there are three possible outcomes for staff in the wake of contracting: transfer to the contractor, redeployment by the client organization, or redundancy. Which combination of these is applied in specific circumstances depends on the nature and size of the contracting organization. In the public sector, a mixture of all three is typically used. A good example is the UK's 'Competing for Quality' programme, which subjected to competition a range of white-collar activities within the British civil service between 1992 and 1995. The value of activities affected by the competitive process was £1.85 billion. Of the 34,765 staff affected by it, 11,924 transferred to a new employer (the contractor), 2, 572 took early retirement or voluntary redundancy, 2,917 were given non-voluntary redundancy, natural wastage accounted for 2,773 employees, and the remaining 14,579 were redeployed within the civil service. This outcome is unusual in that a large proportion (42 per cent) of staff were redeployed elsewhere within the organization. Such large scale redeployment is unlikely to be feasible in smaller organizations—the UK civil service employs over half a million staff—or in those with a more functionally specialized workforce.

Despite this relatively benign staffing outcome, the Policy Review of the Competing for Quality programme revealed considerable dissatisfaction by staff with the process and the outcomes. Of the staff attached to successful in-house bidders, 52 per cent claimed that their job satisfaction had worsened while only 26 per cent said that it had improved compared to the pre-competition era (UK

Cabinet Office 1996: 47). However, the perceived adverse impact on jobs appeared to decline over time, suggesting that in the long run staff acceptance of outcomes is greater than in the short run. Improvements in job satisfaction were generally associated with more interesting work and greater responsibility. Worsening conditions were associated with higher workloads, scarcity of support, and greater insecurity.

Rehiring by the incoming contractor, or retention of staff by the successful in-house bidder, makes good economic sense. Most of the employees involved already have relevant skills for the activity concerned, and are likely to perform well under a more demanding, competitive regime. They are likely to respond constructively to new management initiative to improve working practices and increase productivity. For the incoming contractor the important issue is the identification of those staff to be retained and those who should be offered redundancy. To some extent, this will be dependent on the information provided by the purchasing organization. But such information may not always be made available, as it may be perceived to disadvantage certain staff members, reducing their employment opportunities. Contractors may therefore have to rely on their own selection processes, and this will typically involve interviewing the staff attached to the activity being contracted shortly after the announcement of the winning bid.

The contracting process is fraught with hazards for the purchaser and the contractor alike. One persistent complaint by staff concerns the lack of proper communication regarding the process itself, how it will affect individuals, and what options might be available to them. The Competing for Quality Policy review described it as follows: 'Dissatisfaction with communications throughout the process was amongst the most consistent and forceful of the complaints made by staff. The result of poor communication has been to add considerably to uncertainty and to erode trust between staff, their managers and their colleagues' (UK Cabinet Office 1996: 48). Not surprisingly, the available contracting and outsourcing 'manuals' tend to stress the importance of keeping staff informed through regular communication and participation in the process. This could involve the service provider making a formal presentation to the staff affected about intentions, opportunities (for rehiring), and plans (see, for example, White and James 1996: 60).

Good communication will ease the transition, but will not change the fundamental nature of the change from internal production to outside provision. Change that brings uncertainty will be feared, and such fear can easily turn into resistance. In general, good communications and adequate provisions to safeguard the staff affected will forestall industrial trouble. But as Case Study 8.2 illustrates, sometimes resistance to change is unavoidable and has to be confronted by the organization.

An interesting point highlighted by the Kellogg case study is the role of unions in the contracting process. Unions generally oppose contracting *policy*, on the grounds that it is detrimental to their members' interests. It is also not

Case Study 8.2. All change at Kellogg's

In 1994 Kellogg's share of the Australian breakfast cereal market was 47 per cent, yet it was feeling the latent threat from competitors. The company was hampered by inefficient production techniques despite ten years of gradual change: a study showed that manufacturing costs at Kellogg's Sydney plant were the second-highest of its twenty-one worldwide plants, and 50 per cent higher than one of its local competitors. Although the age of plant and machinery was part of the problem, work practices and labour costs were largely to blame. The company had difficulty getting the six unions on site to agree to any significant changes.

The company was seen as a model of a cooperative approach. Its communication and consultation processes with unions were regarded as exemplary. However, the strict job demarcations created by the six different unions involved caused problems: production workers were not allowed to undertake minor repairs, and maintenance staff refused to wear pagers. As a result, production would often cease for up to forty-five minutes until repairs would be undertaken, leading to food spoilage.

After several failed rounds of negotiations with the unions, and the rejection of proposals agreed to by the workers, Kellogg's embarked on a covert operation code-named Project Dory, to contract out plant maintenance, security, and cleaning. In December 1994, Kellogg's approached a maintenance contractor for help in developing a detailed proposal and retrenchment plan. The covert operation was justified by management on the grounds that it feared sabotage of equipment or contamination of produce in light of previous disagreements with unions.

On a Friday evening in July 1995, a total of 140 workers received redundancy notices from their employer, delivered by courier. The company offered generous redundancy packages and guaranteed alternative jobs with the contractors for all cleaning and security staff, and most of the maintenance staff. After a full week's break in production, three selected contractors took over maintenance, security, and cleaning operations. Changes to work practices, production processes, and corporate culture were instituted. The number of staff was reduced significantly and savings are believed to be running at approximately $A2.5 million per annum. New organizational units are responsible for production, simple maintenance, and quality control. The number of unions at the plant was reduced to one —the National Union of Workers—facilitating streamlined industrial relations, and helping to restore Kellogg's reputation for cooperation and communication.

Sources: Workplace Change (1996), Industrial Relations & Management Letter (1995).

in the unions' interests, as it may be associated with the loss of membership, particularly amongst those employees who transfer to the incoming contractor. Where several unions have recognition within one workplace, tensions and conflicts often arise between them, as each tries to strike a better bargain for its members. This leads to protracted negotiations at best, and outright standstill at worst. The Kellogg case study is an example of the latter, forcing the company to resort to covert operations for what should have been a negotiated transition to a new regime.

Nevertheless, trade unions can play a constructive role in negotiating favourable terms for their members as the quid pro quo for a smooth transition process. For while unions are philosophically opposed to contracting, they are apt to recognize the point at which ideological opposition should give way to pragmatic negotiation. That still leaves the client organization with a choice between a negotiated transfer or a clean break with its employees.

Clean break or negotiated transfer?

With a 'clean break', staff are given redundancy notices—and payments—and are then free to seek alternative employment opportunities. For a large proportion of staff previously employed by the client this means being re-employed by the contractor, but most likely on different terms and conditions. The staff affected in this way are often perceived to have engaged in 'double-dipping': they have claimed their entitlement to redundancy while having secured an employment transfer with the incoming contractor.

The rights and wrongs of this outcome are debatable, and some public sector jurisdictions have come out strongly against it. Double-dipping is seen to be unfair to those who cannot avail themselves of the twin benefits. It is also not strictly necessary as a means of securing employee transfer, where a negotiated transfer is both feasible and acceptable to staff. Nevertheless, the counter-argument is that a transfer from the public to the private sector entails some loss of job security, and possibly some other benefits of public employment. This argument is based on the presumption that, prior to contracting, public sector employees could expect to have 'jobs for life'. The redundancy pay-out could thus represent compensation for the loss of security of tenure.

But double-dipping creates an incentive problem for the 'negotiated transfer' strategy. If a large enough number of employees believe they can obtain voluntary redundancy *and* subsequently secure a position with the incoming contractor, the negotiated transfer will become unacceptable to the majority of staff. In this case only the clean break strategy becomes viable. For essentially this reason, the Australian Industry Commission (1996: 390–1) concluded that as far as public sector contracting was concerned: 'staff who accept a voluntary redundancy package offered as part of a decision to contract out a government's service should be precluded from working with the external contractor on the relevant outsourcing contract for a specified period.'

The advantages of the clean break approach are: administrative simplicity, reduced negotiation time, and equality of treatment among staff based on the scale of redundancy payments applicable in the organization. The two main disadvantages of the strategy are, first, the potential opposition by staff and unions and, second, the cost of the redundancy pay-outs which can be large enough to render the financial case for contracting a marginal one. They are typically much more generous than the incentive payments made to staff under the negotiated transfer approach.

Negotiated transfers involve formal arrangements between contractor and purchaser to transfer staff over to the contractor's payroll on agreed terms and conditions. Those terms are usually stipulated in the tender documents and become a condition of the contract. They are, however, preceded by intense negotiations with the preferred tenderer and staff representatives including unions. Under this scheme staff who agree to transfer receive a severance payment—substantially lower than full redundancy, but enough to compensate for the loss of continuity of employer. Those who do not wish to transfer are eligible for full redundancy, with or without the restriction on double-dipping.

The advantages of a negotiated transfer are that it provides continuity of employment to staff and ensures that services are delivered with minimum disruption. Another important advantage is that with fewer redundancies, the costs of contract implementation are significantly reduced, even allowing for the transfer payments discussed above. Lastly, the prospective contractor faces greater certainty about the transfer of skilled staff than under the clean break approach.

As for the disadvantages, negotiated transfers can easily get bogged down in protracted negotiations which are costly in terms of management time and effort. Another problem with the scheme is the restriction placed by the client as to who should be transferred. The most restrictive case is when all current employees are to be included in the transfer. This means the contractor has the responsibility of dealing with excess staff, a factor which is likely to result in an increase in the contract price. Nevertheless, negotiated transfers are favoured by public sector clients because they resolve the redundancy problem in two basic ways: by minimizing the numbers that are made redundant, and cutting the financial costs of funding those redundancies.

For a prospective contracting client, the worst of all possible outcomes would be to negotiate a transfer and then find that redundancy payments must be paid as well. This is precisely what happened when the Government Cleaning Service (GCS) in New South Wales was contracted out to three private sector firms. A significant aspect of Case Study 4.2 was the award of redundancy payments despite the transfer of all employees and their entitlements, including wage rates and conditions, to the contractors.

This occurred because of union objections, despite state government efforts to negotiate terms that were favourable to employees, including continuity of current rates of pay without loss of superannuation or sickness benefits entitlements. In 1993, the Federated Miscellaneous Workers' Union applied for redundancy to the NSW Industrial Relations Commission on behalf of the workers transferred on the grounds that they had been made redundant by the state government. The presiding judge decided in favour of the unions on the basis that two important features of redundancy were present in this case: the decision to terminate had been made by the employer and that termination was unrelated to the employee's performance at work. In summing up, the judge stated that: 'on balance, and I must say with some reservations, I have concluded that it is appropriate that an award of redundancy pay should be made in favour of the former GCS employees' (Jensen and Liebenberg 1995: 28).

Although the appellant had sought redundancy pay based on the voluntary redundancy scale determined by the NSW government, the judge was of the view that a lower rate was justified. Even so the judgement cost the government an estimated $A25 million, but this amount was still notably less than the annual saving achieved by contracting. The judgement was upheld following an appeal.

Two features of this case make it highly unusual. First, the transfer of employees was large by any standard, involving some 7,500 workers. Secondly, there were political overtones to the court battle between the union and government. The union had always been opposed to the contracting decision, arguing that internal restructuring of the GCS could achieve similar performance improvements. However, the lesson of this case is that negotiated transfers stand or fall on the terms and conditions attached to them. Indeed, in the public sector it would appear that they do not need to change significantly to make a transfer look like a redundancy.

Terms and conditions of transfer

International evidence suggests that contracting can have a negative effect on terms and conditions of employment, particularly where a transfer from the public to the private sector is concerned. According to Ascher (1987: 110): 'public sector arrangements for holiday and sickness pay, disciplinary procedures and pensions are better than those offered by many contractors.' However, the Industry Commission (1996: 169–75), which reviewed the rather limited information available, suggested that, more often than not, these changes reflected a move towards industry standards and away from general public sector pay and conditions. The point is that public sector pay is often out of line with specific industry norms which tend to be market-driven. This means that sometimes terms will be better in the private sector; at other times the differences may be insignificant.

The issue remains controversial, however, and understandably so. If savings from contracting are achieved directly at the expense of workers then there is no net efficiency gain, only a transfer of wealth. What little research has been done to try to separate efficiency from pecuniary effects suggests that the bulk of the savings stems from the former (Cubbin et al. 1987). A similar conclusion was reached by Walsh (1991) in the context of UK local authority service contracts. Another often heard complaint about contractors is their wider use of part-time and casual labour. Once again, this reflects general labour market trends, rather than a distinctive approach associated with contractors.

Protecting employees' terms and conditions in a negotiated transfer is good management practice. It creates a more cooperative industrial climate, signalling to the transferring employees that their management is taking care to safeguard their interests. To the incoming contractor it makes for a smoother transition. And although the costs of this arrangement are higher than under a less restrictive transfer—in effect the contractor loses the freedom to align terms with prevailing market conditions—these higher costs will be reflected in a higher contract price. However, the contractor will have discretion over the number of persons employed on the contract, and can raise productivity through multi-tasking (recall the firemen example discussed above) and other innovative work practices.

Protection of terms and conditions is typically not indefinite. It usually applies to the first contract term which means that, in the longer run, terms and conditions are likely to be more fluid, giving the contractor greater room to manœuvre. By this time the contractor should have optimized the deployment of staff on the contract so that the lifting of this restriction could provide opportunities for further cost reductions. A good example of such transfer is given in Case Study 8.3—the contract between the Norrell Corporation and IBM.

Protection of terms and conditions is easier to implement with a negotiated contract. In a competitive tendering environment, bidders need to know in advance not only what the current terms and conditions are, but what accrued liabilities for other staff entitlements have accumulated in the past. This immediately raises the costs of bidding, since the purchaser will be expected to provide large amounts of information regarding these matters, and respond to enquiries from every bidder who wishes to ascertain the true costs of the contract. Detailed negotiations will still be required with the preferred tenderer, as it is unlikely that every aspect of a negotiated transfer can be resolved prior to contractor selection.

Continuity of employment on pre-existing terms and conditions may be adroit change management on the part of the outsourcing client, but European legislation has attempted to make it mandatory.

TUPE

In 1977, the European Community enacted the 'Acquired Rights Directive' (ARD), whose purpose was to provide continuity of the employment relationship, including terms and conditions, in the event of a 'transfer of undertaking'. The ARD was conceived to provide protection to employees in cases of mergers or acquisitions. However, the definition of a transfer of undertaking remained shrouded in uncertainty, and has been debated at length in the European and national courts.

In 1981 the ARD was implemented in the UK as the 'Transfer of Undertakings

---

Case Study 8.3. Norrell Corporation

When IBM entrusted the running of its offices to Norrell Corp.—experts in the field of office management—it insisted its staff be offered employment at the same terms and conditions. But, because Norrell could do the job with fewer staff, IBM still saved money: Norrell's founder and CEO, Guy Millner, argued the company's core competency is running offices, resulting in greater expertise and efficiency.

In 1992, when IBM signed the $75 million per year contract with Norrell, IBM was employing 3,750 office workers in its head office. IBM's high-cost structure and generous pay-scales made certain simpler operations—for example, management of secretarial pools, processing of office and travel expenses, and fielding phone calls for marketing and field support divisions—rather expensive.

IBM, previously known for its 'lifetime employment' policy, was concerned about public relations: it did not want to be seen as mistreating its staff. Norrell accepted the terms and conditions of employment, and took over the operation of IBM's corporate headquarters.

Despite having to pay staff more than they normally would, Norrell still made substantial savings for IBM, simply because Norrell's staff were more efficient at office management than IBM's had been. In fact, Norrell runs the same office with 20 per cent fewer staff. Efficiency was also boosted by altering the way the office was run: software was standardized, paperwork was cut down, and scanners were used in preference to retyping documents.

When the contact was renegotiated in 1994, IBM dropped the condition that the pay of former IBM staff be maintained at IBM levels, allowing for salaries to be adjusted to Norrell's pay-scale (a gap of about $15,000 per year for an executive secretary); IBM is saving another $20 million each year as a result.

Source: Klebnikov (1995).

(Protection of Employment)' Act or TUPE for short. This legislation was subsequently amended by the Trade Union Reform and Employment Rights Act 1993, which removed the condition that an 'undertaking' had to be a commercial one. In other words it broadened the coverage of TUPE to include public sector activities and contracted-out services. The effect 'was to bring the momentum of compulsory competitive tendering [in British local government] to a shuddering, if temporary, halt' (Milne 1997: 11). The initial uncertainty over the implications of TUPE slowed contracting down, particularly in the UK public sector. But once its effects were better understood, the business of contracting was back on track.

The principal effect of TUPE is to ensure minimum standards are maintained in negotiated transfers. But it also adds complexity to voluntary arrangements where terms may be superior to those mandated by TUPE. For example, under the legislation employees have no right of choice between transfer and redundancy. The legislation is designed merely to assure the continuity of employment. Furthermore, allowing some staff to accept a redundancy package can put the whole TUPE process in doubt, since it applies only in cases where an entire undertaking is transferred or a coherent part of such undertaking. An incomplete aspect of the legislation is its treatment of pension rights. Under TUPE, organizational policies are not the subject of continuity, only the rights are. Therefore, it is up to the purchaser to ensure that pension benefits provided by the supplier to transferees meet its requirements.

The right to continuity of employment also means that entitlement to redundancy payments, in the event of severance of the employment relationship with the new employer, remains unaffected by the transfer. This raises the prospect of a large potential redundancy liability for the contractor. This liability would be realized if, at the end of the contract term, the contractor wished to make some staff redundant. There are two ways of dealing with this aspect of TUPE: the purchaser indemnifies the provider for such redundancy liabilities or, in case it does not, the liability is built into the purchase price.

It should be evident from the above that TUPE leaves many issues to be resolved by the parties, not least of which is the question of whether the legislation applies to a particular contract. It does not in all cases. 'The uncertainty over TUPE and its implications has concerned staff, and may have heightened fears of private sector employment. In the event, around three quarters of transferred staff said that their rate of pay and hours were the same' (UK Cabinet Office 1996: 51). As this appraisal of TUPE highlights, even in cases where it applies, terms and conditions may vary somewhat compared to previous employment. For competing tenderers, the concerns naturally tend to be centred on costs: 'Where TUPE did apply, 66 per cent [of companies] said that it had a major impact on increasing cost, 27 per cent that it had a major impact on reducing quality, and 54 per cent that it constrained innovation' (UK Cabinet Office 1996: 62).

TUPE applies only to UK employment transfers, and there have been many cases of successful transfer under TUPE auspices. The National Physical Laboratory example discussed in Chapter 5 is a case in point. Nevertheless, the ambiguities and gaps in the legislation make it something of a minefield for the unwary. Test cases and legal challenges mean that the practical implications of the legislation are altered frequently. However, there are few countries where employment legislation is simple, and employees' rights defined in every circumstance. Such legislation is also subject to frequent change, and demands careful handling by management and specialist resources by organizations contemplating a contracting initiative.

Managing transition

The demands on management can be separated into two distinct components: laying the foundations for transfer of activities from in-house to external providers; and managing the transition process when the activity, and in many cases the staff, move across organizational boundaries. The first component is the contracting strategy writ large. In the early days contracting used to be seen as the first choice for companies in financial distress: it was simply a way of saving money. Such a strategy therefore needed little justification from management. More recently, and with far more contracting undertaken in the public sector, the line of argument has shifted. It is now a question of what the appropriate level of activity is within an organization, given that the market can provide specialists who could perform better. The drive is towards greater specialization and 'core competencies', driven in the private sector by greater competition and in the public by rising expectations.

Nowhere is the relationship between greater competition and contracting more evident than in the international air transport industry. In this sector, the deregulation of airlines and the opening of global markets has unleashed a fierce wave of competition. This has manifested itself in acquisitions and international alliances which have created veritable behemoths from once national airlines. British Airways (BA) was one of the first to seize upon the globalization trend, growing in size and improving its customer service significantly. By mid-1996 it achieved the enviable status of being the world's most profitable airline, but while profits were up, labour productivity had effectively reached a plateau. The incoming chief executive, Robert Ayling, who took over from Sir Colin Marshall, envisioned a radical plan to maintain, even increase, BA's prominence and profitability. But he has had difficulties persuading staff, and their union representatives, of the merits of his plan. Case Study 8.4 describes the strategy in detail, the reactions to it, and the steps management have taken to keep it alive.

The radical nature of the organizational changes proposed in the case was bound to cause unrest. They would need careful handling and prolonged negotiations. But Mr Ayling's style is apparently more confrontational, described by *The Economist* (1997*b*: 71) as a 'sledgehammer'. The same article suggested that such heavy-handedness was deliberate, perhaps even desperate. But an article by the same newspaper two weeks later suggested that things could have been handled differently. This illustrates the dilemma that confronts management when it seeks major organizational change: strong-arm tactics signal determination and commitment to change, but risk raising the ire of employees and fomenting unrest. A softer, more collegial style will be better received initially, but may be resisted long-term if management's resolve is in doubt. This may be why both approaches are often used: the first to make the proposed changes credible; the second to quell the unrest that it leads to. British Airways' handling of the dispute discussed in the case study appears to conform to this pattern. After an initially aggressive stance, Mr Ayling adopted a more conciliatory style.

Most contracting strategies are not of such radical nature, and involve only an 'adjustment' to the organizational boundary. That means contracting one or more specific services over a period of time. The problem for management

Case Study 8.4. British Airways: the virtual airline

British Airways is one of the world's largest, and certainly most successful, airlines. With a fleet of 283 aircraft, it was able to post a record of 24 million passengers on international flights in 1994, which is 6.5 million more than its closest rival. After a highly successful privatization in 1987, British Airways has gone from strength to strength, recording an unbroken string of profits since then. With profits of £560 million in 1995/6, it has become the world's most profitable airline—wresting that title from Singapore Airlines in late 1996.

Despite this apparent financial strength, for the first quarter of 1995/6 costs rose 5.9 per cent while yield only rose by 5.2 per cent. According to Boeing analysts, the amount of money airlines make per passenger mile is falling at a rate of 1 per cent per year. In real terms, worldwide airline revenues are falling at about 2 per cent per year, despite the fact that air travel is expanding at around 7 per cent per year.

In order to stay on top, British Airways' CEO, Robert Ayling, therefore announced an ambitious plan to save an additional £1 billion on cumulative operating costs by the year 2000. In order to achieve such a goal, Ayling has outlined a few key initiatives which continue the trend which has seen British Airways lean towards becoming the first of the new generation of 'virtual airlines'.

The first part of Ayling's plan is to cut the workforce, since staff account for 30 per cent of BA's running costs: voluntary redundancies have been offered to approximately 5,000 workers (10 per cent of its British workforce), and the number of senior management executives has been cut from 25 to 11. However, these measures will only cut costs by around 2 per cent, saving perhaps £140 million per year. BA also wants to streamline the basic pay of short-haul European cabin staff, consolidating special allowances and wages.

Unfortunately, Ayling has had trouble convincing staff—and the powerful Transport & General Workers' Union which represents many of them—of the merits of his plan, which is seen as antagonistic and heavy-handed. A three-day strike was called on 9 July 1997—the start of the peak summer travel season—and wiped out 70 per cent of BA's flights from London's Heathrow airport. An effective strike can bring any airline, even one as powerful as BA, to its knees in six weeks as travellers seek to avoid delays and disruption.

The second part of British Airways' strategy is to outsource. It has signalled to its staff that the only operations essential to its business are pilots, cabin crew, and marketing; everything else can be outsourced. Engine maintenance has already been contracted; the property division has been sold; BA Engineering (currently operating as a profit centre) is also a candidate for sale. Baggage handlers and ticket processors have been warned that, if an external contractor can do the job more cheaply than internal teams, these functions too will be outsourced. BA is looking at outsourcing its IT functions, as the US-based Delta Airlines has done. Outsourcing vehicle maintenance and catering (BA is one of the few airlines still to rely on its own kitchens) is also under consideration.

Ironically, BA appears to be emulating its bitter rival, Richard Branson's Virgin Atlantic. Virgin owns few of the support systems available at BA; instead it hires them. For example, Air Florida provides Virgin's computerized reservation service; British Caledonian provides maintenance for Virgin's aircraft. Ayling has commented that if restructuring BA means borrowing methods used by newcomers to the market, then that is what BA will do.

Sources: The Economist (1997*b*), Ramesh (1996).

in these situations is how to implement the transition from in-house to the contractor without disruption in supply and industrial unrest. The important elements to successful transition management may be grouped under three headings: communications, planning, and support.

The importance of communication is stressed by almost every practitioner (and consultant) who has been involved with contracting. Immediately after a management announcement to contract out a service, fear and uncertainty by staff concerning their future employment are greatest. To mitigate this, the objectives, effects, and proposed timetable of the contracting initiative should be laid out. This can be done through written communications, but if the numbers make it possible, management presentations to employees would add weight to the message. Communications should continue throughout the period leading up to the contractor taking over operations. They should involve all stakeholders, but especially trade union representatives, who should be won over at an early stage. Some outsourcing manuals even suggest that a communication plan should be devised and stuck to. Once the winning contractor has been appointed and contractual matters resolved, it is useful to have a staff presentation. Not only does this give staff an opportunity to acquaint themselves with their future employer, it also provides a forum for further questions not previously addressed by the contracting client.

But communication has its pitfalls too. One human resources specialist from Arthur Andersen told the story of a client organization which ill-advisedly commented on the number of employees that would be transferred to the contractor before arrangements had been finalized. This indiscretion cost the company more than $US10 million in settlement of workers' claims. The lesson from this experience is that while communication is essential to good transition management, it needs to be tempered by a recognition that impending negotiations could be compromised.

The transition process starts with the announcement of the preferred contractor. It does not end until the transfer of staff and the activity has been completed—until the provider has taken over the operation. It is useful to distinguish contracts which are essentially new, from those which take over an activity from the customer or a competitor who lost the bid. The first case is the easiest to manage; the last potentially most difficult because it involves a competitor who may be reluctant to assist in the transition process. However, most well-established service providers are aware that the damage to their reputation from non-cooperation with an incoming contractor makes such a strategy extremely short-sighted. In practice, few contractors find that their counterparts put obstacles in their way when contracts turn over.

Transition planning must include the incoming contractor as well as the client organization. Indeed, the contractor should be asked to provide a clearly articulated transition plan as part of the tendered proposal. Most experienced service providers have well-developed transition or 'phasing-in' processes, which have been refined over many contracts. These normally include a timetable for events such as presentations, staff interviews prior to transfer, and meetings with the client and other stakeholders. The client's and contractor's transition plans (and that of the losing incumbent, if applicable) need to be compatible. Specifically, they need to be meshed in such a way that the roles of the client and contractor management become part of seamless, coordinated process. The difficulties will vary depending on the nature and size of the activity, the experience of the contractor and client in implementing handovers, and the attitudes of employees. The central importance of transition planning lies in the attempt to identify and manage every significant step associated in the movement of staff and resources from one organization to another. Despite the best-laid plans, events are not perfectly predictable and unanticipated problems may arise during transition. But that does not mean that planning has little value. Without such plans, the protagonists could quickly lose control of the process, with entirely unpredictable and costly consequences.

Lastly, the role of support systems for staff affected by organizational change has been highlighted by recent contracting experience. Support includes advising staff of their options, career counselling, and assistance with superannuation and other entitlements which may be affected. In recent times, it has also encompassed outplacement services, which help staff made involuntarily redundant find alternative employment. The support role is another facet of a package of measures which includes the safeguarding of terms and conditions of employment. Developing such a package has traditionally been undertaken by the client organization. But sometimes purchasers shift the responsibility for staff support to the contractors, particularly as regards post-transfer counselling and career management.

An interesting development which facilitates the support function for purchaser and provider alike has been the emergence of career management specialists. Chapter 5 (Case Study 5.2) included a general description of their activities, and an assessment of their expanding role. But what is noteworthy about the latter is the position some such specialists have taken on both sides of an increasingly fluid labour market. On the supply side, they assist former employees who are seeking jobs by assisting with skills development, including interview techniques. On the demand side, they utilize their knowledge of the pool of available personnel to respond to demands for particular types of skills in specific industries. It is much more than simply an employment agency function, and the way it works is shown in Fig. 8.1.

Impact on customers and suppliers

Contracting creates new but permanent interfaces between the client, and in some cases the client's client, and the provider. Consider the contracting of transport operations in the city of Adelaide in South Australia, which took

Excess labour demand   **Excess labour supply**

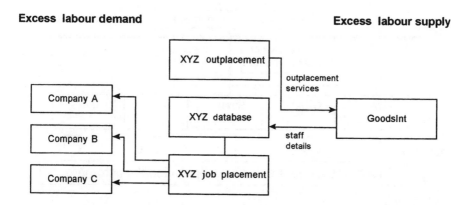

Note: GoodsInt has contracted the provision of its IT services, thus creating some redundancies for staff not transferred to the incoming contractor. HR specialist XYZ is retained to provide outplacement services to those employees. At the same time, details of the staff seeking new employment are recorded in the XYZ database, which is linked to the HR specialist's job placement service function. New jobs are then found, through XYZ job placement services, amongst companies A, B, and C which face shortages in the IT area.

Fig. 8.1. Matching demand and supply of labour through human resources specialists

place in 1996. The client is the South Australian Passenger Transport Board, which defines its role as the planning and overseeing of an integrated transport system in the metropolitan district of Adelaide. The Board contracts with service providers for the operations of buses, trams, and trains but not the ticketing and information systems. The way the system is set up is shown in Fig. 8.2.

The ultimate customers—the client's clients—are the users of the transport system, the urban travellers. The services are provided by contractors and the management and coordination of the entire system is undertaken by the Board. The interfaces that need active monitoring and management are those between the Board and the service providers, and between the latter and the travelling public. As can be seen from the figure, there are also lateral interfaces between the various service providers who need to liaise on a regular basis to comply with the demands of the Board. In a system of such complexity—the Board operates a total of eighteen transport contracts in the metropolitan area and ten in rural areas—if the management of those interfaces fails, then the functioning of the entire system will be jeopardized.

The difficulties sustaining customer–supplier relationships vary according to the complexity of the delivery mechanisms that are put in place. But even with the relatively simple replacement of the in-house IT support provider by an external specialist, things can go wrong. The problem here is

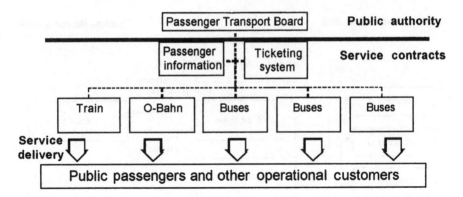

Source: Serco Institute

Fig. 8.2.   An illustration of contractual interfaces in a transport system

that there are numerous *internal* clients for IT support within the client organization. Keeping all of them happy all of the time can be a testing juggling act for the service provider. And if performance falls below expectations, the blame will fall on the management for contracting out the service instead of maintaining the in-house operation. With a complex national network such as the British Rail system which operates through a multiplicity of separate franchise companies, maintenance contractors, an owner of the rail infrastructure, and a government regulator, the resources demanded for system-wide coordination among customers and suppliers could be far greater.

Critics of contracting claim, with some justification, that the problems of coordinating complex networks involving many interfaces make integration a preferred solution. But with advances in information technology and the low cost of data processing and remote communications it is now possible to manage complex networks of independent units much more effectively than hitherto. The superiority of integrated over distributed systems operated by independent contractors is less clear-cut. Private sector examples would confirm this view. Benetton has managed to keep customers and suppliers happy for a long time using essentially such a system. Shell relies on a 'mutually supportive network' of forecourt franchisees to deliver retail goods and food services at its filling stations. But see Grant (1995: 322–3) for the view that where system-wide coordination is required, integration offers a more effective means of achieving it.

The management and coordination of complex networks of customers and suppliers remains one of the big tasks on the organizational change agenda. It must be factored into the change management plan in every organization that is about to embark on a contracting initiative.

Conclusion

Contracting improves organizational performance by creating change along three principal fronts: reducing staff numbers; introducing new skills and working practices; and modifying individual incentives, employment terms, and attitudes to the workplace. But resistance to change is ubiquitous, and nothing quite resists change like organizational inertia. It stops the restructuring of economic activities from being either rapid or smooth. Economists tend to view this problem as essentially 'friction' in the system; sand in the wheel of progress. But management theorists regard change as the biggest challenge that continually faces business organizations (Kanter 1983). Successful implementation of organizational change is costly in terms of management time and effort. It is difficult to estimate this cost in advance, and anecdotal evidence suggests that it is typically underestimated.

Another problem is that the probability of success in implementing change through contracting, particularly in the public sector, may be significantly influenced by the political environment. For example, in January 1998, the tendering process for services managed by the NSW Rail Access Corporation was suspended by the state government after several contracts had already been awarded. The alleged reason was concern over potentially substantial job losses (Riley 1998). It is clearly impossible to specify the quantum of management resources required to push change through. But of all the demands placed on management by the introduction of contracting, the exigencies of organizational change are likely to be the heaviest.

Guide to further reading

For a discussion of organizational structure and change from an economics perspective Milgrom and Roberts (1992) is a useful first stop. A comprehensive treatment of staffing issues in the public sector is to be found in the Industry Commission (1996) report, and also, in the British context, in the UK Cabinet Office (1996).

Other useful references on human resource issues include White and James (1996) and Wray (1996). OECD (1997) contains a range of international case studies and advice on implementation. Also relevant is the OECD (1993) report on market-type mechanisms in the public sector.

There are many texts that discuss change management in general terms, but Kanter (1983) is a provocative starting point. Other relevant contributions include Rothery and Robertson (1995) and Ascher (1987).

APPENDIX TO PART III:
QUESTIONS IN CONTRACTING STRATEGY

This appendix contains a list of questions concerning important elements of the contracting strategies analysed in Part III. They are intended as topics for discussion or as focal points for further analysis. Most of the questions are addressed to the purchaser (client), but some that are of relevance to the provider (contractor) have also been included. The list is not exhaustive, but focuses on the topics discussed in the text, the location of which is indicated, by chapter and section, immediately after each question.

Client–purchaser	Contractor–provider
What are this organization's distinctive capabilities? And what productive activities should it be in? (Chapter 5: who benefits from specialization?)	
In which activities is competitive, market mediated mode of provision likely to be superior to in-house provision? (Chapter 5: specialization and competition)	Which markets are ripe for development, where the benefits of specialization can turn producers into purchasers? (Chapter 5: patterns of specialization)
Will the organization's capacity to add value to a particular product or service be eroded by contracting out an activity critical to it? (Chapter 6: value migration)	Should service providers specialize by function/activity or by type of client? (Chapter 5: patterns of specialization)
How should the service providers be selected? Through open tender, selected tender, or direct negotiations? (Chapter 6: competitive tendering — bidding for contracts)	When bidding for contracts in a competitive environment, beware the winner's curse. (Chapter 6: winners and losers)
Should the client organization rely on one service provider, or should the activity contracted be split between several? (Chapter 6: alternative sourcing methods)	Would service providers be willing to work in partnership with potential competitors in serving one client, as in the case of BP? (Chapter 6: alternative sourcing methods)
On which type of pricing mechanism should the contract be based—fixed-price, fixed-price plus incentive, schedule of rates, gainsharing, or appropriate mix? (Chapter 6: the contract price)	

Client–purchaser	Contractor–provider
Can service characteristics be specified with sufficient precision for the bids to be comparable and contracts enforceable? (Chapter 6: competitive tendering — bidding for contracts. Discussed further in Chapter 9)	
What type of performance monitoring regime should be built into the contract(s)? (Chapter 7: monitoring performance)	Does the performance monitoring system proposed by the client have implications for the way the provider allocates resources within the contract? (Chapter 7: monitoring performance)
What kind of incentive or penalty systems (if any) should be built into the contract? (Chapter 7: controlling risks)	
What are the risks to the client organization associated with a particular contract? Can they be identified and quantified? (Chapter 7: controlling risks)	
How are those risks to be optimally allocated between the purchaser and provider? (Chapter 7: allocating risks in contracts)	Will the client give the winning tenderer the opportunity to modify risk allocation in a way that benefits both parties? (Chapter 7: allocating risks in contracts)
Should the service provider be required to purchase contract-specific physical assets? What are the likely consequences of such a strategy for the length of contract and the price? (Chapter 7: allocating risks in contracts)	What are the financial risks for the contractor of being required to purchase contract-specific physical assets? (Chapter 7: allocating risks in contracts)
How should flexibility be built in— through an explicit, classical contract in which much is spelled out, or through a relational contract in which there is room for contractual variations and evolution on a give and take basis? (Chapter 7: which contract—classical or relational?)	How does the scope for flexible, alliance-type contracts vary between clients, in particular between those in the private and the public sector? (Chapter 7: flexibility and which contract—classical or relational?)
How is the impact on staff of the contracting initiative to be handled? What kind of communication policy is required to minimize adverse reaction? (Chapter 8: impact on staff)	

Client–purchaser	Contractor–provider
What are the relative advantages for staff and the organization of a clean break versus the negotiated transfer approach? (Chapter 8: clean break or negotiated transfer)	Can the contractor support the client organization through a negotiated transfer of the client organization's staff if required? (Chapter 8: clean break or negotiated transfer)
Is a negotiated transfer preferable to a clean break? If so, what are the implications for the price of the contract of the terms and conditions of transfer from the client to the provider? (Chapter 8: terms and conditions of transfer)	
How will the contractor manage the transition of activity from client to vendor? (Chapter 8: managing transition)	Has a transition plan been formulated by the client? Can the contractor support such a plan? (Chapter 8: managing transition)
What impact will the new contractual arrangements have on customers and suppliers? What kind of new interfaces will be required to achieve adequate coordination? (Chapter 8: impact on customers and suppliers)	

STRUCTURAL CHANGE

In this part we look at the structural changes that have resulted from the economy-wide application of contracting. The public sector is, perhaps, the one that has been most profoundly affected by it, and about which the controversy concerning the appropriate scope of private and public production continues to smoulder. Chapter 9 considers the issues relevant to public sector contracting, including potential benefits and problems. The emphasis is on application, and the identification of the limits to contracting activity. Chapter 10 then follows with an analysis of structural changes in three major economies, the UK, USA, and Australia, and the role that contracting for services has played in bringing about those changes. This is done by using national accounts statistics to examine shifts in employment and output between sectors at a reasonably disaggregated level.

Chapter 11, 'The Future of Contracting', takes a forward look at contracting trends, not by gazing at a crystal ball, but by asking whether contracting is a fad. The chapter also examines the downsizing phenomenon and the ongoing confusion between its role and that of contracting. Lastly Chapter 12 contains some lessons from experience and conclusions regarding what we already know, and how much more we still need to find out.

9

Public Sector Contracting

The good news is that—while privatization is by no means the universal corrective that more fervent proponents assert—there are real opportunities to make public undertakings more efficient and accountable by enlisting the private sector.

(John Donahue, 1989)

Since the late 1970s, the pace of public sector reforms has quickened in many OECD countries. The United Kingdom led the charge, the watershed coming in May 1979 with the election of a Conservative administration under the leadership of Margaret Thatcher. Initially, public sector reform in the UK meant simply privatization. The nationalized industries had become a financial burden on the public purse, particularly after the oil price shocks of 1973/4, and were perceived as unresponsive behemoths. Privatization was seen not only as a means of improving their performance, but also as a way of curbing the power of the trade unions.

The British privatization programme has become a model which has been followed enthusiastically by other countries. After a slow start, Australia and New Zealand have followed suit, the latter widely acknowledged to have undertaken the most thoroughgoing public sector reforms of the English-speaking world. In the USA, which has always had a relatively low level of government ownership of utilities such as the water, electricity, and gas industries, the reforms have been more recent. They have permeated both the federal and local governments. The Clinton administration has reportedly reduced public employment at the federal level by some 332,000, to approximately 1.9 million. This has been achieved largely by contracting activities previously undertaken by government, so that while federal employment has fallen substantially, federal budgets have not.

The significance of these public sector reforms can be gauged by examining the movements in public sector employment during the period in question. According to OECD figures, between 1985 and 1995 government employment as a percentage of total employment fell from 17.6 to 15.2 per cent in Australia; from 16.1 to 14.3 per cent in New Zealand; and from 21.7 to 14.2 per cent in the

UK. However in the USA it only fell from 15.3 to 14.0 per cent during this period, reflecting the fact that many of the public sector reforms have occurred since the mid-1990s. It is evident that public sector employment has fallen most steeply in the UK. This may reflect not only the incidence of privatization, but also the relatively large size of the UK public sector as it was in the mid-1980s.

The purpose of this chapter is to consider the circumstances in which contracting for public services is likely to be beneficial, and those in which it should be avoided. It will review the international empirical evidence and discuss what lessons can be learnt from past experience. It will also consider the controversy that surrounds the fundamental issue of the extent to which market forces should be permitted to take over activities traditionally undertaken by the government. Amongst other issues considered are: who is accountable when services are supplied under contract, what are the employment effects of contracting and how should competitive neutrality between private and public sector providers be safeguarded?

The role of contracting in public sector reform

Public sector reform runs along a continuum. At one end, there is the 'organizational improvement approach' which involves redesigning or re-engineering internal processes and information systems, clarifying responsibilities and outcomes, and operating within a more precisely defined set of objectives. The purpose of such reforms is to improve performance from within, without changing the external conditions in which the organization operates. At the other end there is privatization: setting the public corporation free from government control (and protection), and subjecting it to the rigours of a fully commercial environment coupled with competition. In between, there are a variety of reforms which involve market-oriented arrangements such as corporatization, internal markets, and market testing and contracting out of publicly funded services.

Corporatization creates corporate governance structures that closely resemble those of private sector enterprises. This entails the formation of a board of directors of the public enterprise, enhancing managerial freedom, and reducing political interference. This model was conceived as part of the public sector reforms implemented in New Zealand. While it replicates the management and governance *structures* of the private corporate sector, the corporatized entities remain in full public ownership, are answerable to governments via the responsible minister, and are subject neither to the threat of takeover nor to bankruptcy.

Reforms which create an internal market within a government-administered and -funded sector are expected to generate incentives and constraints leading to improved resource allocation and enhanced efficiency in service delivery. Such reforms have been implemented in the UK's National Health

Service (NHS). The way the system operated was by separating the purchasers from the providers of medical services. The purchasers are mainly the local health authorities who hold the purse strings; the providers are essentially the hospitals, community services trusts, and private suppliers of health care services. The latter were required to compete for the available 'business', with contractual transactions between purchasers and providers replacing the old administrative arrangements. Interestingly, such contracts had no legal status and were therefore not enforceable in the courts—the contractual system had to be self-enforcing, reflecting its 'internal' nature.

Turning to privatization and contracting out, the distinction between the two has been a source of some confusion. Indeed, in the USA, 'privatization' can and does mean contracting out. In 1989 John Donahue of Harvard University published a book entitled *The Privatization Decision*. In Britain that would be interpreted as a book about the sale of publicly owned assets to the private sector. But in America it refers to 'enlisting private energies to improve the performance of tasks that would remain in some sense public' (Donahue 1989: 7). Thus despite having privatization as its title, Donahue's book is principally about contracting for public services.

This difference in interpretation, as Donahue points out, stems from the fact that the USA (but not Canada) has never had major state-owned enterprises. By contrast, the European, Australian, New Zealand, and other 'mixed' economies have always had (and still have) a major share of economic activity run by the state. In these countries, the nationalized industries comprised mainly the public utilities, communications, and transport undertakings. Many parts of these sectors have been, or are being, privatized in what has become a worldwide boom in the business of disposing of public assets. Between 1984 and the end of the 1980s, the British government raised a total of £37 billion from asset sales. But it is important to note that privatization entails a change in *ownership*, and need not involve a change in the competitive environment in which the erstwhile public enterprises operated. Indeed Bishop, Kay, and Mayer's assessment of the UK privatization programme was that it failed to introduce competition in sectors where it would have been both feasible and beneficial to do so (1994: 13–14).

Contracting out is defined as the application of competition to a set of economic activities which were previously immune to it. Its distinctive feature is what economists refer to as *ex ante* competition: that is, competition *for* the market instead of competition *in* it. It involves the selection of a contractor for the supply of goods or services to commence at a predetermined *future* date. The market is defined by the contract specification and the tendering process resembles an auction. In principle, contracting provides the public sector client with a fair measure of control over the activities undertaken by the provider: monitoring performance, imposing penalties, and renewing contracts. Such a level of control is not available with privatization: once ownership is transferred to private shareholders, the principal form of control over the enterprise is through regulation.

Historically, contracting was the Cinderella of the public sector reforms: neither as glamorous nor as profitable to the government as privatization. Yet in November 1986, in an editorial article entitled 'Good and Bad Privatisation', the *Financial Times* dubbed contracting for services as the 'good' privatization, bringing competition and efficiency rather than merely transferring ownership of existing public assets. Contracting for public services may have begun with 'brush-and-flush' activities—blue-collar services such as refuse collection, and street and building cleaning. But in recent years the policy reach has been extended to a variety of high-tech, white-collar services. Prominent examples include the contracting of the National Physical Laboratory discussed in Chapter 8, the vehicle driving theory testing service, and the UK's ballistic missile early warning system. In general, the range of services now contracted by the public sector is very wide, and although not as pervasive as the privatization programme, contracting for public services has gained currency as a major instrument of public sector reform.

Another feature that distinguishes privatization from contracting concerns the role of physical assets. In the former, they are paramount: selling British Telecom involves transferring tangible, physical assets from the public to the private sector. With contracting, physical assets and their ownership generally play a minor role in determining contractual terms and outcomes. As will be discussed later in this chapter, the significance of ownership of physical assets depends largely on the type of service being contracted. With privatization, one objective at least is to raise revenue for the government through asset sales. The purpose of contracting is to bring about a change, through *ex ante* competition, in the behaviour of management and personnel performing specified service functions. If successfully implemented, such changes should result in lower costs without a loss of quality. The result would be a financial saving to the government in the provision of services to the community, achieving better value for taxpayers' money.

Potential benefits of public sector contracting

There are essentially four ways in which contracting can reduce costs and/or buttress quality of publicly funded services. They are: separation of purchaser from provider, drawing up comprehensive service specifications, the introduction of competition, and the provision of feedback on contractual performance. Each of them will be examined in turn.

Separation of purchaser and provider roles. For some services, the separation between purchaser and provider has always existed. This is particularly true of community and welfare services funded by governments and provided by private, often non-profit, organizations. The relevant government department acted as the agent-purchaser on behalf of the ultimate clients—the recipients of the service. But such separation has not been the norm in government departments or municipalities which produce and deliver services in-house. Demand and supply of the services are typically managed in the same unit; for example refuse collection and disposal services may be coordinated through the works and services department of a city council. Such arrangements can create problems because the section that manages the supply of the service also has to be responsive to, and representative of, demand. If users complain about the quality of the service directly to the service provider and there is no alternative supplier, they may normally expect little or no response. Things are likely to improve when a purchasing department can exert leverage on behalf of the service recipients, enforcing contractual agreements and service standards where appropriate.

The Australian government's Department of Finance (1995) reviewed purchaser–provider arrangements in Australia, New Zealand, and the UK. It came to the conclusion that the split in functions led to improved client responsiveness and reduced 'capture' of government decision making by those with a vested interest in those decisions. In other words, the separation of functions resulted in greater weight being given to the client's needs and less to supplier interests.

From a managerial point of view, there are merits in specializing in one or other side of the activity: if management is concerned solely with productive efficiency and quality of service, the result is usually superior to the alternative arrangements just described. Separation of demand and supply is the fundamental characteristic of markets, and it can be equally effective when applied to public services. When contractors are appointed, such separation becomes inevitable; when in-house teams are allowed to compete for contracts the separation takes on special significance: not only does it ensure that the client's needs are properly represented, it also allows for 'fairness' in the competition between in-house and external providers.

A good illustration of the consequences of genuine separation comes from Auckland City Council in New Zealand. Auckland is the country's largest city with a population of approximately 1,000,000. In 1991, following a major review of the Council's activities, the entire Works and Property Maintenance Department was singled out for contracting. Auckland City Council had effectively decided to become a major purchaser of services on behalf of its citizens, but it also retained an internal capacity for service delivery. This was done by creating an in-house business unit as a provider of works and property services. The unit was functionally and organizationally separate from the purchasing arm of the Council. It was initially successful in winning approximately 15 per cent of the Council's contracts. But this early success was not sustainable and the unit was eventually disbanded after it failed to win contracts against private sector competition. By 1997 Auckland City was a major purchaser of services, with more than 260 separate contracts in place.

This case highlights the real implications of separation between purchaser and provider: the in-house service provider may fail to win contracts, for any number of reasons, just like a private contractor. If the separation is to be effective, the in-house provider should be left to go out of business if its performance warrants it. To do otherwise may not only affect short-term costs or quality of service, but will also undermine the integrity of the competitive process in the long run.

Purchaser–provider separation may create special problems where specifying the appropriate level of service is difficult, and where the provider must exercise discretion *in situ* about the needs of the client as, for example, in aged care and disability services. However, the problem of safeguarding quality of service in these environments has been a permanent cause of concern to public sector organizations, irrespective of the mode of service delivery. It is not clear that purchaser–provider separation makes matters worse, particularly when it is remembered that welfare services such as aged care have been successfully contracted by governments for many years.

Specifications. Developing comprehensive and meaningful service specifications is no easy task. Yet it is a very important one, for without them competition may stall and the contract may come to a sticky end. It is instructive to note that most of the services that were put up for contracting in the UK in the 1980s for the first time had no prior specifications. Levels of service delivery were based on custom and practice, highlighting the problems that arise when market discipline is entirely absent. Comprehensive specifications had to be drawn up from scratch, and evaluation of appropriate service levels had to be reconsidered. It could not simply be assumed that the service provided in the past represented an optimal level of service: there was no logical basis for such an assessment.

Furthermore, specifications may be of two different types: input (task based) or output (performance based). In general, performance-based specifications that spell out outputs or outcomes are preferred. But in cases where output or outcomes are hard to define, it may be more effective to use a task-based specification. This type of contract is often used in cleaning contracts, since the output of 'cleaning activities' is difficult to define precisely. According to the Australian Industry Commission's extensive study of contracting in the public sector: 'Many of the improvements in quality appear to derive from better specification of the service by the purchaser, improvements in monitoring and the ability to use external expertise' (Industry Commission 1996: 9).

The precision with which service specifications are set down, while important, is not the critical factor in the process. It is the determination of outcomes required by users that is the central consideration. Experience shows that specifications tend to be dynamic; users' needs change and specifications have to follow suit. But the discipline of identifying and tracking those needs, while ensuring they are met in a consistent and rigorous way, is the principal merit of establishing a formal process for developing specifications.

Competition. Why is competition *for* the market appropriate contractor selection mechanism? Why not introduce several competitors simultaneously and have traditional, *ex post* competition in the market? The reason is that many publicly provided services have natural monopoly characteristics—least cost production requires that there be only a single service provider at any one time. It is surprising how commonplace these natural monopoly attributes are. For example, the provision of school meals would be inefficient if several caterers competed simultaneously within the single school kitchen. It is therefore more efficient to have one caterer within the premises supplying meals for the duration of the contract.

If contractor selection is by means of competitive tender, bids would be solicited from professional catering companies to supply school meals of a specified quality and quantity. Bid prices would reflect the caterers' estimated costs of providing the service, and would also vary according to their expectations about the intensity of competition. By choosing from amongst the lowest bids submitted, cost can be reduced relative to the status quo. This will be true irrespective of whether the winning tenderer is an in-house team, or a private contractor.

But how can the purchaser be confident that the bid prices are truly competitive and that the lowest among them represents good value for money? Both the theoretical and empirical evidence point overwhelmingly to the conclusion that competition reduces prices. Recent research in auction theory shows that the more bidders there are in a competitive tender, the greater will be the downward pressure on prices (see Bulow and Klemperer 1996 for theoretical results). And although the empirical findings have been disputed by critics of government contracting, the statistical evidence which was reviewed in Chapter 3 supports the conclusion that, on average, competition tends to reduce prices. However, it is interesting to note that the savings generated by competition—most frequently observed to lie in the 10–30 per cent range—accrue to the client whether the provider is publicly or privately owned. This means that even in-house teams can muster the necessary productivity gains when competition looms. Therefore it appears that competition, not ownership, has the dominant influence on economic performance.

This conclusion is not clear-cut, however. Recent evidence by Szymanski (1996) indicates that in-house teams under contract to English local authorities regularly returned savings of 10 per cent. By contrast, private contractors were generating savings nearer 20 per cent. What do these results mean? It could be that ownership matters or, perhaps more likely, that competitive neutrality between private and public bidders is not being enforced. If in-house teams persistently under-perform compared to their private sector counterparts, yet continue to win competitive tenders, competition is not being effective. In due course, private contractors may stop bidding altogether for contracts they believe are destined to remain in the public sector. Maintaining competitive neutrality is a laudable ideal but not always easy to implement. The issue will be considered in more detail later in this chapter.

The benefits of competition tend to be greatest where the supply side of the market is well developed—that is where there is a reasonably large pool of potential service providers. But this does not mean that open tendering is always the best way to proceed: it is costly to review a large number of bids. These costs can be reduced by calling for expressions of interest first. But reducing the number of final bidders raises concerns about the likelihood of collusion. While collusion may be attempted in some instances, it is proscribed by competition legislation. The penalties for collusive practices can be very large, and successful prosecutions for price-fixing are not unknown. Purchasers can protect themselves further by extending the domain from which they solicit bids. This may reduce the likelihood that bidders will know one another, discouraging collusive behaviour. However, it is clear that there is a trade-off between reducing the probability of collusion and increasing the costs of evaluating the bids.

Managing competition effectively is not always easy. In particular, there is a tendency for public sector clients to focus on observable factors, namely price, and to give less weight to the more intangible aspects of the bid such as the contractor's reputation for quality. This can have serious implications. It could bias the selection process in favour of contractors who submit unrealistically low bid prices which may, in turn, have other undesirable effects. Successful contractors may subsequently attempt to renegotiate prices upward, after the contract has been let. Alternatively, they may attempt to 'shade quality' in an effort to reduce the gap between revenues and costs.

Monitoring contractor performance. An essential requirement of successful contracting is the monitoring of contractual performance, as discussed in Chapter 7. One might have expected formal monitoring to take place even in the absence of contracting, but it appears that it was rare in public sector services prior to the introduction of contracting. There are two possible reasons for this. First, without adequate specifications, and with the provider and purchaser effectively the same entity, monitoring may not have seemed particularly necessary. Significant performance problems would normally have come to light through complaints from service recipients. Second, with the introduction of profit-oriented private contracts into public services, concerns have been raised that pressure to cut costs may result in lower quality. This has placed special emphasis on ensuring that contractors do not shade quality, and that service standards are maintained. The 'quality shading' hypothesis has been much debated in the theoretical literature. Because of the difficulty of specifying service standards precisely in advance, it may be hard to establish whether the standards desired by the client are being met once the contract has been let. This can create a situation of potential contract failure, where the client believes the requirements are not being met but does not have the information with which to enforce them.

As might be expected, empirical evidence is scant in this area. However, official reports (see for example Walsh 1991) suggest that the introduction of contracting brings greater emphasis on explicit inspections and maintenance of quality standards. Others, however, acknowledge the difficulties that monitoring presents for public sector clients. In a recent report, the US General Accounting Office (1997: 17) made this telling comment concerning six major contracting out initiatives in state and local governments: 'Officials . . . said that performance monitoring was their weakest link in their privatization process.'

Despite the difficulties with monitoring, the presence of a formal process for recording performance information enhances accountability in public service provision. To the extent that such a process did not exist prior to contracting, the introduction of performance monitoring is an important element of public sector reform. But it also raises questions about the burdens that formal contracts place on public sector clients, questions that go to the heart of the issue of the merits of contracting.

Problems of public sector contracting

Contracting of public services remains controversial, but some areas tend to be more contentious than others. No one is much concerned about the contracting of cleaning, catering, or even refuse collection services. The contracting of these activities is just as prevalent in the private sector, and appears to raise no moral or ethical issues. But passions are aroused when the discussion turns to contracting of prisons, welfare, and other human services where personal contact between client and provider is extensive, and where the provider needs to exercise judgement, force, care, and compassion as part of the service delivery. In such circumstances, people's intuition seems to suggest that some of the merits of contracting outlined above turn into definite drawbacks: competition drives costs relentlessly down with potentially detrimental consequences for quality; the separation of the proximate client (the government agency) from the provider makes things worse by further clouding the effect on ultimate service recipients. Precise specification and rigorous performance monitoring will be difficult to implement in these circumstances. According to the sceptics, the important aspects of quality cannot be properly specified in the contract and are therefore not monitorable.

Recent research suggests that this problem, known as the non-contractibility of quality, may be serious enough to tilt the balance in favour of in-house provision. Other problems which may have the same effect, and which are considered below, include the question of ownership of physical assets, the issue of public sector accountability, and the effect of contracting on employees.

Non-contractibility of quality. In certain activities it is difficult if not impossible to specify the requirement in a manner that leads to observable and verifiable outcomes. The treatment of prisoners is a good example, particularly as regards the use of force in maintaining order and discipline within the correctional facility. The best that can be done is to stipulate the use of 'appropriate force', depending on the actual situation faced by the guard(s). Although this concept has a well-understood meaning in the law-enforcement community and in the judiciary, it is still insufficiently precise from a contractual point of view. There is no universal yardstick by which the appropriateness of alternative actions might be judged. More importantly, situations in which an assessment of appropriateness may be required, such as a prison riot or break-out, could be quite rare and therefore difficult to observe until it is 'too late'.

In these circumstances it is easier to specify inputs than outputs (or outcomes). The way this is achieved in the prison context is to require that the contractor adhere to industry standards and obtain accreditation from a certifying body. In the USA, the American Correctional Association (ACA) issues standards for 'good' prisons, and provides accreditation to those that meet them. The standards cover such areas as staff training and experience, safety procedures, security, inmate facilities, food quality, and intake of calories. To obtain ACA accreditation, a correctional facility must meet 38 mandatory standards and 90 per cent of the non-mandatory ones. There are 463 ACA standards in total for adult prisons and, not surprisingly, only a small proportion of all private or public prisons in the USA are ACA accredited.

Of course, a client may demand full accreditation or specify that certain standards required for accreditation be met, even if accreditation is not required. In this case it is up to the contracting organization—the client—to monitor and enforce those standards. It cannot rely on the accreditation process for enforcement, only for determination of what constitutes good practice. Recent theoretical research suggests that it is in this area that problems arise. Because certain aspects of quality are non-contractible and incentives for cost reductions are present (the profit motive), there may be significant opportunities for the contractor to reduce costs without violating the formal contract provisions. Yet these reductions would have a deleterious impact on quality. This is quality shading of a subtle kind: the contractor reduces costs in a manner which has a negative effect on quality and which would not be desired by the client, but the client may not be able to observe this deterioration, nor to correct it through legal enforcement if it is suspected.

The proposition that 'contractors have an opportunity to reduce costs in ways that may lead to a substantial deterioration of quality' has been demonstrated theoretically by Hart, Shleifer, and Vishny (1997: 1148). They apply their theoretical propositions to real world cases and focus on prison management as a case of non-contractibility of quality. In particular, they cite the failed private contract at the Elizabeth detention centre in New Jersey as a case in point. The events are outlined in Case Study 9.1, and the reader may reflect on the nature and significance of this contractual failure in terms of the issues just covered.

Case Study 9.1. Contract failure in Elizabeth, New Jersey

There has been much debate recently in the United States about the efficacy of using private companies either to own or simply to manage correctional facilities. Most of the objections to private prisons revolve around the quality of service provided, especially with regard to health care, violence towards inmates, and rehabilitative services. Despite this, private prisons have grown quite rapidly from approximately 1,200 prisoners in 1985 to 50,000 prisoners in 1994, which represents approximately 3 per cent of the total prison population in the United States.

Like all service-based contracts, prison contracts encounter the problem of how adequately to account for intangible outcomes in the writing of the contract. While many of these factors can be incorporated into the contract, some cannot. In the case of prisons, this causes some unique problems. For example, how should a contract specify the level of force that a prison guard can use during a prison riot? To consider how the writing and enforcement of contract specifications can create contract failure, consider the much-publicized example of a detention facility run by Esmor Correctional Services Corporation in Elizabeth, New Jersey.

Esmor has been one of the firms to prosper during the recent growth in private prisons. The firm has eleven prison contracts across four states and its total revenue in 1994 was $US24.27 million. In October 1992, the US Immigration and Naturalization Services put out a request for tender for a detention facility in Elizabeth, New Jersey. The main purpose of the facility was to house illegal immigrants who were awaiting deportation. Despite growing concern over another facility in New York managed by Esmor, the $54 million contract to manage the Elizabeth detention facility was awarded to Esmor in August 1993. Esmor's main competitor for the contract complained at the outcome, claiming that Esmor's bid price, which was $20 million lower, was based on guards' pay rates which were 'unrealistically low'.

Nine months after the contract was operational, a riot broke out in the facility and the Immigration and Naturalization Service conducted a thorough analysis of the factors that contributed to the riot. The subsequent report was quite scathing about Esmor's performance. It stated that 'It appears that the level of salary was not realistic and could not . . . insure the availability of well-qualified applicants.' The report went on to state that 'It is evident that many, if not most, of the guards hired by Esmor did not meet the requirements of the contract or were only marginally qualified.' Furthermore, the report concluded that inmates were subjected to abuse and harassment by the guards and that some detainees were locked in punishment cells for no reason. The contract with Esmor was subsequently terminated.

Sources: Hart et al. (1997), Sullivan and Purdy (1995).

The Esmor case represents an unambiguous failure in the quality standards provided by the contractor. What is less clear is whether the quality in question was of the non-contractible type. After all, the Immigration and Naturalization Service (INS) report found that the guards hired by Esmor 'did not meet the requirements of the contract'. But surely the level of training and experience of the guards should have been equally apparent to the client as it was to the INS inspectors who wrote the report? There may be many aspects of the quality of prison management services that are non-contractible, but the quality of the personnel seems eminently verifiable and should therefore have been verified by the purchaser.

There is no doubt that quality standards, and the incentives for quality shading, can impose significant constraints on contracting. Donahue (1989: 45) was giving sound advice when he counselled: 'arm's-length contracts with outside suppliers are more attractive . . . the more precisely requirements can be specified in advance.' But precision is a matter of degree, and quality is often a matter of judgement. Ultimately the public sector client has to determine whether there are sufficient countervailing forces to mitigate the propensities of contractors to engage in quality shading. Such forces might include the ability to switch contractors at relatively low cost, effective monitoring of contractors' activities, and relying on the contractor's desire to safeguard an expensively acquired reputation and to secure future business by meeting client expectations.

While quality issues will remain at the forefront of the contracting out debate for a long time yet, it is instructive to note what the Australian Industry Commission (1996: 120) had to say on the matter: 'The problems of securing quality outcomes for these type of services have been a constant source of concern for governments regardless of the method of service delivery.'

Ownership of physical assets. As was mentioned at the beginning of this chapter contracting brings *ex ante* competition to the provision of services. The transfer of physical assets associated with a particular service activity is incidental to the process and, in principle, asset ownership should have no influence on contracting outcomes. In practice it does. Its effect depends on the activity being contracted, and the value and 'specificity' of the physical assets required to produce the service. This can raise the costs of achieving efficient contracting outcomes, and reduce competition.

Consider three types of public services which are frequently contracted by governments: building cleaning, refuse collection, and prison management. These services are associated with low, moderate, and high levels of physical assets respectively. We can use these practical examples to illustrate the effects that these assets have on contracting. In the case of cleaning, the level of physical capital required is negligible—the service is labour intensive. Who should own the physical assets—the vacuum cleaners, brooms and brushes— is a relatively trivial issue. In this industry, ownership of equipment is almost universally left in the hands of the service provider. The equipment is not specific to any particular contract, hence the physical assets are transferable across different contracts or activities.

Refuse or garbage collection requires a moderately high level of capital investment, because of the need for specialized vehicles. Now consider what happens under the alternative modes of ownership: public or private. In the former case the vehicle would be owned by the client and leased (or loaned) to the contractor for the term of the contract. This may seem an efficient outcome, in that the client retains control over the physical assets, but problems can arise with respect to maintenance and renewal. The contractor will have little incentive to maintain the vehicles to a standard that extends their economic life beyond the contract term. Moreover, the contractor will have little or no incentive to invest in the operational enhancement of the vehicles, what economists refer to as 'relationship-specific investments', because the contract term may be too short to make this sunk expenditure worthwhile. The potential problem with public ownership of assets is therefore one of under-investment—equipment may be allowed to run down, particularly in the run-up to contract termination.

Unsurprisingly, we observe that equipment ownership tends to be left with the service provider in most refuse collection contracts. And because the equipment is not specific to a particular contract, it can be used elsewhere once the contract reaches the end of its term. This means that contract duration does not need to allow for a long period of capital amortization, and contracts can be retendered with reasonable frequency.

Prison management services, in which the ratio of physical to 'human capital' is extremely high, raise significant contractual problems. If the incarceration facility remains in public ownership and is leased or loaned to the privately contracted prison manager, incentive problems emerge once again. The manager may skimp on maintenance expenditure and avoid relationship-specific investments which enhance the facility and improve the quality of service. The lack of incentive stems from the knowledge that the benefits from these outlays are limited by the duration of the contract: if the contract is lost to another service provider at the rebid stage, the benefits go with it. Hence the shorter the contract duration, the stronger the incentives to hold back on investment expenditures.

In the alternative case, where the facility is owned by the contractor, other problems arise. Given the sheer magnitude of the investment involved, the contract will have to be of a very long duration to secure profitability for the service provider. Enforcement of contractual performance may be compromised if both parties know that early termination of the contract will require buy-back of the facility by the state which is both expensive and complex. Also, with contract durations of twenty to thirty years not uncommon in such circumstances, the salutary effect of competition is going to be all but absent. In conclusion, both ownership solutions present problems for contracting of prison management services.

Asset ownership has become a more troublesome issue as public sector clients have turned to contractors for the financing of infrastructure. Public sector borrowing constraints have led departments to seek private finance wherever possible, and this has had a significant impact on contracting initiatives. For example, the recent UK Ministry of Defence contract for helicopter training services required the provider to purchase the thirty-eight helicopters that were previously attached to this activity. This purchase represents a substantial financial transfer to the Ministry of Defence, reducing its capital requirements considerably. But the price for this arrangement is a very long contract duration which restricts the application of competition from the provision of this service.

Another example, this time in the prison management field, comes from Fazakerley near Liverpool in England. Under what is known as BOO-type contract—build, own, and operate—the UK government recently entered into a twenty-five-year, joint-venture agreement with Tarmac and Group 4 to finance, construct, and manage a new 600-bed prison. A similar contract was awarded to the Securicor company to build and operate a prison in Bridgend, Wales. Both of these deals were conceived and brought to fruition under the Private Finance Initiative (PFI)—a policy formulated by the UK Treasury to enlist private funding for investment in public infrastructure. The PFI is currently being reviewed, but looks set to be extended as funding constraints continue to impede the realization of public sector projects.

The downside to these otherwise laudable partnerships between the private and the public sectors is the diminution of competition through the inordinate lengthening of contracts. Ironically, even some of the service providers agree that, from the point of view of both client *and* contractor, an optimal contract length would lie somewhere between three and seven years. Long enough to let the contractor achieve real improvements in service delivery, but not so long that it instils complacency and stagnation. Consideration should therefore be given to ways of achieving a balance between both objectives: private financing and the promotion of competition. One possibility would be to decouple the financing from the management activities, as appears to be the practice in the hospitality industry. Under such a scheme, the financing and ownership of the infrastructure would be separately contracted for, not combined with the contract for management services. In this way the management contract can be made much shorter, and subjected to competition every few years. The infrastructure contract would be of a length sufficient to yield a fair rate of return to the financing and building companies. The management of the facility can change hands, if appropriate, every few years while the ownership of the facility does not. Such arrangements are frequently used in the hotel industry, where management teams from rival hotel chains displace one another.

Public sector accountability. One important aspect of democratically governed societies that is allegedly endangered by contracting is accountability. In the traditionally hierarchical public service, accountability operates through bureaucratic channels up to senior administrative and political levels of control. Under the Westminster system of government, accountability is understood to mean a capacity to call an authority or department to account by having its senior officials answer and explain their conduct. Where maladministration is judged to have occurred, sanctions may be brought to bear on bureaucratic personnel. Only in rare cases would a government minister resign for actions taken by his department's officials.

Clearly, contractual relationships do not operate in the same way as administrative channels. Commentators on the public policy side of the debate have suggested that: 'Managers in the public service generally felt that accountability within the organization is improved by contracts, but that accountability to the public is not' (Deakin and Walsh 1996: 42). This raises the question: what does accountability to the public mean? Donahue's answer is that: 'It means evaluating alternative arrangements for carrying out public business by the yardstick of *fidelity to the public's values*, whatever they may be' (1989: 12). Such a yardstick is very wide indeed, and does not provide a basis for practical implementation.

One route to the resolution of this problem is to draw a clearer distinction between responsibility and accountability. When a public sector organization transfers responsibility for service provision to other parties through legally enforceable contracts, it does not relinquish accountability for them. In other words, irrespective of the mode of service delivery chosen by the agency, it must remain accountable to the government (and thus the public) for the performance of the service functions delegated to it. This point is not always well understood by government agencies. They can sometimes treat the appointment of a contractor in the same way as the relegation of an activity to another government department.

An interesting illustration of this problem was highlighted in a recent report by the ombudsman's office of the Commonwealth of Australia. The case involved a contractor hired by Australia Post to deliver mail, a common and usually trouble-free practice. In the process of delivery, the contractor damaged a pensioner's letter box. When the pensioner turned to Australia Post for compensation, the response was that the matter was strictly between him and the contractor. The contractor, however, offered only a third of the cost of the repair, essentially because his property damage insurance policy required under the mail delivery contract was not effective for such small claims (the excess on the policy was greater than the cost of repair). The ombudsman was able to report subsequent progress in this matter: 'Australia Post has since amended its contracts to provide that where a dispute arises, it can (after its own assessment) make a compensatory payment to the consumer and then seek recovery of any damages from the contractor. Australia Post has now made this a condition of its new contracts and reports that it and its suppliers have found no difficulty in its implementation' (Commonwealth Ombudsman 1997: 72).

This incident was used by the ombudsman to highlight the potential loss of accountability associated with contracting. It was a small matter, and the financial sums involved were insubstantial, but the case took on special significance because of Australia Post's attempted abrogation of its accountability to the public. If the problem lay with the inadequacy of the contractor's insurance arrangements, then that had to be fixed. It was up to the contracting organization to resolve the matter in a manner that protected the interests of the actual injured party, as well as any future ones.

Where service delivery by a public sector organization is concerned, as in the case just described, contracting can bolster accountability in three ways. First, it promotes a review of current service levels and the drawing up of revised, improved service specifications. Second, it introduces performance monitoring systems which would not have been put in place in the absence of contracting. Third, it focuses attention on mechanisms for redress in cases where the public, individuals or organizations, have suffered loss or damage. It should be remembered that traditional channels of accountability, although preferred by some, can be pretty opaque. Recent experience suggests that, if properly implemented, contracting need not reduce accountability, and may even constitute an improvement on the status quo ante.

Effect on employment. The impact of contracting on overall employment levels in the economy is not well researched, but there is currently no evidence that links unemployment levels to the intensity of contracting in the private or the public sectors. What is clear, however, is that the costs of contracting are not uniformly distributed among the stakeholders of the organization. The employees directly affected by contracting may be those who bear the greatest costs: they face disruption to their current activities, uncertainty about future job prospects, and possibly a worsening of terms and conditions of employment. This has the potential to arrest the contracting process in its tracks, particularly if it is met with union opposition. Although not officially documented, many public sector organizations opt for internal restructuring, benchmarking, and re-engineering instead of contracting because they believe that they can achieve efficiency gains without raising the spectre of costly industrial disputes.

The financial and intangible costs associated with employment issues can place contracting in the balance. In some cases, the initiatives are abandoned altogether because of internal and external opposition; in other cases the contract is implemented but is less than successful because of simmering resentment which manifests itself in a lingering non-cooperative attitude by staff. In a few isolated cases, disgruntled employees have allegedly resorted to sabotage in order to destabilize contractual relationships between the purchaser and provider (see Hall and Domberger 1995: 122–4).

Following a contracting decision, there are three possible outcomes for the staff affected: redeployment within the contracting organization, transfer to the contractor, and redundancy. The approach to these options varies widely, both internationally and between domestic jurisdictions, as was discussed in the previous chapter. But continuity of employment usually dominates employee concerns over whether terms and conditions will be the same after contracting. For this reason many public sector organizations have stipulated that winning tenderers must take on a minimum proportion of, or even all, existing staff employed on the activity prior to contracting. The rationale is that the cost of redeployment may be lower for the contractor, who has other contracts which provide employment opportunities for suitable staff. For the purchaser, the advantage of this strategy is that fears about redundancy and loss of jobs can be allayed at a very early stage. A good example of how this can be successfully achieved, without legislative constraints, comes from an English 'Royal County' (see Case Study 9.2).

Case Study 9.2.   Staff transfer at Berkshire County Council

The county of Berkshire is situated in south-east England, and has had long associations with the monarchy because Windsor Castle lies within its boundaries. 'The Royal County', as it is known, is one of the most densely populated regions in England and has a growing population which has reached almost 800,000 people. Because of its close proximity to London, Berkshire is also a major business and commercial centre, with many multinational companies such as Hewlett Packard, Sony, Oracle, and Mars located there.

On 1 April 1993, Berkshire County Council contracted out its highways and planning department, which included over 300 staff and senior management. The contract itself was then the largest contract for professional services awarded by any UK local authority. The services involved cover professional and technical advice in environmental concerns, planning, and engineering. The contract was awarded to the Babtie Group.

At the time, the UK's Compulsory Competitive Tendering legislation was being extended to cover many white-collar activities—such as financial services and payroll. But Berkshire County Council decided to contract these services before the introduction of the legislation. It did so for two reasons: first, to maximize flexibility with the aim of achieving the greatest savings possible. The Council believed that demand for service providers might be so large once the legislation was enacted that the price would rise and competition would be limited. Secondly, Berkshire wanted to make sure that the service provider selected would be able to absorb the county's existing staff. And the Council felt this would be best achieved by negotiating directly with the service providers prior to the legislation coming into force.

As a result, every Berkshire employee who wanted a position with the private contractor was able to obtain one. As of 1995, the Council had contracted about 50 per cent of its total financial operations, including payroll, income collection, accounting functions, and a significant proportion of internal audit.

Sources: Economist Intelligence Unit (1995), Berkshire County Council.

The treatment of redundancies and redeployment varies widely, and it is inappropriate to suggest a 'best practice' approach. Circumstances and budgets vary considerably and policies must be adapted to local conditions. However, the importance of communications with staff regarding the implications arising from contracting initiatives cannot be overstated. This message, articulated in virtually all contracting guidelines and manuals, is eminently justifiable: fear and uncertainty are exacerbated by lack of information. Indeed, effective communication of impending changes seems one of the hardest things to achieve in the context of contracting, as suggested by the recent Cabinet Office review of the Competing for Quality programme (UK Cabinet Office 1996: 48–51). These difficulties could be related to the persistence of what Kirkpatrick and Martinez Lucio (1996: 6) call the 'older traditions of official secrecy' in the public service.

Private–public sector competition: a level playing field?

As a consequence of the growth of contracting, the public and private sectors are increasingly competing head to head for the provision of government-funded services. This is an unusual sort of competition, since the traditional role of the public sector is to step into service provision only where the private sector is deficient—in cases of market failure. Nor have these competitive encounters been free from controversy. Following the introduction of the 1988 Local Government Act which made competitive tendering for services compulsory in English local authorities, in-house teams were permitted, indeed encouraged, to submit tenders against private competition. Of the first round of contracts, valued at almost £2 billion, 76 per cent were won by in-house teams. The private sector's response to this outcome was to cry foul play. Complaints of unfair competition were widespread, and private contractors alleged that evaluation of bids by local authorities was often biased in favour of in-house bids. Table 9.1 shows the proportion of in-house contracts across the different services for the first and second round of contracts. It is interesting to note that in the second round the overall proportion of in-house successes declined substantially, suggesting some convergence towards parity between the private and public sector provision.

Much of the work of the Department of the Environment, which had responsibility for the implementation of CCT, was directed at issuing guidelines and directives to local government that would counter any in-house advantage. For example, a required rate of return had to be factored into in-house bids to ensure that they took account of their cost of capital, in the same way as would a private contractor. The OECD's *Best Practice Guidelines for Contracting out Government Services* makes it clear that: 'In-house bids should in all respects be treated the same as outside bids. Special care needs to be

Table 9.1. Compulsory competitive tendering in UK local government, 1991–1994

Activity	1991		1994	
	Contract value (£m)	Proportion in-house (%)	Contract value (£m)	Proportion in-house (%)
Refuse collection	516.9	73.5	539	64.4
Building cleaning	366.2	62.7	332	40.8
Grounds maintenance	315	77.9	492	57.8
School catering	345.5	85	542	72.5
Sports and leisure	143.8	88	150	84.8
Street cleaning	132.4	81.2	190	63.7
Vehicle maintenance	144.1	80.2	151	74.9
Total	1963.9	76.1	2396	58.8

Sources: UK Department of the Environment, Audit Commission, Institute of Public Finance.

taken to ensure that the costing of the bid is complete, i.e. that it incorporates all items of cost faced by private sector contractors' (OECD 1997).

The 'unfair' advantages to in-house bids stem from two main sources. First, there are cost advantages which include incomplete allowance for the cost of capital, rental of premises and equipment, and exemption from certain taxes and charges such as payroll taxes. Second, there are informational advantages: the in-house team may have better knowledge of the client's requirements, based on long-term experience and unhindered access to the client's representatives. Admittedly, the cost advantages may be mitigated, or even be nullified, by the higher pay rates often awarded in the public sector. And the information advantages may be less valuable when set against the private sector's access to new technology and innovation. But it should also be noted that the private sector can, and sometimes does, cross-subsidize bids to eliminate competition when entering a market. A case was reported in Japan where a contractor bid 1 Yen for a local government contract believing that winning would provide competitive advantage in subsequent tenders well worth the losses made on this contract.

Some jurisdictions have come to the conclusion that in-house bids are more trouble than they are worth, and have ruled them out. But the majority have not. Why then do governments believe that the benefits of having in-house bids outweigh the costs? To be sure, including the bid of the in-house provider increases the competition by one, but the real reason appears to have more to do with policy implementation than with the promotion of competition. Contracting policy is founded on the beneficial effects of competition and has been promulgated on that basis. There are those, however, who would argue that the critical aspect of the policy is the transfer of activity from the public to the private sector. But that argument is harder to sustain and would generally be met with much stronger political and administrative opposition. Allowing in-house bids reaffirms the view that competition is the key, rather than whether services are provided by private or public contractors. It therefore legitimizes the policy. It has meant that the ideological opposition to contracting is less intense than it otherwise would have been, and it has facilitated the usually difficult transition from bureaucratic service provision to a market-type mechanism (see Industry Commission 1996: 398–9).

When in-house bidders are unsuccessful a private sector contractor takes over the activity and that is that. If they are *very* successful, they may seek further expansion by tendering for outside work, typically contracts for similar services put out by other public sector organizations. The scope of competition with the private sector is therefore extended beyond the home base, creating further problems of competitive neutrality. The private sector would argue that such expansion is facilitated by the special advantages conferred by the public sector, namely access to cheap capital when expansion is internally funded, and immunity to commercial risk. For these reasons some jurisdictions have restricted the scope of in-house activities to competing for in-house contracts only.

Some public sector organizations see corporatization as the solution to this problem. Corporatization turns the in-house team into a legally separate entity, but it is owned by the public sector 'client' and is therefore clearly a public sector competitor. A more promising approach is to consider the management/staff buy-out option (MBO), where an in-house team is experienced and bold enough to enter the private sector fray. In terms of the issues discussed above this is perhaps the best solution, but it has not been widely used. Some MBOs have been documented, particularly in the IT area, where demand is strong and commercial opportunities abound. But in general, successful in-house teams would prefer to face private sector competitors from the relatively secure base of public ownership.

The limits to public sector contracting

A recent collection of case studies by the OECD (1997) suggests that a very wide range of activities are being contracted by the public sector: international airport operations by the city of Indianapolis in the USA; information technology functions by the UK's Inland Revenue Department; case management services for the unemployed by the Department of Employment, Education, Training and Youth Affairs in Australia; building cleaning services by the Copenhagen National Hospital, Denmark; catering services by the Turkish Ministry of Finance; internal audit functions by the New Zealand Audit Office; printing services by the Dutch Tax and Customs administration; and residential care for handicapped children by the Icelandic government. Looking at this list, and given the earlier examples discussed in this chapter, one might well wonder whether the boundaries between the public and private sectors have been breached beyond recognition. Are there any 'inherently governmental functions' remaining? If so, what are they and what are the criteria by which they are defined?

Some commentators, for example Boston (1995), suggest that, in theory at least, all functions of the state are contractible. But he also states that it is 'in the public interest for governments to have at their disposal in-house, non-partisan policy advisers capable of providing expert advice across the broad range of policy issues'. His list of inherently governmental functions includes policy making and advice, planning, regulation, law enforcement, and emergency services. The criterion invoked to define these functions appears to be the 'public interest', but without a meaningful definition of this criterion the argument becomes circular.

Donahue's approach to the search for the limits of contracting is based on motivational factors. Whom would you trust to provide a service required by the public and funded by taxation, he asks: a profit-motivated contractor or a civil servant committed to the public service? In some activities one is likely to be indifferent because motivational factors are likely to play no role, say in printing services, or catering, or transport. But in welfare or prison services, which require considerable discretion, care, and judgement, one would be inclined to favour the civil servant. Donahue (1989: 87) expresses it in the following way: 'The public's business becomes much easier to accomplish if agents display a combination of informed fidelity to the public interest, initiative, and integrity that can be summarized by the word *honor*, a term that is admittedly complex, but is also too important to neglect.'

There is immense value, then, in the intrinsic motivation by public servants to pursue the public interest. The limits of contracting could reasonably be defined by reference to it. That means that services that not only rely on the appropriate skills, but demand a strong sense of the public good, should be provided by government employees. This would indeed apply in aged care and welfare services, as well as prison management. The problem, however, is that the intrinsic motivation of government employees cannot always be relied upon to fulfil public objectives. In the absence of external pressures, other motives intercede and weaken the agent's commitment to the public interest. As Donahue himself concedes: 'The potential for chronic inefficiency, then, is a special peril for collective endeavors' (1989: 51). This inefficiency typically manifests itself in services which are of high cost and low quality. It has also prompted the search for alternative delivery mechanisms, and cast some doubt on the intrinsic motivation principle as the basis for setting the limits of contracting.

In 1997, Oliver Hart and his colleagues at Harvard and Chicago Universities considered this issue in a paper entitled 'The Proper Scope of Government'. Their analysis is firmly rooted in economics: it assumes that both government employees and contractors are motivated by self-interest. Government employees are not effectively compensated for cost or quality improvements in service provision because of the nature of ownership and employment in the public sector. The incentives for cost or quality improvements by them are therefore weak. Those incentives are correspondingly stronger for private service providers, because they can appropriate a larger share of the benefits. However, it is also assumed that certain public services have significant elements of non-contractible quality. This has the effect of creating 'significant opportunities for cost reduction that do not violate the contracts, but that, at least in principle, can substantially reduce quality' (Hart et al. 1997: 1152). In other words, public sector purchasers would have difficulty in establishing that the private contractor was *not* providing the quality of service stipulated in the specifications.

In these circumstances in-house provision would be preferable, even though it would probably result in higher costs and indifferent quality. And the same conclusion would apply to other public services where non-contractibility of quality was significant. The limits of contracting are thus established by reference to behavioural differences between the public and the private sectors under particular conditions.

Systematic evidence on this matter is very scarce. But the numerous contracting initiatives that have been undertaken internationally, in complex services close to core areas of government, should provide an empirical basis for judging. There are good reasons to suggest that countervailing factors exist which would reduce the quality problems discussed above: contractors' concerns about their reputations, the presence of *ex ante* competition, and continual improvements in monitoring and evaluation of contractual performance. It is too early to tell whether these effects dominate, or whether such contracts will be prone to failure. It seems clear that some of the more innovative public sector contracting initiatives of recent times are by their nature *experiments* in alternative modes of service delivery. Time must elapse before the outcomes of such experiments become known and their implications assessed.

A few senior public sector managers recognize the experimental nature of some of their contracting activities. The last case study in this chapter (Case Study 9.3) describes the activities of one such manager, the mayor of the city of Indianapolis. Although he may appear overly enthusiastic about the city's activities, highlighting the successes and downplaying the setbacks, he openly acknowledges the fact that some initiatives are experiments in redrawing the boundaries between the public and the private sectors. That is a rare admission indeed.

Guide to further reading

For recent surveys of contracting in the public sector see Domberger and Rimmer (1994), Domberger and Hall (1996), and Domberger and Jensen (1997).

Case Study 9.3. Doing business with government

It is little wonder that making government more efficient is suddenly a top priority in city halls: budgetary constraints have tightened over the last five years while citizens continue to demand higher levels of service from government. In response to this, Indianapolis mayor Stephen Goldsmith has encouraged cooperation between the public and private sectors, primarily through outsourcing, arguing the need to 'tear down the wall between public and private' (1997). Since 1992, more than 70 services have been subjected to competitive tendering, the operating budget has been cut by 7 per cent, and the workforce has been reduced by almost 40 per cent. Along the way, a great deal has been learnt about the pitfalls and possibilities of making government work harder and smarter.

To illustrate Indianapolis's experience with outsourcing, consider its printing and copying business. Before 1993, the city spent $1.4 million annually running three print shops and operating more than 200 copiers. Each print shop operated independently: no coordination existed between them at all. Each made its own decisions about personnel, purchased its own supplies, and maintained its own equipment. After opening up the entire printing and copying business to competition from the private sector, total costs were reduced by $400,000 per year, or nearly 30 per cent. The winning contractor, Pitney Bowes Management Services, consolidated the print shops into one copy centre. Today, 78 per cent of the city's copying is done at the Pitney Bowes copy centre, saving a great deal of secretarial and clerical time. Further unexpected savings were realized when Pitney Bowes offered its expertise in a 'red tape' initiative to reduce the number of forms produced and needed by city departments.

Another example of Indianapolis's innovative private sector solutions to specific problems is in the controversial area of prisons. Like most large cities, Indianapolis's jail is overcrowded, holding approximately 300 inmates over capacity. When Indianapolis opened up the construction of a new jail to private proposals, the Corrections Corporation of America (CCA) submitted a novel idea that solved the capacity problem: they proposed to design, build, and operate a 670-bed jail. The government will rent 264 of these beds over the short term, with the option to rent more as needed. CCA is free to rent the city's unused capacity to other governments—paying the city $3 for each bed rented to someone else. Further, CCA guarantees to pay for at least 240 rented beds per day, whether anyone actually rents them or not. This system will save the city $20 million in construction costs and $1.4 million in annual operating expenses. As Mayor Goldsmith said: 'both parties benefit the most when government purchases output instead of inputs.'

Private sector managers need to understand and address the political risks involved in competition and privatization. In the private sector, bad decisions often can be written off; but voters and the media can make one bad decision fatal for an elected official. Understandably, public figures are cautious about transferring any responsibility to the private sector. Given the reluctance to outsource, the question must be asked: How far can privatization go? According to Goldsmith, 'The answer is certainly an experiment in process.'

Source: Goldsmith (1997).

Bennett and Ferlie (1996) is a useful summary of internal market reforms in the health service, and Corry (1997) provides an overview of public expenditure control in the age of New Labour. For a US perspective on contracting in the government sector see Prager (1994).

Hart et al. (1997) is an important contribution to the issue of non-contractibility of services and the limits to contracting out. For a British perspective on contracting in local government services, see Patterson and Pinch (1995).

For a thorough and comprehensive coverage of the economics of privatization see Vickers and Yarrow (1988), or their more recent reassessment in Vickers and Yarrow (1991). Schmidt (1996) is another useful if somewhat theoretical contribution to privatization in an incomplete contracts framework.

The classic reference on bureaucracy and how it works is Wilson (1989). For a cost–benefit framework applied to contracting out see Wisniewski (1991). For a comprehensive discussion of the broader social and economic impacts of competitive tendering and contracting there is no better source than the Industry Commission (1996) report, especially chapters B4 and B5.

10

Contracting and the Service Economy

> The most important concomitant of economic progress [is] the movement
> of working population from agriculture to manufacture and from manu-
> facture to commerce and services.
>
> (Colin Clark, 1951)

Contracting out of manufacturing activities is commonplace in the corporate
world. Following the pioneering development of subcontracting networks by
Japanese automobile manufacturers in the 1950s, their American and
European counterparts also turned to contracting for the production of motor
vehicle parts and subassemblies. In the high-tech electronics industries,
'contract manufacturing', as it has become known, is now *de rigueur*. 'Original
equipment manufacturers' (OEMs)—firms that sell finished goods under their
own name such as IBM and Hewlett-Packard—are turning to the likes of SCI
Systems and Solectron Merix to manufacture the parts and components of
their finished products. The OEMs concentrate on marketing and product
development.

Contract manufacturing is widespread in a variety of industries, from textile
finishing (Benetton) to telecommunications (Motorola). And as pointed out by
Quinn, Doorley, and Paquette (1990), manufacturing activities essentially
comprise a 'chain of services', whether produced internally or farmed out to
specialist contractors. Such activities include the sorting of components,
producing and assembling parts, and quality control through inspections and
testing. Yet there is a fundamental difference between services which culmi-
nate in the delivery of tangible output—a brake assembly for a car, say, or a
hard-drive for a PC—and services which yield no such output. Interestingly,
the most rapid expansion in contracting has been of the latter type: support
services which produce no material output but which are essential to the
smooth functioning of organizations. Such services include information
systems development and maintenance, security, financial services, and
payroll and human resource management.

Not so long ago, they would have been considered an integral part of any
organization, whether public or private. Purchasing such services from outside

providers would not normally have been considered, except as a last resort in the search for internal economies when organizations got into financial trouble. Today, contracting for such services is becoming much more acceptable, with significant implications for the growth of service industries.

This chapter will present arguments and evidence suggesting an important connection between the growth of contracting and the evolution of the services sector in the industrialized economies. It will also consider possible links between this trend and the question of service sector productivity, which has been the subject of intense debate in business and policy circles.

The nature and significance of services in the economy

In 1691, Sir William Petty—a seventeenth century scholar and mathematician— made the important observation that economic development entails a shift in resources from agriculture to manufacturing, and from manufacturing to services. This proposition was dubbed 'Petty's law' by the economist Colin Clark (1951: 395–6), who documented the long-run drift in employment between sectors in countries at different stages of development. Behind the inexorable movement of labour towards services, economic forces were at play: according to Petty 'There is much more to be gained' by manufacturing than by 'husbandry' (agriculture), and more from 'merchandise' (services) than from manufacture.

Simplistic though this may sound, the empirical regularities suggested by Petty and highlighted by Clark are borne out by international statistics. Even the present-day efforts of goods manufacturers to develop or acquire effective distribution channels reflect a wider preoccupation with the service side of the business. Compaq's $9 billion bid for Digital Equipment Corporation is seen by some as an attempt by the PC manufacturer to find new ways to sell and service computers.

By dividing the economy into three major sectors—agriculture, industry, and services—long-term employment and output trends can be measured and compared. The sectors are made up as follows:

- agriculture, which includes forestry and fishing;
- industry, which comprises mining (extractive) and manufacturing industries, electricity, gas and water, construction;
- services, which are made up of wholesale and retail trade, hospitality services, transportation, storage, communications, finance, insurance, real estate, business services, community, social and personal services, and government services.

This sectoral classification is the one reported in the OECD statistics of output and employment for member countries. The definition of services under this classification is somewhat restricted: it excludes construction and the 'utilities'.

In some circumstances they are lumped in with services, although the techno-logical characteristics of electricity, gas, and water are more akin to industry, which provides a rationale for their inclusion in that sector (see Uno 1989). While there is no universally accepted definition of services, adopting a mini-malist classification has the merit of avoiding overstatement of service growth. However, the vast body of evidence now available on the evolution of the services sector suggests that the overall trends are insensitive to the choice of definition.

Table 10.1 shows the distribution of employment between sectors in five of the G7 economies as well as Australia since 1870. Although the numbers differ

Table 10.1. Distribution of employment as a percentage of total employment, six industrial economies

Country/sector	1870	1960[a]	1984	1995
UK				
Agriculture	23	5	3	2
Industry	42	46	32	24
Services	35	49	65	73
USA				
Agriculture	50	8	3	3
Industry	24	31	25	24
Services	26	61	72	73
Australia				
Agriculture		8	6	5
Industry	n.a.	35	28	23
Services		57	66	72
Germany				
Agriculture	50	14	5	3
Industry	29	48	42	38
Services	22	38	53	59
France				
Agriculture	49	21	8	5
Industry	28	36	32	26
Services	23	43	60	69
Japan				
Agriculture	73	33	9	6
Industry }	27	30	34	34
Services }		37	57	61

Note: n.a. = not available.

[a] Australia: 1972.

Sources: Elfring (1989: table 1), OECD labour force statistics.

across countries, there are striking similarities in the trends experienced by these economies. First among these is the long-term decline in agricultural employment. This reflects the shift of jobs away from the land, where a significant proportion of the population was active in the latter part of the nineteenth century. The USA, Germany, and France had around 50 per cent of their labour force engaged in primary sector activities at this time; in Japan, the corresponding figure was a large 73 per cent. By 1995, the proportion of the labour force in agricultural and related activities had declined in all countries, with the exception of the UK, to between 3 and 6 per cent. In the UK, agricultural sector employment was down to a mere 2 per cent of the working population.

Industrial sector employment shows a rise and then a gentle decline in the five countries represented in the table, Japan being the only exception. Thus by 1995, UK industrial employment had declined to 24 per cent, starting from 42 per cent in 1870 and reaching a high point of 46 per cent in 1960. More moderate industrial declines are observed in the USA and Germany, whose corresponding employment proportions rise to 31 and 48 per cent, and then fall to 24 and 38 per cent respectively. Only in Japan does manufacturing employment rise from 30 per cent of the total and remain steady at 34 per cent through to 1995.

As for services, the trend in employment is uniformly upward in all six countries. In the UK, the USA, and Australia, the proportion of total employment accounted for by this sector exceeded 70 per cent in 1995, reflecting the skew in the level of economic activity now dedicated to the production of services. These trends are reflected not only in employment, but also in output levels. Fig. 10.1 shows the proportion of Gross Domestic Product (GDP) classified as services in the same group of countries since 1962. Over this period, the proportion rises in every case, although Japan's services output appears to have levelled off since 1980. In the remainder, the proportional growth of services output between 1962 and 1995 is in the region of 20 to 30 per cent. Over the same period, agriculture and industry experienced a corresponding proportional decline (not shown in the figure).

What factors underlie this continuous long-run growth? Economists have suggested three explanations, two of which will be considered here. They are not necessarily competing hypotheses: each may provide a partial explanation of the overall phenomenon. First, demand for services generally is what economists call 'income-elastic'. This means that demand for the output of the services sector rises more than proportionately with income: a doubling of income will lead to more than doubling of the demand for services. Empirical studies tend to support this hypothesis. For example, studies of the demand for leisure services such as travel, tourism, and hospitality indicate a high income elasticity of demand. This means that demand is strongly correlated with the rise in consumer wealth, but that it is also sensitive to cyclical upswings and downswings.

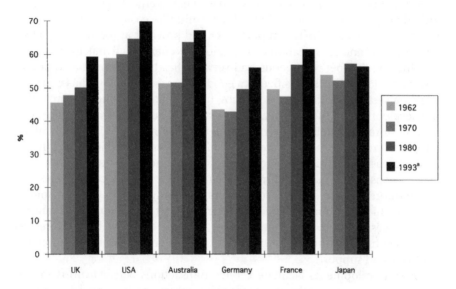

^a 1993 figures, except: 1991 for USA; 1992 for Germany and Australia.

Source: OECD statistics.

Fig. 10.1. Growth of services as a percentage of GDP

Second, with the growth of income and output, it becomes economically efficient for services once provided within households or firms to be supplied by outside specialists—to be contracted out. Legal, accounting, and data processing services would be typical examples of such contracting in the company sector, and restaurants, day-care, and house maintenance services are corresponding examples for households. This hypothesis about the growth of services implies a change in the way services are produced, rather than their overall volume. The shift from internal to external production has an important implication for the measurement of economic activity: services that were invisible to government statisticians when they were produced in-house are now captured as a separate market activity. They appear as new service transactions in the national accounts even though they may not represent new services actually produced and sold.

Does this mean that the officially recorded growth in services arises entirely from changes in measurement? The answer is undoubtedly no. Greater specialization in the production of services, fostered by contracting, makes possible reductions in cost through scale economies, improvements in quality through innovation, and the development of new service products. In time, this will lead to new demand, over and above the replacement of services previously produced in-house, resulting in an expansion of real output of this sector.

Although services have traditionally been characterized as intangible—they are things you cannot get hold of, which cannot be easily stored, and which require direct contact between purchaser and provider at the point of sale—technological and organizational innovation has changed all that. Increasingly, the dividing line between goods and services has been blurred: a computer program sold on disk is classified as a good, whereas on-line purchases of software are service transactions. Advances in information technology, including the development of the Internet, mean that knowledge-intensive services can now be stored and delivered on demand: the customer can simply download information as and when required. With highly sophisticated information and data processing facilities, interactive information exchange between remotely located customers and centrally located suppliers becomes feasible. Furthermore, instead of being sold separately, many services are now sold as bundles which combine the goods and the services components. For example, word-processing and data management services can now be delivered as bundles combining the goods (hardware) with the other service components (software and support).

These developments facilitate service transactions between firms in two ways. First, they generate efficiency gains by promoting specialization in productive activities, both in the private and the public sectors, along the lines suggested in Chapter 5. Secondly, they allow for low-cost customization of services—differences in specifications can now be accommodated to suit purchaser requirements without them incurring punitive prices. In 1968, the American economist Victor Fuchs published *The Service Economy*. In this major study he concluded that although some of the service sector expansion could be accounted for by the growth in demand for services used in the production of *other* goods and services—intermediate demand—much of that increase had other causes. The analysis below suggests that, since the publication of that study, the increase in transactions between firms has had a greater impact on the growth of the service sector.

Producer services: the growth of intermediate transactions

Much of the recent growth in services stems from inter-firm transactions—the outputs of service providers are used for production purposes rather than for final demand. Evidence in support of this proposition is provided in Table 10.2. This table disaggregates the growth of service sector activity by individual industry group—five such groups in total for each of the six countries included in the preceding analysis. It allows more accurate pinpointing of the location of service activity growth since 1962. It can be seen from the table that the only subsector to exhibit long-term proportional growth in all countries is the 'finance, insurance, real estate and business services' category, with Germany being the (arguable) exception. As for long-term proportional decline, with the

Table 10.2. Distribution of service activities as a percentage of total services

Country/sector	1962	1970	1980	1993[a]
UK				
Wholesale and retail trade, restaurants, and hotels	22.9	19	22.8	21.1
Transportation, storage, and communication	16.3	15.5	12.7	12.4
Finance, insurance, real estate, and business services	20.2	22.5	29.5	36
Community, social, and personal services	18.9	20.7	8.6	10.1
Producers of govt. services[a]	21.7	22.3	26.3	19.5
USA				
Wholesale and retail trade, restaurants, and hotels	28.8	29.4	26.2	25.2
Transportation, storage, and communication	9.6	10.7	10	10
Finance, insurance, real estate, and business services	29.1	28.6	31.6	34.7
Community, social, and personal services	8.9	9	12.9	13.3
Producers of govt. services[a]	23.6	22.3	19.2	16.8
Australia				
Wholesale and retail trade, restaurants, and hotels	32.6	30.4	29.6	25.5
Transportation, storage, and communication	13.8	15.1	9.8	11.3
Finance, insurance, real estate, and business services	26.8	27.1	31.8	32.7
Community, social, and personal services	19.5	20.5	23	24.6
Producers of govt. services[a]	7.3	7	5.7	5.9
Germany				
Wholesale and retail trade, restaurants, and hotels	28.2	27.3	20.5	18.4
Transportation, storage, and communication	13.3	13.3	9.8	10
Finance, insurance, real estate, and business services	18.2	19.2	22.3	21.9
Community, social, and personal services	17.7	18.3	23.7	31.5
Producers of govt. services[a]	22.7	21.9	23.7	18.3

Table 10.2. *continued*

Country/sector	1962	1970	1980	1993[a]
France				
Wholesale and retail trade, restaurants, and hotels	26.9	26.5	24.7	21.9
Transportation, storage, and communication	10.8	11.5	10.3	12.5
Finance, insurance, real estate, and business services	23.2	28.3	29.5	29.9
Community, social, and personal services	14.2	12.5	7.6	9.7
Producers of govt. services[a]	24.8	21.2	28	25.9
Japan				
Wholesale and retail trade, restaurants, and hotels	22.3	25.8	24.9	24.9
Transportation, storage, and communication	9.8	12	11.1	11.3
Finance, insurance, real estate, and business services	25.2	22.2	25.9	27.5
Community, social, and personal services	17.9	22.9	22.7	24.7
Producers of govt. services[a]	25	17.1	15.4	11.6

[a] 1993 figures, except: 1991 for USA; 1992 for Germany, Australia.

Source: OECD statistics.

possible exception of France, the 'government services' sector exhibits such a trend across the five remaining countries. This pattern is not as consistent over time as the growth in business services; the decline in government services is arrested or even reversed in some countries in 1970 or 1980 before declining again in 1993.

The evidence presented in Table 10.2 also accords with what is known about developments in the public sector in several countries. Privatization of nation- alized industries and contracting out of services have reduced the productive capacity of the public sector, transferring some of it to the private. Many of the activities previously produced in the government sector and included under such categories as public administration are increasingly provided by the private sector. This could account for the increase in the business services category noted above as well as the decline of 'community and social services', traditionally a public sector activity, particularly in the UK.

Closer analysis of inter-firm transactions in goods and services requires much more detailed data. Input–output tables are the most accessible source of such information. They provide a detailed snapshot of the transactions between every sector of the economy in a single year, at a highly disaggregated level. They represent the most complete description currently available of the structure of the economy. For that reason they are also time-consuming and expensive to compile. For example, the 1990 UK input–output tables were only published in February 1995. The input–output tables of the UK, USA, and Australia will be used here to trace the evolution of inter-firm service transactions over time.

Input–output tables reveal the degree of interdependence in the economy: the extent to which specific industries buy intermediate inputs, including producer services, from the remaining sectors of the economy. Intermediate inputs are goods or services produced *and* used by firms in the production of output destined for final consumption. Thus producer services are intermedi- ate service inputs which are used by firms in support of their productive activ- ities. For example, building maintenance and computer support constitute producer services. Now consider the simplified input–output table for the UK shown in Table 10.3. This is a consolidated table, which means that individual industries, of which there are a total of 123, have been aggregated into eight major industry groupings. The numbers under the column headings refer to the number of individual industries aggregated into a single such grouping. Thus the (1–3) under the heading 'Agriculture' means that this group is made up of three industries, namely agriculture, forestry, and fishing. Manufacturing contains over eighty individual industries, from number 10 (extraction of metal ores and minerals) to number 90 (other manufactured goods).

The numbers in the table correspond to millions of pounds sterling at 1990 prices. It can be seen that the row headings span the same eight industry groups as those along the column headings, as well as an additional row labelled 'other inputs'. Reading down the columns gives the value of *purchases* by a particular industry group from all other industry groups. These are

Table 10.3. A simplified input–output table for the UK, 1990 (£m)

Industries	Agriculture (1–3)	Energy (4–9)	Manufacturing (10–90)	Construction 91	Distribution (92–5)	Transport (96–102)	Business services (103–14)	Other services (115–23)	Total intermediate
Agriculture	2,874	—	9,130	3	444	31	—	88	12,570
Energy	554	22,494	5,608	596	2,326	2,209	1,658	711	36,156
Manufacturing	3,828	3,208	62,312	14,710	12,262	4,312	7,897	3,549	112,078
Construction	242	28	1,006	22,991	631	146	1,701	951	27,696
Distribution	887	1,267	12,633	2,869	4,131	2,681	2,266	773	27,507
Transport	273	1,345	8,896	888	11,498	8,145	10,129	1,392	42,566
Business services	688	1,543	21,137	8,083	14,692	7,246	35,794	30,171	119,354
Other services	383	349	3,804	401	1,014	966	3,010	6,139	16,066
Total intermediate	9,729	30,234	124,526	50,541	46,998	25,736	62,455	43,774	393,993
Other inputs incl. imports	9,982	35,077	164,123	39,325	78,511	44,346	90,501	113,483	575,348
Total inputs	19,711	65,311	288,649	89,866	125,509	70,082	152,956	157,257	969,341

Note: Numbers in parentheses show which of the 123 input–output industries are consolidated into that group.
Source: UK Central Statistical Office (1995).

referred to as intermediate purchases. In the final row the value of 'other inputs' purchased by this industry group, not included among intermediate purchases from other domestic industries, is also given. These represent mainly purchases of labour services, capital and imports from abroad. Reading across the rows of the table shows the value of *sales* by a particular industry group to the others. These are known as intermediate sales by industries, sales of goods and services which do not go to final demand but to other producers.

For purposes of illustration, consider the third industry along the row and column of the table—the manufacturing industry group. Reading *down* the manufacturing industry column shows how much it purchased from agriculture, energy, and the other sectors in the table in order to complete its own production activities. Of particular interest is the intersection of this column with the row labelled business services. It shows that manufacturing industry purchased business services valued at £21,137 million in 1990. This represents just over 7 per cent of the total value of inputs purchased by this industry group. Now reading down the 'business services' column it can be seen that this group made intermediate purchases from its own industry valued at £35,794 million. This represents about 24 per cent of total input purchased. There is nothing unusual in an industry group purchasing its own output for purposes of producing *final* output. It should also be remembered that this category represents an aggregation of a dozen separate industries such as banking and finance, and insurance. The banking industry needs and does purchase insurance in the course of its business activities. Therefore this figure represents mainly intermediate purchases *between* the more disaggregated industry categories comprising 'business services', as well as some purchases *within* each of them.

Reading across the 'business services' *row* shows the value of sales by this industry group to all other sectors of the British economy, summing to a total of £119,354 million. Dividing this number by the total value of inputs purchased by UK industries—£969,340 million—and expressing the result in percentage terms comes to just over 12 per cent. This indicates that intermediate purchases of 'business services' by all production sectors in the economy amounted to approximately 12 per cent of all input purchases, including imports and labour. Intuitively, the more business services are purchased from external providers, and the less they are produced in-house or not produced at all, the lower is this percentage likely to be. But how can it be determined what proportion of service activity which is transacted represents new business as opposed to activities previously undertaken in-house?

There is no easy method of providing an exact answer to this question. One way of establishing a reasonable approximation is to distinguish 'new' from 'traditional' services. For example, an increase in the level of intermediate transactions in cleaning services is likely to represent growth in the extent of contracting, since such services are necessary to every establishment and organization and must have been undertaken internally. However, the growth in computer maintenance transactions is more likely to reflect a greater proportion of maintenance activity not previously undertaken in-house, as computing services are a *relatively* new type of corporate support service. But even such 'new' services are typically provided in-house until the benefits of contracting to outside specialists become widely perceived. Hence it is reasonable to assume that the bulk of the growth in producer services reflects the replacement of activities undertaken internally by intermediate transactions.

A close inspection of input–output tables over a reasonably long period, say twenty years, would highlight significant changes in the structure of the economy. Specifically, it would permit an analysis of the extent to which inter-industry service transactions have grown, and thus provide a measure of the increase in contracting activity by this sector. Similarly, it would allow an examination of the degree of inter-industry transactions in goods which, for example, may change over time because domestic firms may source parts and components from suppliers abroad instead of purchasing them domestically.

Table 10.4 extends the information provided in Table 10.3 across both time and countries. It shows, in a highly condensed form, the value and proportions of intermediate transactions in both goods and services for the UK, USA, and Australia. For each country the data, which were derived from the detailed input–output tables, are approximately twenty years apart. This means that a fair degree of industrial restructuring and sectoral trends can be observed from these statistics. The values of intermediate goods and services transactions in the table were compiled by adding the individual values for all industries from the 'domestic use matrix' in the input–output tables showing 'who uses what'. These values are then divided by total input usage by all industries to derive the proportions, expressed as percentages, for each relevant grouping. The groupings are aggregated into major sectors, similar but not identical to the

Table 10.4. Changes in intermediate goods and services as a percentage of total inputs, UK, USA, and Australia

Goods and services	UK		USA		Australia	
	1971	1990	1967	1987	1974	1992
Agriculture, energy, and construction	5.8	7.3	7.7	7.1	7.3	6.7
Intermediate goods	22.2	12.1	22.3	16.6	19.6	15.6
Intermediate services	10.6	21.2	15.8	19.9	17.3	19.8
Other inputs including imports	61.4	59.4	54.2	56.4	55.8	57.9
Total	100	100	100	100	100	100

Note: Calculated from input–output tables, using the domestic use matrix.
Sources: UK Central Statistical Office (1975, 1995), US Department of Commerce (1977, 1994), Australian Bureau of Statistics (1981, 1996).

breakdown shown in Table 10.1. Here there are four categories of interest: purchases from the agriculture and mining industries but also including energy, water, and construction; purchases of manufactured goods; purchases of services; and other purchases which include labour and imports.

By making pair-wise comparisons of the figures for each country, the changes in the degree of interdependence amongst industries can be assessed. There are two particularly striking results. First, in all three countries the proportion of intermediate goods purchased has fallen over the twenty-year period under investigation. The change is quite dramatic in the UK where the proportion of intermediate goods to all input purchases falls from 22.2 per cent in 1971 to 12.1 per cent in 1990. The fall is more moderate in the USA and Australia, but significant nevertheless. Second, in all three countries the value and proportion of intermediate services rises substantially. In the USA it rises from 15.8 per cent to 19.9 per cent and in the UK from 10.6 per cent in 1971 to 21.2 per cent in 1990. Qualitatively similar increases are recorded for Australia.

What inferences may be drawn from these statistics? The decline in intermediate (producer) goods is consistent with the increase in overseas manufacturing activities by firms in all three countries. As suggested earlier, parts, components, and even complete goods are increasingly produced in low-cost locations overseas. The shift away from domestic sourcing would be reflected in a decline of domestic purchases of intermediate goods and an increase in imports. As for services, their increase suggests a rise in the volume of bought-in services, a rise which is consistent with the growth of contracting and outsourcing. In this context it is instructive to note a statement made in the article accompanying the 1990 UK input–output tables. The statement refers to the expansion of service industry categories since the publication of earlier tables: 'The number of input–output groups was expanded for the 1990 balances and the table presented here to 123. The expansion was concentrated in the service sector, where business services and other services have been divided up' (UK Central Statistical Office 1995: p. xii).

The expansion of the service categories in the tables is of special significance. It reflects the fact that domestic transactions between these service sectors and other industries, which may have been of trivial amounts in the past, are now large enough to merit a separate classification. This is quite appropriate in the context of the rise of the services sector, which is where most of the growth of contracting by the private and public sectors appears to have taken place. A potential weakness of this analysis is that it does not take into account international transactions in services, which are clearly on the increase (see Inman 1985). However, to the extent that intermediate services can be imported, insurance being a good example, the figures in Table 10.4 would *underestimate* the growth of service transactions.

Three decades ago Fuchs (1968) used input–output analysis to identify the causes of service sector employment. More recently, two Canadian economists, McFetridge and Smith (1988), used the same data sources to estimate the

extent to which service sector growth is mirrored by the increase in contracting. One of the measures which they devised to capture this correspondence,
and which they considered to be amongst the most reliable ones, was the ratio
of intermediate service transactions to the value of industrial wages and
salaries. The rationale behind this measure is that as contracting increases,
there is a reduction in the number of employees carrying out internal service
functions, and an increase in payments to external providers. Thus, aggregated
over all industries in the economy, the growth in service contracting would be
accompanied, other things being equal, by a rise in the ratio of the value of
services purchased to wages and salaries paid (see McFetridge and Smith 1988,
for further discussion).

Fig. 10.2 reports this ratio for the three countries discussed above. The ratio
was computed from the input–output tables used in the previous analysis. For
each country, there are two values recorded for the ratio, approximately twenty
years apart. The ratio does indeed rise during the period under observation in
all three countries. It is particularly large for the UK, more than doubling
between 1971 and 1990, but it also shows a noticeable increase for the USA and
Australia. These results support the proposition that contracting for services,
especially producer services, has been on the increase internationally.

Looking beyond mere measurement of the scale and scope of services to the
effect this restructuring has on industrial efficiency, there could be significant
implications for productivity. If, as the analysis in this section suggests, the
observed increase in the size of the service sector is due in large part to the

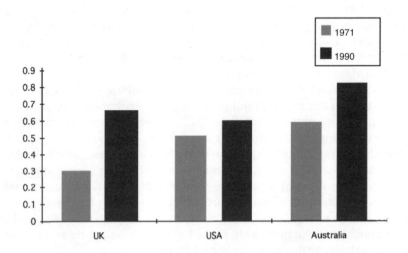

Sources: as for Table 10.4.

Fig. 10.2. Changes in the ratio of the value of intermediate services to wages and
salaries

growth in contracting, then efficiency gains would be expected and these should translate into productivity improvements. Yet paradoxically, official statistics suggest that the service sector is the laggard in the productivity stakes, raising concerns about the impact on economic welfare of the rise of services and the decline of manufacturing.

Contracting for services and the productivity puzzle

Deindustrialization is the unflattering term given to the decrease in manufacturing employment and the rise of services. The shift is taken by many as evidence of economic decline, although others regard it as a concomitant of economic progress. *The Economist* (1995*b*: 15) recently rejected the view that 'the production of material goods, as opposed to ephemeral services, is the only true source of wealth and jobs'. Nevertheless, disquiet about the shift from manufacturing to services in the industrialized economies remains real enough. There are two main reasons for this: restricted export potential and low productivity growth relative to manufacturing.

The rise in exports of manufactures is a sure path to economic prosperity, as attested by the post-war success of the German and Japanese economies. Manufactured goods form the greater proportion of world merchandise trade, although international trade in services has been on the increase in recent years. Services are not generally as exportable as manufactures, due to their nature and the restrictions to trade put up by importing countries. Both of these trade impediments are diminishing, because of the technological changes discussed above and the deregulation achieved under the auspices of the World Trade Organization (WTO). Despite these developments, however, conventional thinking still raises doubts about the capacity of services to make up for the impact that a fall in manufacturing exports would have on the balance of payments.

The slower productivity growth of services compared to manufacturing is the other major concern. Since the rise in real incomes is strongly associated with increases in productivity, the growth of the sector in which productivity is lagging relative to the rest of the economy is seen as having a potentially negative effect on wealth creation. Indeed, in his original research on the growth of services in the USA, Fuchs (1968) suggested that the main reason why that sector was becoming large relative to manufacturing and primary industries was because of its sluggish productivity. The sector in which output per worker is rising less fast is the one which will require more manpower to produce a growing volume of output. This, according to Fuchs, was why service sector employment rose much faster than manufacturing in the USA during the period he investigated—1929 to 1965. Over this time frame he estimated that the annual rate of labour productivity growth was 3.4, 2.2, and 1.1 per cent respectively in agriculture, manufacturing, and services. This was the period during which the employment share of services rose from 40 to 55 per cent, mainly at the expense of jobs in manufacturing.

International comparisons of productivity rates tend to confirm these early findings for the USA. Although labour productivity for the industrialized economies as a whole has fallen since the mid-1970s, the *relative* weakness of service sector productivity has remained stubbornly constant across both time and countries. Research by Gordon (1996) on the measurement of service sector productivity provides interesting comparative data. For the period 1979 to 1992, annual labour productivity for the manufacturing sector was 2.50, 2.78, and 4.42 in the USA, Australia, and in the UK respectively. The corresponding figures for service sector productivity were 0.64, 1.85, and 1.11. In all three countries services appear to be lagging significantly behind manufacturing. In the USA and the UK there is a yawning—fourfold—gap between them, with the productivity revival in UK manufacturing strikingly in evidence.

Is there a connection between this productivity puzzle and the growth of contracting for intermediate services? At first sight there appears to be an outright contradiction since contracting generally reduces costs, and therefore should be expected to raise productivity. On further reflection, however, there are three reasons which may explain this apparent contradiction. First, it is quite conceivable that the benefits of contracting are being captured by manufacturing, where service activities previously undertaken in-house are now more efficiently done outside. For this to be observable in the statistics, the value added per labour hour in manufactures must increase as a direct result of the contracting of service activities. To establish such a link one would need firm-level data which would examine the effect of contracting 'events' on productivity. Such disaggregated data is not available from official sources. But the general proposition is worth investigating, as much of the growth of services is the direct result of intermediate purchases by manufacturing industry.

Second, although contracting for services is not new, it accelerated rapidly in the 1990s. But as noted by Robert Solow, a Nobel laureate in economics from MIT, the impact of restructuring and new technology on productivity may take a considerable time to show through. Solow observed that the huge investments in information technology made by service industries during the 1980s had little effect on productivity, which remained well below 1 per cent per annum. For similar reasons, the effect of contracting on service productivity may be subject to some delays, although the evidence on efficiency gains discussed in Chapter 3 does not support this contention.

The third way of resolving the contradiction is the simplest, and the most convincing: the productivity statistics are biased downwards. The problems of accurately identifying price and output movements in service industries are legion, particularly in the 'hard-to-measure' categories which include construction, wholesale and retail trade, finance, insurance, and real estate (see Griliches 1992). It is these difficulties which lead to distortions in the reported productivity figures. So severe was this problem perceived to be that in 1996 the US Senate Finance Committee appointed an advisory committee, the Boskin Commission, to report on the biases of the consumer price index. The reported bias was substantial, with flow-through effects for the measurement of real output and productivity. The problem is especially acute in services. Alan Greenspan, the chairman of the US Federal Reserve Board, commented in November 1997 that: 'the measured growth of real output and productivity in the service sector is implausibly weak . . . Indeed the published data indicate that the level of output per hour in a number of service-producing industries has been *falling* for more than two decades' (speech delivered at the Center for Financial Studies, Frankfurt).

Anecdotal evidence suggests that efficiency gains have not been confined to producer services. Technological innovation and greater competition have also raised labour productivity in services provided to consumers: in the banking industry (telephone banking), in air transport (electronic ticketing), and in many other service industries utilizing information technology to reduce labour costs. But it is in the producer services sector that the greatest structural change has occurred. This change is characterized by greater specialization and fragmentation of productive activities. It leads to the emergence of new sectors, and the shrinking of others. In the process, business activity is reorganized in an efficiency-enhancing manner.

Contracting and producer services: which causes which?

The transformation of producer services from in-house operations to purchasers from specialist providers can only be sustained if contractual arrangements are robust—if contracts don't fail. Previous chapters have highlighted the conditions that must be met for these transactions to succeed. But mistakes will be made, and some transactions will be unsuccessful not because contracting is inherently problematic, but because of ineffective implementation. There is a need to distinguish between contractual breakdowns which are isolated instances of poor contract design or management, and those cases where contractual failure is endemic. In the latter case, repeated contract breakdown would reflect 'market failure'—the inability of voluntary transactions to yield mutually beneficial outcomes to buyers and sellers. In the long run, such transactions will either be modified or disappear.

But in many cases the transactions are essentially experimental; despite having formal contracts drawn up, there may be little if any practical experience to determine the nature of long-run outcomes. The experimental nature of contracts for some public sector activities was candidly acknowledged by the mayor of Indianapolis, Stephen Goldsmith, in the case study reviewed in the previous chapter. Also, in that chapter the Esmor correctional facility case stands as an example of failure, but views are divided as to whether this is evidence of systematic failure or poor contract management. As further evidence on the contracting of prisons and other 'controversial' services accumulates, such transactions will cease to be experimental and the truly non-contractible activities will have been identified.

Successful contracting has the potential of creating whole new industries. Once the first few successful contracts are established, others will follow. The increased demand will elicit an expansion of supply, so that gradually a specialist service sector develops with more producer and government services being farmed out to contractors. The development of UK-based service providers Serco and Capita Managed Services followed essentially such a pattern. The growth in supply generates further efficiency gains, as described in Chapter 5, and allows contractor reputations to take hold. This encourages the more recalcitrant purchasers to go where their less risk-averse counterparts have gone before—to contract out. In this way the expansion of the service sector becomes a self-sustaining process, a particular example of the general phenomenon described by the American economist Allyn Young as: 'the division of labour depends upon the extent of the market, but the extent of the market also depends upon the division of labour' (Young 1928: 539) .

This quotation, which echoes the famous words of Adam Smith, indicates why contracting can be both cause and effect in the growth of the producer services industry. Once the process gets under way, and contracting is perceived as being a successful method of acquiring services, the level of interaction is such that it becomes meaningless to try and argue which is the cause and which is the effect.

Guide to further reading

Inman (1985) is a very useful general reference on recent developments in the services sector. It contains a contribution by the elder statesman of service industry analysis, Victor Fuchs, as well as other interesting papers by Baumol, Fischer Black, Kendrik, and Kravis. Inman's introductory chapter, as editor of the volume, is a particularly useful summary of what follows.

Griliches (1992) examines the complexities of measuring output in the service industries, and is the originator of the 'hard-to-measure' hypothesis. Another contribution to the measurement literature is Uno (1989).

The growth of services has been the subject of intensive research in recent years. Insightful contributions include Daniels (1993) and Giarini (1987), which includes several interesting articles including one by Bhagwaati on 'International Trade in Services'. Other references worth consulting are Marshall (1988), Quinn and Gagnon (1986), Gershuny and Miles (1983), Riddle (1986), and Elfring (1989).

Useful articles and statistical updates on services are published regularly by the OECD and the IMF. The study by Andrew Wyckoff (1996) is an interesting exploration of the influence of services on macro-economic stability.

11

The Future of Contracting

In 10 or 15 years, organizations may be outsourcing all work that is 'support'
rather than revenue-producing . . . In many organizations a majority of the
people who work for it might be employees of an outsourcing contractor.

(Peter F. Drucker, 1995)

Is contracting a fad?

Popular management and business thinking tends to place contracting
(outsourcing) in the same category as other modern management tools such
as business process re-engineering, benchmarking, and total quality management. The trouble with these once-fashionable techniques is that, eventually,
they lose their lustre. They seem to go the way of all fads: eagerly espoused,
reluctantly reassessed, quietly abandoned. The first question to be addressed
in this chapter therefore will be: is contracting just another fad?

Before attempting to answer that question it is also relevant to ask: what is
wrong with fads? Do they not reflect the natural cycle of a new tool or remedy
which is applied vigorously at first, but whose beneficial impact diminishes as
the original problem subsides and another one emerges? Not so, say Hilmer
and Donaldson (1996), who have conducted a study of the rise and fall of
management fads. According to them, the problem with such fashions is that
they are frequently 'false trails'; remedies which are not relevant to specific
corporate problems. In their search for solutions, managers apply the new
tools somewhat indiscriminately, in the expectation that it will lead to performance improvement regardless of its pertinence to the problem at hand. It is
therefore not surprising when such improvements turn out to be either short-
lived, or well below initial expectations. The authors refer to this phenomenon
as 'instant coffee management: just open the jar and add water, no effort
required'.

This view may be somewhat simplistic, but it is a reasonable description of
the reasons behind the herd mentality that new-fangled management techniques can create among practitioners. The spread of these new techniques
would be well described by the mathematical relationship which is used to

represent the diffusion of technical innovation. Known as the S-curve, it rises initially at an increasing rate, reaches a point of inflexion, and thereafter increases at a decreasing rate reaching a kind of plateau. Interestingly, the S-curve is also used to represent the diffusion of epidemics and, intriguingly, an influential financial newspaper recently referred to the phenomenon as 'an epidemic of outsourcing' (reference omitted).

This description has rather sinister implications, but whether depicted as an epidemic or a fad, the common characteristic attributed to the phenomenon is its ephemeral nature. What evidence is there to suggest that this may be the case? Take the public policy debate first. Public sector contracting is seen as a trend spurred on by the New Right—a political philosophy that draws on public choice theory. According to the theory, market-type mechanisms for public service provision are the principal way of reforming inefficient bureaucratic agencies (Kirkpatrick and Martinez Lucio 1996). The privatization movement in the USA is very much predicated on this intellectual foundation. However, like all political ideologies its influence is likely to wane over time. Hence some observers contend that the 'tide of contracting-out may have passed its high water mark' (Milne 1997), a passing that is often related to which mainstream political party is in office.

But this conclusion may be wrong. Today's political parties, whether on the left or right, appear to be committed to fiscal rectitude and efficient government. For example, Britain's Labour Prime Minister, Tony Blair, made the following statement regarding the policy of compulsory competitive tendering of local government services instituted by the previous Conservative administration: 'There can be no monopoly of service delivery by councils; the 1970s will not be revisited. Delivering quality services means that councils must forge partnerships with communities, agencies and the private sector . . . there will be zero tolerance of failure: there is no room for poor performance, whether it is in our schools, children's homes, or collecting rubbish' (*Guardian* 1997). Although it is not clear from this statement precisely what policy is being advocated, what is evident is that contracting and market testing are not being ruled out as efficiency drivers.

Similar policy positions are being espoused, in varying degrees, by state and federal governments in the English-speaking industrialized economies and beyond, as was indicated in Chapter 9. An examination of the changing public sector landscape suggests that using the market to provide services efficiently and effectively is no longer a matter of political dogma, but rather one of economic common sense. As far as public sector contracting is concerned, the evidence would indicate that it is less of a fad and more of a fact of life. That does not mean that there are no limits to public sector contracting, but that those limits are yet to be reached.

As for the private sector, demand side pressures stemming from deregulation and globalization of markets are forcing firms to seek efficient service solutions. Technological change is also altering the supply side of the market, leading to the development of specialist service providers in areas such as IT and telecommunications, to name but two. Chapter 10 on the service economy highlighted the structural changes in the economy as a whole which reflect these developments. The services sector has evolved to the stage where many activities previously undertaken in-house are now routinely contracted out. This is unlikely to change much in the future, given the robust state of these service industries and the steady demand for their output. This evolution, which with the aid of detailed industrial statistics could be traced several decades back, is likely to continue. Its pace, however, is hard to predict.

To some observers, whether contracting is a fad will be seen to depend on its relationship to another management fashion: downsizing. Downsizing is widely used in the drive to cut costs, but it is coming under increasing criticism from management experts for being short-sighted and unsustainable. To the extent that contracting and downsizing are perceived identical, they will also be thought to suffer the same fate. The relationship, if any, between the two deserves close examination.

Contracting: a handmaiden to downsizing?

Contracting and downsizing are frequently used as synonyms, but this is incorrect. Contracting refers to the change in organizational boundaries resulting from decisions to contract out activities undertaken within the organization or the reverse. Downsizing refers to the reduction in size of the organization brought about by large-scale layoffs and redundancies—significantly reducing the number of people employed. The effects of downsizing are striking and immediate. Whereas contracting leads to a change from an internal to an external employer, with a small reduction in staffing, downsizing involves sacking a selected number of employees at a stroke. The numbers involved in downsizing are far larger than with contracting: IBM slimmed down its workforce from 406,000 employees in 1987 to 202,000 in 1995; General Electric started downsizing in the early 1980s, reducing its workforce of 402,000 by over a quarter. Throughout 1997, announcements of large-scale layoffs continued among some of America's largest corporations, including well-known names such as Woolworths (9,200) and Citicorp (9,000).

Downsizing is affecting the public as well as the private sector. Despite having one of the smallest ratios of government expenditures to GDP among OECD countries, the US administration has pledged itself to small and efficient government. Its new charter was described by Alice Rivlin, director of the Office of Management and Budget, in terms of the following questions: 'What should government do and pay for, what should it pay for but not do, and what should it neither do nor pay for.' The answers to these questions provide the guiding principles which should determine the scope of government activity. Since 1993 the federal administration has reduced the size of its workforce by over 330,000 people, to the lowest level it has been since the 1930s. On the face of it, a clear example of downsizing. On further examination, however, it is something quite different. While the size of the federal workforce has declined, the size of the federal budget has not. And most of the jobs have not been lost, but transferred to the private sector. Thus, the administration has been contracting out rather than downsizing; its overall expenditure as a percentage of national income has not changed much. What has is that now a far greater proportion of activity is funded by the government but undertaken by external contractors. This is a case of government paying for services which it does not produce. It brings into sharp relief the fundamental difference between contracting and downsizing.

The confusion between downsizing and contracting is disturbingly common. Claims that firms are shrinking in order to concentrate on their core business serve to perpetuate this confusion. Have firms shrunk by reducing expenditure on workforce and activity, or have they transferred the workforce and activity to a contractor? In the first case it is difficult to see why reducing the number of employees helps the organization concentrate on core business. Presumably the same number of activities is undertaken as before, only now there are fewer personnel to discharge those functions. To be sure, some activities may have been eliminated altogether, but they would have been redundant, and would have had no influence on core business.

On the other hand, contracting does reduce the number of support and intermediate activities undertaken by the organization, activities which remain essential to the value chain, but which are conducted more efficiently outside. But this makes it all the more evident that contracting and downsizing are not the same thing: the former involves redrawing organizational boundaries and relinquishing activities to the market. The latter is simply a scaling down of activities through labour force reductions; it does not fundamentally change the structure of production.

Stephen Roach, chief economist at Morgan Stanley investment bank in New York, and once a leading champion of downsizing, has since expressed misgivings concerning the long-term efficacy of downsizing. Roach's initial stance was that American corporations in the 1970s were bloated and relatively inefficient, a condition which was reflected in poor productivity performance particularly in the services sector. To meet the challenge of global competition, American business needed to invest in new technology and engage in capital–labour substitution. Downsizing was the method by which it would be achieved, helped by massive investments in information technology in services. Writing in the business magazine *Forbes* (1994), Roach claimed that American service industries were being reborn out of the IT revolution, and that this was 'at the heart of America's stunning turnaround on the productivity front'.

Of course, the productivity miracle was not mirrored in the official statistics, as was discussed in Chapter 10. But this, according to Roach and others, was a problem of measurement rather than one of performance. The official statistics understated productivity growth, particularly in services, and therefore could not be trusted to yield a true reflection of productivity outcomes which were believed to be far better. This line of argument was held until 1996, when Roach (1996: 82) radically changed his position: 'Instead of focusing on investment in innovation and human capital—the heavy lifting required to boost long-term productivity—corporate strategies have become more and more focused on *downsizing* and compressing labour costs. . . . A major rethinking is in order' (italics added). The fundamental criticism of downsizing was that it led to a one-off reduction in costs, not a sustained increase in the *rate* of productivity growth.

The disillusionment with downsizing should not come as a surprise. Pruning excess human resources from the organization is a way of ensuring that labour costs per unit of output are at a minimum. It does not by itself lead to a continued reduction in labour costs, not unless the downsizing is repeated at regular intervals, something which obviously cannot persist indefinitely. Hence the view that it is unsustainable, and the emphasis on investment in innovation and human capital. These have the potential to increase productivity by the application of new production techniques which embody new knowledge and new technology. In a similar vein, Porter (1996) has cautioned corporate management not to confuse operational effectiveness—efficiency in production—with the selection and implementation of business strategies. Downsizing may be acceptable as a means of achieving the former, but certainly not the latter.

Unlike downsizing, contracting can lead to sustainable productivity improvements for reasons that have already been explored in earlier chapters. The pressure of competition induces suppliers to search for greater efficiency in their effort to retain clients. Gainsharing contracts are designed to ensure that the search is continuous, rather than intermittent, depending on the frequency with which the contract is up for renewal. The importance of the distinction between downsizing and contracting lies in the very different consequences they have on the functioning of organizations.

Whither contracting?

In the private sector there seems to be few manufacturing activities or support services which are not considered candidates for outsourcing. In the public sector, it would seem that there is little, with the exception of defence and the police, that cannot be farmed out to private contractors. So where and when will the bounds of contracting be identified? No definitive answer can be given based on current trends. Over the past twenty years a large number of contracting experiments have been taking place, in both private and public sectors. A large number of them can be judged a success by conventional criteria of cost and performance. But many others are still in gestation and the outcomes will not be properly known for some considerable time.

This is true of the very long-term contracts involving the acquisition of large-scale assets by the contractor. Contracts for information technology in the private sector such as the one between Xerox and EDS, and for prison management services in the public sector, are but two relevant examples. It remains to be seen whether virtual organizations can sustain the network of contracts upon which their success is based. Relationships between Benetton and members of its extensive network have not always been trouble free, and it remains to be seen whether British Airways can successfully slim itself down to become the quintessential 'virtual' airline.

In the newly privatized market for electricity in the UK, where the industry was broken up into generators, suppliers/distributors, and transmission companies, contracts between parties at different levels in the vertical chain of production have come under strain. The problem is that market participants want supply contracts that match closely the life of their fixed assets. The generators of electricity want long-term supply contracts with the distribution companies to ensure that their assets are fully utilized during their economic lives. In the absence of such contracts, generators have resorted to the alternative—vertical integration—to overcome these problems. This is essentially why Scottish Power acquired a distribution/supply company, and was not prevented from doing so by the UK Secretary of State for Trade and Industry.

The outer bounds of contracting will be discovered wherever contracting experiments consistently fail. By consistently it is meant that contracts have not failed because of random errors of design or implementation, but because of systematic factors which make contractual solutions non-viable. As the evidence on contracts is gathered, it is important to identify correctly the causes of failure, otherwise the evidence is apt to be misleading. For example, the contract failure at the Esmor correctional facility in New Jersey has been attributed to the inherent problems of contracting prison management services. On the other hand, there is evidence which suggests that the client failed to monitor the contractor adequately, and that such monitoring was not beyond its capacity. Placing this event into one or either category—mistake or inherent non-contractibility—is not a straightforward matter.

Paradoxically, at a time when organizations are contracting or downsizing, or both, some of the largest mergers in the corporate history are being announced. This may indicate that the tide is turning and that organizations are reintegrating once more, seeking the advantages associated with large scale. But there is another, equally plausible explanation. The same competitive forces that are spurring the contracting process may also be promoting merger activity. The key point is that the majority of these mergers are horizontal—between firms in the same output markets—rather than between firms at different levels of a value chain leading to a single market. Horizontal mergers are intended to attenuate the forces of competition. Their objective is increasing the market dominance of the merged entity, thus gaining some market power.

If this proposition is true, then the contracting and merger movements are not inconsistent with one another, and may indeed be mutually supportive. Firms which increase their dominance in output markets and enhance internal efficiency by purchasing goods and services in the markets for intermediate inputs are getting the best of both worlds. And as long as competitive pressures persist in output markets, and capital markets work efficiently in displacing managements which do not maximize shareholder value, both trends are expected to continue. Certainly, as cases of inappropriate contracting come to light in the future and the limits become better defined, there may be a turning point in the contracting trend. But until such time there is no good reason to expect the current patterns of contracting activity to show any significant change.

Guide to further reading

On the question of management fads Hilmer and Donaldson (1996) provide an interesting and accessible discussion. On the role of market-type mechanisms in the public sector the special issue of *Public Administration* edited by Kirkpatrick and Martinez Lucio (1996) is an excellent collection of articles. For another perspective on the same topic see Boston (1995).

For a discussion of the economic forces driving structural change in the private sector see Woodall (1996). The productivity and downsizing debate are discussed in Roach (1996) and in earlier issues of *Forbes* magazine. Porter (1996) discusses the distinction between operational effectiveness and business strategy, and its relevance to management tools such as downsizing and contracting.

12

Conclusions

'I can see nothing' said I . . .
'On the contrary, Watson, you can see everything. You fail, however, to reason from what you see.'

(Sir Arthur Conan Doyle, 1922)

The central purpose of this book has been to develop a framework within which contracting decisions can be properly understood and soundly implemented. There is much more to contracting, it was argued, than the latest business tool to find favour with management. Among the popular fallacies that have no place in management thinking are that strategic contracting or outsourcing decisions can be based on a simple cost–benefit calculation; that a strategy that suits one organization will necessarily suit another; and that there is a uniformity of outcomes after the decisions are implemented.

Benefits and costs of contracting decisions depend crucially on how the strategies are designed and implemented. That is why it is necessary to look beyond the arithmetic to the cost and benefit drivers. The methodology developed in this book tries to do just that. For example, specialization and economies of scale in the provision of certain services can be significant, but how much the client benefits from them depends largely on the mechanisms used to capture the value generated. These issues were discussed in Chapters 5 and 6 respectively. Similarly, to ensure that cost savings are not gained at the expense of quality of service, controls have to be put in place—contractor performance has to be managed. Examples of this, discussed in Chapter 7, included the way Sun Microsystems kept suppliers up to scratch. Finally, none of the benefits would be realized if organizational change cannot be handled smoothly. Because the outcomes of such processes are not always predictable, it is difficult to know in advance what the costs will be. These issues were discussed in Chapter 8, which included examples of radical approaches to organizational change. The Semco case study, which turned out to be relatively effortless, was contrasted with British Airways, an organization which is still trying to push change through.

The key theme of the book, then, is that decision makers need to plan and implement contracting policies which will result in reasonably predictable outcomes. And because every organization's resources, skills, and priorities differ, each is likely to approach the contracting decision somewhat differently. As in so many management matters, one size does not suit all when it comes to contracting, and the path organizations choose to take regarding the make or buy decision will vary. Their perceptions of the merits of such decisions will also change over time. Take the banks, for example, which viewed their IT systems as their 'crown jewels' to be firmly kept in-house. Today they are much more ready to let contractors manage their IT operations.

But some are more risk averse than others. Consider the case of the Commonwealth Bank of Australia which announced, in August 1997, the award of an IT services contract worth $A500 million a year for a period of ten years. The contract was with Electronic Data Systems (EDS), the US-based multinational IT service provider. The difference with this transaction was that the bank took a 35 per cent equity stake in EDS Australia. Why? Such action is a form of insurance for the bank in terms of the quality of service provided to it. It also means that if additional savings are generated over time, they will flow back to the client through its shareholding in the provider. Of course, there is another side to the coin, namely the risk that if the provider runs into trouble, the client stands to suffer a financial loss. And selling IT services to other banks may be difficult because of perceived conflicts of interest. Such a 'strategic partnership' with a service provider is relatively rare in the banking industry at this juncture. But it illustrates the increasing diversity of approaches that are taken to contracting for support services.

Another important aspect of contracting strategies is that the outcomes for different organizations are by no means uniform, and depend on a range of factors. Among them, size and duration of contracts are particularly important. In the context of IT outsourcing, as was mentioned earlier in this book, very large and very long-term contracts are prone to develop problems. The level of control and flexibility required by the typical client at agreed prices may simply not be sustainable. Evidence to that effect comes from the renegotiated IT contract between Xerox and EDS after one year into a $12 billion, ten-year contract, and the agreement between Kodak and Digital which was restructured after difficulties emerged.

By way of conclusion, four 'lessons' from the contracting theory and experience discussed in this book are worth noting. First, one of the most powerful effects of the switch from in-house production to external supply is the change in incentives. They are effectively the factors that motivate contractors to work harder in lowering costs. This immediately brings the question of performance to the fore. Efficiency gains will not result in performance shortfalls provided quality can be readily observed and monitored by the client. Which gives a special role to the availability of information. In some circumstances it is not possible to specify formally the full range of service characteristics, which makes monitoring and enforcing contracts particularly difficult. This problem, known as the non-contractibility of quality, has been at the centre of the current debate on the contracting of certain public sector services such as prison management. Ultimately, whether services should be brought back in-house on account of this problem depends on the significance of the non-contractibility issue. We do not yet have an empirical answer to this question.

Second, there is a link between the way contractual arrangements are implemented and the benefits that are subsequently derived. But the link is not always clearly visible, and implementation costs are easily underestimated. These are often difficult to predict in advance, and depend crucially on how organizational change is managed. Careful, if costly, implementation also yields benefits. For example, the design of an effective performance management system may be costly, but it may help avoid problems later on when monitoring gets under way. Indeed, the benefits of contracting cannot be measured just in terms of cost reductions, but should encompass the quality, reliability, and value derived from the agreement.

Third, contracts are relationships, and as such they are governed by factors that affect all relationships. Nowhere is this made clearer than in a research paper by Lyons and Mehta (1997: 43) in which the results were reported of interviews with leading British industrialists on contractual issues. One manager made the following observation: 'Never sign a contract with someone you don't trust.' The paradox in this statement is clear: it should not matter whether you trust your partner if everything is agreed in writing and is enforceable. On the other hand, if you trust your partner why go to the trouble of a formal contract? What the statement alludes to is the fact that many aspects of every contract between purchaser and provider are relational: they cannot be defined explicitly and therefore trust and reciprocity become central to the success or otherwise of the arrangement.

It is important to note that, as in all relationships, circumstances are bound to change and new or unexpected developments can impose strains on an otherwise stable relationship. It may take a long time to build up trust, but very little to destroy it. As long as the pay-offs to the relationship are perceived to be stable or growing, there will be an incentive to sustain it. But if the pay-offs are seen by one of the parties to have declined, the relationship may be put at risk.

Lastly, contractual relationships can be thought of as lying along a spectrum which runs from spot transactions at one end, to vertical integration at the other. In between lie arrangements such as partnering contracts, franchises, and joint ventures. Virgin, the British 'virtual conglomerate' which straddles retailing, travel, cola, and music businesses, is perhaps the best exponent of joint-venture agreements where one party provides the brand name and marketing flair (Virgin), and the others provide production facilities and capital. When circumstances change, a move along the spectrum of contractual relationships may be an appropriate response. One such example has been observed in the market for electricity in the United Kingdom. As competition has become more intense with the removal of the domestic electricity consumers' franchise, the structure of contracts between electricity generators and distributors has changed. As pointed out by Jenkinson and Mayer (1996: 7), one major generator has entered into a fifteen-year contract with an electricity distribution company on the basis that it bears a significant part of the risks of competition in the market for domestic electricity. From a contractual point of view this appears to be 'broadly equivalent to vertical integration, as the generator is essentially taking an equity stake in the supply business'.

Our knowledge about the role of contracting in the economy, and why contracts evolve the way they do, is already considerable. And our understanding of what makes some contracts successful and others a failure is bound to improve over time. Yet more time is required to gather additional evidence; some contracts have such a long gestation period that the results will not be known for quite a number of years. But with so many contractual experiments being undertaken in the private and in the public sectors, the empirical harvest is going to be a very rich one indeed.

GLOSSARY OF SELECTED TERMS

advantage, competitive the ability of a firm to add more value to a given good/service than a competitor

asset specificity a characteristic of assets which have value only in the context of a specific business relationship. Cf. *relationship-specific investment*

auction, English a bidding scheme which is open, where each bid is announced, and participants in the auction can respond to other bids

auction, sealed bid a bidding scheme in which bids are submitted in writing and cannot be seen, and therefore responded to, by other participants in the auction

competitive tendering the process of calling for and receiving submissions (*tenders*) from prospective service providers, and choosing one or more of these on the basis of a formal evaluation.

complementary asset an asset necessary to the exploitation of another's distinctive capability; e.g. a bauxite mine and a smelter are complementary assets because neither is particularly useful on its own. Cf. *asset specificity*

complementary goods goods in a relationship whereby an increase in the price of one adversely affects demand for the other; e.g. a rise in the price of cassette recorders lowers the demand for audio cassettes

contract, contingent a long-term legal agreement in which some contract provisions are conditional on future, unknown events

contract, partnering also known as an alliance contract, defines a contractual relationship which stresses common objectives of the transacting parties and sharing of information, and is self-enforcing. See *contract, relational*

contract, relational an exchange relationship which is not fully articulated: the rules of behaviour are implicit, and the enforcement mechanism is the value of the continuing relationship between the parties. Also known as a relationship or implicit contract

contract, spot an intermediate bilateral legally binding exchange agreement, in which the terms are readily observable; e.g. the purchase of a book from a bookshop

contract out to hire an external organization to provide a good or service, rather than providing it *in-house*. Functions commonly contracted out include information technology services, cleaning, and catering. Cf. *competitive tendering; in-house; outsource; tender*

core business the set of activities of an organization which are likely to yield competitive advantage compared to other activities. Core business is another way of defining the firm's distinctive capability or *core competence.*

core competence a firm's distinctive capability; what a company does best. Cf. *core business*

corporate governance the mechanism by which corporations, and their senior managers, are regulated and held accountable to their owners (shareholders). Corporate governance processes involve disclosure requirements and regular reporting of corporate performance

cost–benefit analysis an economic analysis that takes into account both explicit costs and benefits (i.e. those with a market value) and implicit costs and benefits (those without any market value). Often used to evaluate contracting proposals

demand, final demand for a final good/service, i.e. for a good/service that requires no further production. Cf. *demand, intermediate; good, final; intermediate good or service; production, intermediate*

demand, intermediate demand for an *intermediate good/service*, i.e. for a good/service that requires further processing/production before it can be sold. Cf. *demand, final; good, final; production, intermediate*

downsizing the process by which organizations reduce their overall size; typically by making employees redundant and thereby reducing the size of the wage bill

downstream refers to the location of a business process or activity as being further down the *intermediate chain of production* or, in terms of the value chain, closer to the market than if it were *upstream*

effectiveness the degree to which a good, a service, or an activity meets its defined purpose or specification. Closely related to the concept of 'fitness for purpose'

efficiency the measure of the resources required to produce a particular level of output. The higher the level of efficiency, the fewer resources are needed to yield a given output level

efficiency, relative the degree to which an organization requires fewer resources to produce a particular good or service, compared to another. Relative efficiency helps explain the principle of specialization

enabling authorities a term used to describe public sector organizations which facilitate the provision of services by others rather than undertake production themselves

good, final a good that needs no further production/processing before being sold to consumers; eg. a finished car. Cf. *demand, final; demand, intermediate; production, intermediate*

hollowing out the process by which an organisation becomes 'hollow', i.e. loses its *core competence*. Cf. *hollow organization*

hollow organization an organization which, through the *outsourcing* of various essential functions, has lost its *core competence* or distinctive capability. Cf. *hollowing out*

information asymmetry a situation wherein one party to a contract or agreement possesses more information than the other, and this information confers some degree of advantage on the party in possession of it

in-house within the organization in question. The in-house provision of cleaning services, for example, necessitates that the organization employ its own cleaning staff

integration, horizontal the bringing together of a number of firms and/or processes operating at the same stage of production; i.e. a firm buying or taking control of its direct competitor; e.g. a brewery buying another brewery. Also referred to as horizontal mergers. Cf. *integration, vertical*

integration, vertical the process by which a firm enters successive stages in production and marketing, i.e. replacing its own suppliers and/or distributors; e.g. a brewery buying a pub. Cf. *integration, horizontal*

intermediate chain of production the process of discrete activities or functions leading up to the production of final output. Cf. *value chain*

intermediate good or service a good or a service that is used in the production of other goods or services, i.e. that is not consigned to final demand. Cf. *good, final; demand, intermediate*

LATEs (Local Authority Trading Enterprises) companies set up by local authorities in New Zealand for the purpose of trading and conducting commercial activities

market, input the market for intermediate goods or services. Cf. *market, output*

market, output the market for finished goods or services. Cf. *good, final; market, input*

non-contractible unable to be specified and enforced in a contractual relationship. For example, non-contractibility of quality arises when service characteristics required by the client cannot be adequately specified and verified in the contract

output, intermediate see *intermediate chain of production*

outsource to *contract out*, i.e. to hire an external organization to provide a good or service, rather than providing it *in-house*. Functions commonly outsourced include information technology services, cleaning, and catering. Cf. *competitive tendering; tender*

parallel sourcing a purchasing arrangement whereby supplies of a common component or part are sourced from more than one vendor, allowing performance comparisons to be made and reducing dependence on a single vendor

privatization the process of transferring government-owned businesses and assets to private ownership, usually through the sale of a majority stake on the stock market

production, intermediate the production of a good/service whose primary value lies in its use in the production of something else; e.g. the production of a car chassis. Cf. *demand, final; demand, intermediate; good, final; intermediate good or service*

relationship-specific investment an investment made for the purpose of supporting a contractual relationship. Such investment may lose much of its value if the relationship is abandoned. Cf. *asset specificity*

rent (economic) the amount by which the payment of a worker exceeds the minimum amount necessary to keep him in his present employment; the rights, privileges, or licences through which these above-normal profits can be earned. Cf. *rent-seeking behaviour*

rent-seeking behaviour behaviour, whether by firms or individuals, intended to obtain or preserve *rents.*

scale, diseconomies of the situation in which costs per unit of output rise as a result of increases in the volume of production and the rate of output. Cf. *scale, economies of*

scale, economies of reductions in costs per unit of output, achieved by increases in the volume of production and the rate of output. Cf. *scale, diseconomies of*

search costs the costs of obtaining information about a given good, service, or market

specialization describes the concentration of resources in activities which yield superior output or performance for a particular organization. Also related to the adaptation by organizations to particular market needs and niches. Cf. *efficiency, relative*

strategic sourcing the process by which companies make decisions about purchasing parts and components for manufacturing purposes from outside suppliers. Closely related to the decision of whether to make or to buy

sunk investments (sunk costs) costs or specific investments which are incurred in entering a market and which cannot be recovered on exit

tender the bid put forward by an organization for a contract. Cf. *competitive tendering; contract out; outsource*

transaction costs the costs imposed through the use of the market for the provision of goods and/or services, as opposed to *in-house* provision

TUPE transfer of undertakings (protection of employment) regulations. UK legislation which protects employees transferred to contractors by providing certain safeguards to terms and conditions of transfer

upstream refers to the location of a business process or activity as being higher up the *intermediate production chain*, closer to the initial stages of production than to the final output market

value added the value of the firm's production less the value of the materials (but not labour or capital) used in that production. Also known as net output

value chain a breakdown of the production process into discrete functional activities, essentially the same as the *intermediate chain of production*

virtual organization an organization which functions to a large degree by tapping into the skills and expertise of other organizations, and which therefore may appear to have few of its own resources and functional parts. Closely related to 'network organizations'

winner's curse an outcome of a bidding or tendering process in which the winner turns out to have overestimated the value of the contract or underestimated its cost

REFERENCES

ABRAHAM, K. G., and TAYLOR, S. K. (1996), 'Firms' Use of Outside Contractors: Theory and Evidence', *Journal of Labor Economics*, **14** (3): 394–424.

AKERLOF, G. A. (1970), 'The Market for "Lemons": Quality Uncertainty and the Market Mechanism', *Quarterly Journal of Economics*, **84** (3): 488–500.

ALCHIAN, A. A., and DEMSETZ, H. (1972), 'Production, Information Costs and Economic Organization', *American Economic Review*, **62** (5): 777–95.

ALEXANDER, M., and YOUNG, D. (1996), 'Strategic Outsourcing', *Long Range Planning*, **29** (1): 116–19.

ALLEN, G. C. (1966), *The Industrial Development of Birmingham and the Black Country 1860–1927*, New York: Augustus M. Kelley.

ARROW, K. (1973), *Information and Economic Behaviour*, Stockholm: Federation of Swedish Industries.

ASCHER, K. (1987) (ed.), *The Politics of Privatisation*, Houndsmill: Macmillan Education.

ASHKENAS, R., ULRICH, D., JICK, T., and KERR, S. (1995), *The Boundaryless Organization*, San Francisco: Jossey-Bass.

Australian Bureau of Statistics (1981), *Australian National Accounts Input–Output Tables 1974–1975*, Canberra: AGPS.

—— (1996), *Australian National Accounts Input–Output Tables 1992–93*, Canberra: AGPS.

Australian Department of Finance (1995) *Clarifying the Exchange: A Review of Purchaser/Provider Arrangements*, Canberra: AGPS, Nov.

BARNEY, J. B., and HANSEN, M. H. (1994), 'Trustworthiness as a Source of Competitive Advantage', *Strategic Management Journal*, **15**: 175–90.

BENNETT, C., and FERLIE, E. (1996), 'Contracting in Theory and in Practice: Some Evidence from the NHS', *Public Administration*, **74**: 49–66.

BERLE, A. A., and MEANS, G. C. (1932), *The Modern Corporation and Private Property*, New York: Harcourt, Brace and World.

BERNSTEIN, P. L. (1996), *Against the Gods: The Remarkable Story of Risk*, New York: John Wiley & Sons.

BESANKO, D., DRANOVE, D., and SHANLEY, M. (1996), *The Economics of Strategy*, New York: John Wiley & Sons.

BETTIS, R. A., BRADLEY, S. P., and HAMEL, G. (1992), 'Outsourcing and Industrial Decline', *Academy of Management Executive*, **6** (1): 7–22.

BISHOP, M. (1994), 'A Survey of Corporate Governance', *The Economist*, 29 Jan.: 3–18.

—— and KAY, J. (1993), *European Mergers and Merger Policy*, Oxford: Oxford University Press.

—— —— and MAYER, C. (1994), *Privatization and Economic Performance*, Oxford: Oxford University Press.

BOLTON, P., and WHINSTON, M. D. (1993), 'Incomplete Contracts, Vertical Integration and Supply Assurance', *Review of Economic Studies*, 60: 121–48.

BOONE, C., and VERBEKE, A. (1991), 'Strategic Management and Vertical Disintegration: A Transaction Cost Approach', In J. Thepot and R. A. Thietart (eds.), *Microeconomic Contributions to Strategic Management*, Amsterdam: North-Holland (Elsevier Science Publishers): 185–205.

BOSTON, J. (1995) (ed.), *The State under Contract*, Wellington: Bridget Williams.

BRUECK, F. (1995), 'Make versus Buy: The Wrong Decisions Cost', *McKinsey Quarterly*, 1: 28–47.

BRYNJOLFSSON, E. (1994), 'Information Assets, Technology and Organization', *Management Science*, 40 (12): 1645–62.

BUCKLEY, P. J., and MICHIE, J. (1996), *Firms, Organizations and Contracts*, Oxford: Oxford University Press.

BULOW, J., and KLEMPERER, P. (1996), 'Auctions versus Negotiations', *American Economic Review*, 86 (1): 180–94.

—— and ROBERTS, J. (1989), 'The Simple Economics of Optimal Auctions', *Journal of Political Economy*, 97: 1060–90.

Business Week (1996), 'Revolution at Daimler', *Business Week*, 5 Feb.: 56–7.

BYRNE, J. A. (1996), 'Has Outsourcing Gone too Far?', *Business Week*, 1 Apr.: 28–30.

CALDWELL, B. (1995), 'Outsourcing Megadeals', *Information Week*, 6 Nov.: 34–52.

CARLSSON, B. (1989), 'Flexibility and the Theory of the Firm', *International Journal of Industrial Organization*, 7: 179–203.

CASSON, M. (1995*a*), *Studies in the Economics of Trust*, i: *Entrepreneurship and Business Culture*, Aldershot: Edward Elgar.

—— (1995*b*), *Studies in the Economics of Trust*, ii: *The Organization of International Business*, Aldershot: Edward Elgar.

CHESBROUGH, H. W., and TEECE, D. J. (1996), 'When is virtual virtuous? Organising for Innovation', *Harvard Business Review*, Jan.–Feb.: 65–73.

CHILD, J. (1987), 'Information Technology, Organization, and the Response to Strategic Challenges', *California Management Review*, Fall: 33–50.

CHILES, T. H., and MCMACKIN, J. F. (1996), 'Integrating Variable Risk Preferences, Trust, and Transaction Cost Economics', *Academy of Management Review*, 21 (1): 73–99.

CLARK, C. (1951), *The Conditions of Economic Progress*, London: Macmillan Press.

COASE, R. H. (1937), 'The Nature of the Firm', *Economica*, 4: 386–405.

Commonwealth Ombudsman (1997), *Annual Report*, Canberra: AGPS.

CORRY, D. (1997) (ed.), *Public Expenditure: Effective Management and Control*, London: Dryden Press.

CROSS, J. (1995), 'IT Outsourcing: British Petroleum's Competitive Approach', *Harvard Business Review*, May–June, 94–102.

CUBBIN, J., DOMBERGER, S., and MEADOWCROFT, S. (1987), 'Competitive Tendering and Refuse Collection: Identifying the Source of Efficiency Gains', *Fiscal Studies*, 8 (3): 49–58.

DANIELS, P. W. (1993) (ed.), *Service Industries in the World Economy*, Oxford: Blackwell.

DAVIDOW, W. H., and MALONE, M. S. (1992), *The Virtual Corporation*, New York: Harper Business.

DEAKIN, N., and WALSH, K. (1996), 'The Enabling State: The Role of Markets and Contracts', *Public Administration*, 74 (1): 33–47.

DEAKIN, S., and MICHIE, J. (1997), *Contracts, Cooperation and Competition*, Oxford: Oxford University Press.

DEL MONTE, A., and ESPOSITO, F. M. (1992), 'Flexibility and Industrial Organisation Theory', in: A. Del Monte, (ed.), *Recent Developments in the Theory of Industrial Organization*, Houndsmill: Macmillan: 114–47.

DENTON, K. (1994), 'The Power of Flexibility', *Business Horizons*, **July–Aug.**: 43–6.

DIGINGS, L. (1991), *Competitive Tendering and the European Communities*, London: Association of Metropolitan Authorities.

DOMBERGER, S., and HALL, C. (1996), 'Contracting for Public Services: A Review of Antipodean Experience', *Public Administration*, **74** (1): 129–47.

—— —— and LI, E. A. L. (1995), 'The Determinants of Price and Quality in Competitively Tendered Contracts', *Economic Journal*, **105**: 1454–70.

—— and JENSEN, P. H. (1997), 'Contracting out by the Public Sector: Theory, Evidence, Prospects', *Oxford Review of Economic Policy*, **13** (4): 67–78.

—— and RIMMER, S. (1994), 'Competitive Tendering and Contracting in the Public Sector: A Survey', *International Journal of the Economics of Business*, **1**: 439–53.

DONAGHU, M. T., and BARFF, R. (1990), 'Nike Just Did it: International Subcontracting and Flexibility in Athletic Footwear Production', *Regional Studies*, **24** (6): 537–52.

DONAHUE, J. D. (1989), *The Privatization Decision: Public Ends, Private Means*, New York: Basic Books.

DRUCKER, P. F. (1995), 'The Network Society', *Wall Street Journal*, 29 Mar.: A12.

DYER, J. H., and OUCHI, W. G. (1993), 'Japanese-Style Partnerships: Giving Companies a Competitive Edge', *Sloan Management Review*, **Fall**: 51–63.

The Economist (1994*a*), 'Change in the Heartland', *The Economist*, 2 Apr.: 65–8.

—— (1994*b*), 'Farming out the Farm', *The Economist*, 5 Mar.: 77.

—— (1995*a*), 'Dismantling Daimler-Benz', *The Economist*, 18 Nov.: 79–80.

—— (1995*b*), 'Name Calling and its Perils', *The Economist*, 6 May: 15.

—— (1996*a*), 'Unhappy Families', *The Economist*, 10 Feb.: 21–5.

—— (1996*b*), 'Sorpresa', *The Economist*, 2 Mar.: 63–4.

—— (1996*c*), 'Profits of Doom', *The Economist*, 28 Sept.: 28.

—— (1996*d*), 'Full Time Activity: Business Services', *The Economist*, 11 May: 75–6.

—— (1996*e*), 'Making Companies Efficient: The Year Downsizing Grew Up', *The Economist*, 21 Dec.: 93–5.

—— (1996*f*) 'Modest to a fault', *The Economist*, 20 Jan.: 81.

—— (1997*a*), 'Learning to Play the Game', *The Economist*, 17 May: 96.

—— (1997*b*), 'Care for a Downgrade', *The Economist*, 5 July: 63–4.

The Economist Intelligence Unit and Arthur Andersen (1995), *New Directions in Finance: Strategic Outsourcing*, New York: The Economist Intelligence Unit.

ELFRING, T. (1989), 'The Main Features and Underlying Causes of the Shift to Services', *Service Industries Journal*, **9** (3): 337–56.

ENGELBRECHT-WIGGINS, R., SHUBRIK, M., and STARK, R. M. (1983), *Auctions, Bidding and Contracting: Uses and Theory*, New York: New York University Press.

FIERMAN, J. (1995), 'Winning Ideas from Maverick Managers', *Fortune*, 6 Feb.: 66–80.

First Pacific Stockbrokers (1997), *Morgan & Banks*, Australian Equities Research Report, Sydney.

FREY, S. C. J., and SCHLOSSER, M. M. (1993), 'ABB and Ford: Creating Value through Cooperation', *Sloan Management Review*, **Fall**: 65–72.

FUCHS, V. (1968), *The Service Economy*, New York: Columbia University Press.

FUKUYAMA, F. (1995), *Trust: The Social Virtues and the Creation of Prosperity*, London: Hamish Hamilton.

General Electric (1993), *Annual Report,* Fairfield, Conn.: General Electric Company.

GERSHUNY, J. I., and MILES, I. D. (1983) (eds.), *The New Service Economy,* London: Pinter.

GHOSHAL, S., and MORAN, P. (1996), 'Bad for Practice; A Critique of the Transaction Cost Theory', *Academy of Management Review,* **21** (1): 13–47.

GIARINI, O. (1987) (ed.), *The Emerging Service Economy,* Oxford: Pergamon Press.

GINSBURGH, V., and MICHEL, P. (1988), 'Adjustment Costs, Concentration and Price Behaviour', *Journal of Industrial Economics,* **36** (4): 477–81.

GLOBERMAN, S., and VINING, A. R. (1996), 'A Framework for Evaluating the Government Contracting out Decision with an Application to Information Technology', *Public Administration Review,* **56** (6): 577–86.

GOEL, R. K. (1995), 'Choosing the Sharing Rate for Incentive Contracts', *American Economist,* **39** (2): 68–72.

GOLDSMITH, S. (1997), 'Can Business Really do Business with Government?', *Harvard Business Review,* **May–June,** 110–21.

GORDON, R. (1996), *Problems in the Measurement and Performance of Service-Sector Productivity in the United States,* NBER Report No. 5519, Washington.

GRANT, R. M. (1995), *Contemporary Strategy Analysis,* Cambridge, Mass.: Blackwell Business.

GRILICHES, Z. (1992) (ed.), *Output Measurement in the Service Sectors,* Chicago: University of Chicago Press.

GROSSMAN, S. J., and HART, O. (1986), 'The Costs and Benefits of Ownership: A Theory of Vertical and Lateral Integration', *Journal of Political Economy,* **94** (4): 691–719.

Guardian (1997), 'Next on the List: Clean up the Councils', 3 Nov.

HALL, C., and DOMBERGER, S. (1995), 'Competitive Tendering for Domestic Services: A Comparative Study of Three Hospitals in New South Wales', in: S. Domberger, and C. Hall, (eds.), *The Contracting Casebook: Competitive Tendering in Action,* Canberra: AGPS: 99–126 (www.agps.gov.au/products/agip.htm).

—— and RIMMER, S. (1994), 'Performance Monitoring and Public Sector Contracting', *Public Administration,* **53** (4): 453–61.

HAMEL, G., and PRAHALAD, C. K. (1994) *Competing for the Future,* Boston: Harvard Business School Press.

HANDY, C. (1989), *The Age of Unreason,* Boston: Harvard Business School Press.

—— (1995), 'Trust and the Virtual Organisation', *Harvard Business Review,* **May–June:** 40–50.

HARRISON, B. T. (1994), *Lean and Mean: The Changing Landscape of Corporate Power in the Age of Flexibility,* New York: Basic Books.

—— and KELLEY, M. R. (1993), 'Outsourcing and the Search for "Flexibility" ', *Work, Employment and Society,* **7** (2): 213–35.

HART, O. (1989), 'An Economist's Perspective on the Theory of the Firm', *Columbia Law Review,* **89**: 1757–74.

—— (1991), 'Incomplete Contracts and the Theory of the Firm', in O. E. Williamson and S. G. Winter (eds.), *The Nature of the Firm: Origins, Evolution and Development,* New York: Oxford University Press: 138-158.

—— (1995), *Firms, Contracts and Financial Structure,* Oxford: Clarendon Press.

—— and MOORE, J. (1990), 'Property Rights and the Nature of the Firm', *Journal of Political Economy,* **98** (6): 1119–58.

—— SHLEIFER, A., and VISHNY, R. W. (1997), 'The Proper Scope of Government: Theory and an Application to Prisons', *Quarterly Journal of Economics,* **112**: 1127–61.

HAYEK, F. A. (1945), 'The Use of Knowledge in Society', *American Economic Review*, 35 (4): 519–30.

HAYES, M. (1997), 'Solaris Boosts Sun's Sales', *InformationWeek*, 20 Jan.: 32.

HILL, C. W. L. (1990), 'Cooperation, Opportunism, and the Invisible Hand: Implications for Transaction Cost Theory', *Academy of Management Review*, 15 (3): 500–13.

HILMER, F. G., and DONALDSON, L. (1996), *Management Redeemed: Debunking the Fads that Undermine Corporate Performance*, New York: Free Press.

HOEKMAN, B., and KARSENTY, G. (1994), 'Employment and Production-Based Proxies for Trade Specialisation in Services', *Service Industries Journal*, 14 (3): 340–51.

HOLMES, O. W. (1963), *The Common Law*, Cambridge, Mass.: Belknap Press.

HUBER, R. L. (1993), 'How Continental Bank Outsourced its "Crown Jewels" ', *Harvard Business Review*, Jan–Feb.: 121–9.

HUGHES, R. (1987), *The Fatal Shore*, London: Collins Harvill.

Industrial Relations & Management Letter (1995), 'Why Australian "Best Practice" Doesn't Stack Up', *Industrial Relations & Management Letter*, 12 (7): 16–20.

Industry Commission (1996), *Competitive Tendering and Contracting by Public Sector Agencies*, Report No. 48, Melbourne: AGPS (www.indcom.gov.au/).

INMAN, R. P. (1985) (ed.), *Managing the Service Economy*, Cambridge: Cambridge University Press.

Japanese Government Procurement Statistics (1993), Tokyo.

JARILLO, J. C. (1993), *Strategic Networks: Creating the Borderless Organisation*, Oxford: Butterworth-Heinemann.

JENKINSON, T., and MAYER, C. (1996), 'The Assessment: Contracts and Competition', *Oxford Review of Economic Policy*, 12: 1–10.

JENSEN, P. H., and LIEBENBERG, B. (1995), 'Government Cleaning Service: Reforming Business in New South Wales', in S. Domberger, and C. Hall, (eds.), *The Contracting Casebook: Competitive Tendering in Action*, Canberra: AGPS: 13–31 (www.agps.gov.au/products/agip.htm).

KANTER, R. M. (1983), *The Change Masters: Corporate Entrepreneurs at Work*, London: Allen & Unwin.

KAY, J. (1993), *Foundations of Corporate Success*, Oxford: Oxford University Press.

KIRKPATRICK, I., and MARTINEZ LUCIO, M. (1996), 'Introduction: The Contract State and the Future of Public Management', *Public Administration*, 74 (**Spring**): 1–8.

KLEBNIKOV, P. (1995), 'Focus, Focus, Focus', *Forbes*, 156 (6): 11 Sept.: 42–4.

LACITY, M. C., and HIRSCHHEIM, R. (1993), 'The Information Systems Outsourcing Bandwagon', *Sloan Management Review*, Fall: 73–86.

—— WILLCOCKS, L., and FEENY, D. (1995), 'IT Outsourcing: Maximize Flexibility and Control', *Harvard Business Review*, May–June: 84–93.

LAFFONT, J.-J., and TIROLE, J. (1993), *A Theory of Incentives in Procurement and Regulation*, Cambridge, Mass.: MIT Press.

LEIBENSTEIN, H. (1966), 'Allocative Efficiency vs. "X-efficiency" ', *American Economic Review*, 56 (3): 392–415.

LEWIS, J. D. (1995), *The Connected Corporation*, New York: Free Press.

LORENZONI, G., and BADEN-FULLER, C. (1995), 'Creating a Strategic Center to Manage a Web of Partners', *California Management Review*, 37 (3): 146–63.

LYONS, B., and MEHTA, J. (1997), 'Private Sector Business Contracts: The Text between the Lines', in S. Deakin and J. Michie (eds.), *Contracts, Cooperation and Competition*, Oxford: Oxford University Press, 43–66.

MCAFEE, R. P., and MCMILLAN, J. (1987), 'Auctions and Bidding', *Journal of Economic Literature*, **25**: 699–738.

—— (1989), *Incentives in Government Contracting*, Toronto: University of Toronto Press.

—— (1996), 'Analyzing the Airwaves Auction', *Journal of Economic Perspectives*, **10** (1): 159–75.

MCFETRIDGE, D. G., and SMITH, D. A. (1988), *The Economics of Vertical Integration*, Vancouver: Fraser Insitute.

MACLEOD, W. B., and MALCOMSON, J. M. (1993), 'Investments, Holdup and the Form of Market Contracts', *American Economic Review*, 83 (4): 811–37.

MACNEIL, I. R. (1974), 'The Many Futures of Contract', *Southern California Law Review*, **47**: 691–738.

MARSHALL, J. N. (1988) (ed.), *Services and Uneven Development*, Oxford: Oxford University Press.

MELCHER, R. A. (1996), 'Manpower Upgrades its Resume', *Business Week*, 10 June: 55–6.

MILGROM, P. (1989), 'Auctions and Bidding: A Primer', *Journal of Economic Perspectives*, **3** (3): 3–22.

—— and ROBERTS, J. (1992), *Economics, Organization and Management*, Englewood Cliffs, NJ: Prentice-Hall.

—— and WEBER, R. J. (1982), 'A Theory of Auctions and Competitive Bidding', *Econometrica*, **50** (5): 1089–122.

MILNE, S. (1997), *Making Markets Work: Contracts, Competition and Cooperation.*, London: Economic and Social Research Council.

MORRIS, L. (1997), 'Timetable Switch Puts Trains Back on Track', *Sydney Morning Herald*, 17 June: 2.

OECD (1993), *Managing with Market-Type Mechanisms*, Paris: OECD—PUMA.

—— (1997), *Best Practice Guidelines for Contracting out Government Services*, Paris: OECD—PUMA.

OSBORNE, D., and GAEBLER, T. (1992), *Reinventing Government: How the Entrepreneurial Spirit is Transforming the Public Sector*, Reading Mass.: Addison-Wesley.

PATTERSON, A., and PINCH, P. L. (1995), ' "Hollowing out" the Local State: Compulsory Competitive Tendering and the Restructuring of British Public Sector Services', *Environment and Planning A*, **27** (9): 1437–61.

PETERS, T. J., and WATERMAN, R. H. (1982), *In Search of Excellence: Lessons from America's Best-Run Companies*, New York: Harper & Row.

PORTER, M. E. (1990), *The Competitive Advantage of Nations*, London: Macmillan.

—— (1996), 'What is Strategy?', *Harvard Business Review*, **Nov.–Dec.**: 61–78.

POWELL, W. W. (1990), 'Neither Market nor Hierarchy: Network forms of Organization', *Research in Organizational Behaviour*, Greenwich, Conn.: JAC Press, 12: 295–336.

PRAGER, J. (1994), 'Contracting out Government Services: Lessons from the Private Sector', *Public Administration Review*, **54** (20): 176–84.

PRAHALAD, C. K., and HAMEL, G. (1990), 'The Core Competence of the Corporation', *Harvard Business Review*, **May–June**, 79–91.

PUTTERMAN, L. (1995), 'Markets, Hierarchies, and Information: On a Paradox in the Economics of Organization', *Journal of Economic Behavior and Organization*, **26**: 373–90.

QUINN, J. B., DOORLEY, T. L., and PAQUETTE, P. C. (1990), 'Beyond Products: Services-Based Strategy', *Harvard Business Review*, **Mar.–Apr.**: 58–68.

—— and Gagnon, C. E. (1986), 'Will Services Follow Manufacturing into Decline?', *Harvard Business Review*, **Nov.–Dec.**: 95–103.

—— and Hilmer, F. G. (1994), 'Strategic Outsourcing', *Sloan Management Review*, **Summer**: 43–55.

Ramesh, R. (1996), 'BA Strips down to be "virtual airline" ', *Sunday Times*, 22 Sept.

Rappaport, A. S., and Halevi, S. (1991), 'The Computerless Computer Company', *Harvard Business Review*, **July–Aug.**: 69–80.

Reca, J. V., and Zieg, K. C. J. (1995), 'Privatization: An Analysis of Contracting out of Government-Provided Services', *National Contract Management Journal*, **26 (2)**: 51–64.

Ricardo, D. (1817), *On the Principles of Political Economy and Taxation*, in *The Works and Correspondence of David Ricardo*, ed. P. Sraffa, Cambridge: Cambridge University Press, 1962.

Richardson, J. (1993), 'Parallel Sourcing and Supplier Performance in the Japanese Automobile Industry', *Strategic Management Journal*, **14**: 339–50.

—— and Roumasset, J. (1995), 'Sole Sourcing, Competitive Sourcing, Parallel Sourcing: Mechanisms for Supplier Performance', *Managerial and Decision Economics*, **16 (1)**: 71–84.

Riddle, D. I. (1986) (ed.), *Service-Led Growth*, New York: Praeger.

Riley, M. (1998), 'Threat to Jobs Triggers Rail Contract Review', *Sydney Morning Herald*, 31 Jan.: 7.

Ring, P. S., and van den Ven, A. (1992), 'Structuring Cooperative Relationships between Organizations', *Strategic Management Journal*, **13**: 483–98.

Roach, S. (1994), 'Best Case Study of All', *Forbes*, 29 Aug.: 27.

—— (1996), 'The Hollow Ring of the Productivity Revival', *Harvard Business Review*, **Nov.–Dec.**: 81–9.

Rothery, B., and Robertson, I. (1995), *The Truth about Outsourcing*, Aldershot: Gower Publishing.

Sabel, C. F. (1989), 'Flexible Specialisation and the Re-emergence of Regional Economies', in P. Hirst and J. Zeitlin (eds.), *Reversing Industrial Decline? Industrial Structure and Policy in Britain and her Competitors*, Oxford: Berg: 17–70.

Savas, E. (1987), *Privatization: The Key to Better Government*, Chatham, NJ: Chatham House.

Schaff, W. (1996), 'Sun Stresses Service as it Starts to Feel the Heat', *InformationWeek*, 25 Nov. 124.

Schmidt, K. (1996), 'The Costs and Benefits of Privatization: An Incomplete Contracts Approach', *Journal of Law, Economics and Organization*, **12 (1)**: 1–24.

Schumpeter, J. (1943), *Capitalism, Socialism and Democracy*, London: Allen & Unwin.

Semler, R. (1994), 'Why my Former Employees Still Work for Me', *Harvard Business Review*, **Jan.–Feb.**: 64–74.

Sieff, M. (1990), *Management the Marks & Spencer Way*, London: Fontana.

Smith, A. (1880), *An Inquiry into the Nature and Causes of the Wealth of Nations*, 2nd edn., Oxford: Clarendon Press.

Spier, K. E. (1992), 'Incomplete Contracts and Signalling', *Rand Journal of Economics*, **23 (2)**: 432–43.

Steering Committee for the Review of Commonwealth/State Service Provision (1998), Melbourne: Industry Commission (www.indcom.gov.au/).

Stigler, G. J. (1951), 'The Division of Labor is Limited by the Extent of the Market', *Journal of Political Economy*, **59 (3)**: 185–93.

—— (1988), *Memoirs of an Unregulated Economist*, New York: Basic Books.

STORPER, M. (1989), 'The Transition of Flexible Specialisation in the US Film Industry: External Economies, the Division of Labour, and the Crossing of Industrial Divides', *Cambridge Journal of Economics*, **13**: 273–305.

STURGESS, G. (1993), 'Towards Virtual Government', *CTC Newsletter*, Apr. (Graduate School of Business, University of Sydney): 1–2.

SUAREZ, F. F., CUSUMANO, M. A., and FINE, C. H. (1995), 'An Empirical Study of Flexibility in Manufacturing', *Sloan Management Review*, **Fall**: 25–32.

SULLIVAN, J., and PURDY, M. (1995), 'Parlaying the Detentions Business into Profit', *New York Times*, 23 July: 1–28.

SZYMANSKI, S. (1996), 'The Impact of Compulsory Competitive Tendering on Refuse Collection Services', *Fiscal Studies*, **17** (3): 1–19.

THALER, R. H. (1992), *The Winner's Curse: Paradoxes and Anomalies of Economic Life*, New York: Free Press.

TREADGOLD, T. (1996), 'Letting Someone Else Hold the Purse Strings', *Business Review Weekly*, 26 Aug,: 90–1.

TVERSKY, A. (1990), 'The Psychology of Risk', in W. F. Sharpe (ed.), *Quantifying the Market Risk Premium Phenomenon for Investment Decision Making*, Charlottesville, Va.: Institute of Chartered Financial Analysts.

UK Audit Commission (1995), *Making Markets: A Review of the Audits of the Client Role for Contracted Services*, London: HMSO.

UK Cabinet Office (1996), *Competing for Quality Policy Review: An Efficiency Unit Scrutiny*, London: HMSO.

UK Central Statistical Office (1975), *Input–Output Tables for the United Kingdom 1971*, London: HMSO.

—— (1995), *Input–Output Tables for the United Kingdom 1990*, London: HMSO.

UNO, K. (1989), *Measurement of Services in an Input–Output Framework*, Amsterdam: North-Holland (Elsevier Science Publishers).

UPTON, D. M. (1995), 'What Really Makes Factories Flexible?', *Harvard Business Review*, **July–Aug.**: 74–84.

US Department of Commerce (1977), *Revised Input–Output Tables for the United States 1967*, Washington: US Government Printing Office.

—— (1994), *Benchmark Input–Output Accounts of the United States 1987*, Washington: US Government Printing Office.

US General Accounting Office (1997), *Privatization: Lessons Learned by State and Local Governments*, GAO/GGD 97-48, Washington.

US General Services Administration (1995), *Federal Procurement Report*, Washington.

VASILASH, G. S., and BERGSTROM, R. Y. (1995), 'The Five Hottest Manufacturers in Silicon Valley: How Sun Keeps Its Advantage', *Production*, **107** (5): 52–4.

VENKATESAN, R. (1992), 'Strategic Sourcing: to Make or Not to Make', *Harvard Business Review*, **Nov.–Dec.**: 98–107.

VICKERS, J., and YARROW, G. (1988), *Privatization: An Economic Analysis*, London: MIT Press.

—— —— (1991), 'Economic Perspectives on Privatisation', *Journal of Economic Perspectives*, **5** (2): 111–32.

WALSH, K. (1991), *Competitive Tendering of Local Authority Services: Initial Experience*, Department of the Environment, London: HMSO.

WATERSON, M. (1993), 'Vertical Integration and Vertical Restraints', *Oxford Review of Economic Policy*, **9** (2): 41–57.

WELCH, J. (1994), 'Letter to Share Owners', *General Electric Annual Report 1993*, Fairfield, Conn,: General Electric Company.

WHEATLEY, M. (1994), 'Electronics Heading for Sunshine State', *Purchasing and Supply Management*, **Oct.**: 18–19.

WHITE, R., and JAMES, B. (1996), *The Outsourcing Manual*, Aldershot: Gower Publishing.

WILLCOCKS, L., and CHOI, C. J. (1995), 'Co-operative Partnership and "Total" IT Outsourcing: From Contractual Obligation to Strategic Alliance?', *European Management Journal*, **13** (1): 67–78.

—— FITZGERALD, G., and FEENY, D. (1995), 'Outsourcing IT: The Strategic Implications', *Long Range Planning*, **28** (5): 59–70.

WILLIAMSON, O. E. (1985), *The Economic Institutions of Capitalism*, New York: Free Press.

—— (1996), 'Economics and Organization: A Primer', *California Management Review*, **38** (2): 131–46.

WILSON, J. Q. (1989), *Bureaucracy: What Government Agencies Do and Why They Do It*, New York: Basic Books.

WISNIEWSKI, S. C. (1991), 'Analysing the Contracting-out of Government Services: Relevant Cost–Benefit Considerations', *Public Budgeting and Finance*, **11** (2): 95–107.

WOODALL, P. (1996), 'A Survey of the World Economy: The Hitchhiker's Guide to Cybernomics', *The Economist*, 28 Sept.: 3–50.

Workplace Change (1996), 'Bodies for hire: The Contracting out Debate', *Workplace Change*, **2**: 1–3.

WRAY, G. (1996), 'The Role of Human Resources in Successful Outsourcing', *Employment Relations Today*, **Spring**: 17–23.

WYCKOFF, A. (1996), 'The Growing Strength of Services', *OECD Observer*, **200**: 11–15.

YOUNG, A. (1928), 'Increasing Returns and Economic Progress', *Economic Journal*, **38**: 527–42.

NAME INDEX

SUBJECT INDEX